Microsoft® Office 2007
Illustrated Projects™

Carol M. Cram

Capilano College, North Vancouver, B.C.

COURSE TECHNOLOGY
CENGAGE Learning™

Australia • Brazil • Japan • Korea • Mexico • Singapore • Spain • United Kingdom • United States

COURSE TECHNOLOGY
CENGAGE Learning™

Microsoft® Office 2007—Illustrated Projects™
Carol M. Cram

Senior Acquisitions Editor: Marjorie Hunt

Senior Product Manager: Christina Kling Garrett

Product Manager: Brianna Hawes

Associate Product Manager: Rebecca Padrick

Editorial Assistant: Michelle Camisa

Senior Content Project Manager: Jennifer Goguen McGrail

Developmental Editor: Barbara Clemens

Marketing Coordinator: Jennifer Hankin

Composition House: GEX Publishing Services

QA Tester: Susan Whalen

Text Designer: Black fish design

Cover Artist: Mark Hunt

Cover Design: Kun-Tee Chang

For product information and technology assistance, contact us at
Cengage Learning Customer & Sales Support, 1-800-354-9706

For permission to use material from this text or product, submit all requests online at **cengage.com/permissions**
Further permissions questions can be emailed to
permissionrequest@cengage.com

ISBN-13: 978-1-4239-0546-2

ISBN-10: 1-4239 0546-6

Course Technology
25 Thomson Place
Boston, Massachusetts 02210
USA

Cengage Learning is a leading provider of customized learning solutions with office locations around the globe, including Singapore, the United Kingdom, Australia, Mexico, Brazil, and Japan. Locate your local office at:
international.cengage.com/region

Cengage Learning products are represented in Canada by Nelson Education, Ltd.

For your lifelong learning solutions, visit **course.cengage.com**

Purchase any of our products at your local college store or at our preferred online store **www.ichapters.com**

Microsoft and the Office logo are either registered trademarks or trademarks of Microsoft Corporation in the United States and/or other countries. Course Technology is an independent entity from Microsoft Corporation, and not affiliated with Microsoft in any manner. Microsoft product screen shots reprinted with permission from Microsoft Corporation.

Printed in the United States of America
4 5 6 7 8 9 10 12 11 10 09

A Note from the Author

As instructors, what is our goal? I believe that we can and should teach our students to fly—to become independent learners with the confidence to tackle and solve problems. My greatest satisfaction in the classroom comes when my students learn the information, skills, and techniques necessary to function effectively in the workplace and to accomplish tasks related to their own needs and interests.

Several years ago, I was teaching a second-level word processing course to students who had completed the introductory word processing course. These students knew a series of functions and had proven their ability to pass "fill in the blanks" tests. But when I asked the students to produce an attractively formatted business letter, they were at a loss. That's when I realized that teaching a series of functions wasn't enough. Students needed—and deserved—to learn what to do with a software application. They needed to "see the forest" and not just the trees.

I developed a philosophy of teaching software applications that has evolved into the Illustrated Projects series. Each text in this series provides students with step-by-step instructions to create documents or perform tasks appropriate to the software package they are learning. As students complete the projects, they learn how a variety of functions combine together to produce a tangible product.

But the Illustrated Projects approach to teaching software doesn't stop with the projects. In my classroom, the significant learning occurs when students are given the opportunity to create their own version of a project document. That's when I feel a kind of magic creeping into my classroom. Students take the structure offered by a project and then, in the Independent Challenges, adapt this structure to explore practical business applications and to express their own interests. Suddenly, my students are willing to take risks, to solve problems, and to experiment with new features as they work toward the creation of a document that belongs to them. Pride of ownership inspires learning!

I hope you enjoy working with the projects in this book as much as I have enjoyed creating them. And I hope that you too can experience the magic that occurs in your classroom when your students begin to fly!

This book owes everything to the talent and dedication of the Course Technology Illustrated team. I particularly wish to thank Barbara Clemens, the Developmental Editor of this book, for her encouragement and support and her incredible attention to detail. I am honored to call her not only my colleague but my friend. I also wish to thank my husband and daughter for their endless patience and, as always, my wonderful students at Capilano College.

Carol M. Cram

Carol M. Cram, September 2007

Preface

Welcome to Microsoft Office 2007—Illustrated Projects. This highly visual book offers a wide array of interesting and challenging projects designed to apply the skills learned in any Office 2007 book. The Illustrated Projects book is for people who want more opportunities to practice important software skills.

Organization and Coverage

This text contains a total of nine units. Six units contain projects for the individual programs: Word (2 units), Excel (2 units), Access (one unit), and PowerPoint (one unit). Three other units contain projects that take advantage of the powerful integration capabilities of the Office suite. Each unit contains three projects followed by four Independent Challenges and a Visual Workshop. Students will also gain practice gathering and using information available on the World Wide Web in a variety of the projects and independent challenges.

About this Approach

What makes the Illustrated Projects approach so effective at reinforcing software skills? It's quite simple. Each activity in a project is presented on two facing pages, with the step-by-step instructions on the left page and large screen illustrations on the right. Students can focus on a single activity without having to turn the page. This unique design makes information extremely accessible and easy to absorb. Students can complete the projects on their own, and because of the modular structure of the book, can also cover the units in any order.

The two-page spread for each activity contains some or all of the elements shown below.

Road map—It is always clear which project and activity you are working on.

Introduction—Concise text that introduces the activity and summarizes new procedures. Steps are easier to complete when they fit into a meaningful framework.

Troubles and Hints—Troubleshooting advice to fix common problems that might occur and tips for using Microsoft Office 2007 more effectively. These appear right next to the step where students need help.

Numbered steps—Clear step-by-step directions explain how to complete the specific activity. These steps get less specific as students progress to the third project in a unit.

Additional Practice—Provides information on which end-of-unit exercises allow students to practice the same set of skills.

Clues to Use—These boxes provide concise information that either explains a skill or concept covered in the steps or describes an independent task or feature that is in some way related to the steps.

PowerPoint Word Excel and Access

INVESTOR ORIENTATION FOR ORCA ESTATES

Activity:

Update the Presentation

You need to summarize data in the Excel worksheet, copy it, and paste it as a link on Slide 5. Then, you need to change data in the Access database and update the links in Excel and PowerPoint. Finally, you need to print a copy of the completed presentation.

Steps:

1. Switch to Excel, click cell **I14**, then enter and format the labels and formulas as shown in Figure I-18

2. Select cells **I14:J17**, press **[Ctrl][C]**, switch to PowerPoint, go to **Slide 5**, click the **Paste list arrow** in the Clipboard group, click **Paste Special**, click the **Paste link option button**, then click **OK**

3. Apply the **Title Only slide layout**, then size and position the object as shown in Figure I-19

4. Verify that the Total Worth of all the homes in Orca Estates is **$42,540,000** and the total sales are **$21,220,000**

5. Show the **Home Designs table** in Access, increase the price of the homes in records **1** and **4** to **$700,000**, close the table, switch to Excel, then verify that the total in cells **I12** and **J17** is **$23,920,000**

6. Switch to PowerPoint, then verify that the value for Total Sales has been updated to $23,920,000

7. Click the **Slide Sorter View button** on the status bar, click the **View tab**, click the **Fit to Window button** in the Zoom group, then compare the completed presentation to Figure I-20

8. Print a sheet of handouts (6 slides to the page), then save and close all files and applications

Trouble

Make sure you enter formulas where indicated, *not* values, and that you enclose cells I14:J17 with border lines.

Trouble

If the values do not update within a few minutes, click the Office button, point to Prepare, click Edit Links to Files, click Update Values, then click Close.

Additional Practice

For additional practice with the skills presented in this project, complete Independent Challenge 2.

Clues to Use

Reestablishing Links

To reestablish links, you should start with the program that does not contain links and then open the remaining files in the order in which they are linked. For this presentation the order of files is Access, Excel, and PowerPoint.

The Projects

The two-page activity format featured in this book provides students with a powerful learning experience. Additionally, this book contains the following features:

► **Meaningful Examples**—This book features projects that students will be excited to create including a personal resume, a marketing brochure, a proposed budget, an integrated report, and a sales presentation. By producing relevant documents that will enhance their own lives, students will more readily master skills.

► **Start from Scratch**—To truly test if a student understands the software and can use it to reach specific goals, the student should start from the beginning. In this book, students create projects from scratch, just like they would in the real world. In selected cases, supplemental data files are provided.

► **Outstanding Assessment and Reinforcement**—Each unit concludes with four independent challenges and

a Visual Workshop. These Independent Challenges offer less instruction than the projects, allowing students to explore various software features and increase their critical thinking skills. The Visual Workshop follows the Independent Challenges and broadens students' attention to detail. Students see a completed document, worksheet, database, or presentation, and must recreate it on their own.

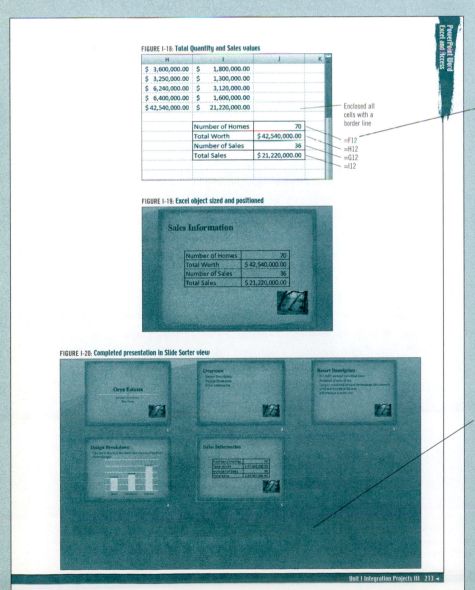

Screen shots—Every activity features representations of what the screen should look like as students complete the numbered steps.

Completed document—At the end of every project, there is a picture of how the document will look when printed. Students can easily assess how well they've done.

Instructor Resources

The Instructor Resources CD is Course Technology's way of putting the resources and information needed to teach and learn effectively into your hands. With an integrated array of teaching and learning tools that offer you and your students a broad range of technology-based instructional options, we believe this CD represents the highest quality and most cutting edge resources available to instructors today. Many of these resources are available at www.course.com. The resources available with this book are:

Instructor's Manual

Available as an electronic file, the Instructor's Manual includes detailed lecture topics with teaching tips for each unit.

Solution Sample Syllabus

Prepare and customize your course easily using this sample course outline.

Figure Files

The figures in the text are provided on the Instructor Resources CD to help you illustrate key topics or concepts. You can create traditional overhead transparencies by printing the figure files. Or you can create electronic slide shows by using the figures in a presentation program such as PowerPoint.

Solutions to Exercises

Solutions to Exercises contains every file students are asked to create or modify in the lessons and end-of-unit material.

Data Files for Students

Data Files contain every file students need to create the projects and end-of-unit material. You can post the Data Files on a file server for students to copy. The Data Files are available on the Instructor Resources CD and can also be downloaded from *www.course.com.*

In this edition, we have included a lesson on downloading the Data Files for this book, see page xii as well as the inside back cover.

CourseCasts—Learning on the Go. Always Available...Always Relevant.

Want to keep up with the latest technology trends relevant to you? Visit our site to find a library of podcasts and CourseCasts, featuring a "CourseCast of the Week," and download them to your mp3 player at *http://coursecasts.course.com.*

Our fast-paced world is driven by technology. You know because you're an active participant—always on the go, always keeping up with technological trends, and always learning new ways to embrace technology to power your life.

Ken Baldauf, host of CourseCasts, is a faculty member of the Florida State University Computer Science Department where he is responsible for teaching technology classes to thousands of FSU students each year. Ken is an expert in the latest technology trends; he gathers and sorts through the most pertinent news and information for CourseCasts so your students can spend their time enjoying technology, rather than trying to figure it out. Open or close your lecture with a discussion based on the latest CourseCast.

Visit us at http://coursecasts.course.com to learn on the go!

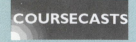

Contents

A Note From the Author iii
Preface iv

Read This Before You Begin

Frequently Asked Questions

What are Data Files?

A Data File is a partially completed file that you use to complete the steps in the units and exercises to create the final document that you submit to your instructor.

Where are the Data Files?

Your instructor will provide the Data Files to you or direct you to a location on a network drive from which you can download them. Alternatively, you can follow the instructions on page xiii to download the Data Files from this book's Web page.

What software was used to write and test this book?

This book was written and tested using a typical installation of Microsoft Office 2007 installed on a computer with a typical installation of Microsoft Windows Vista. The browser used for any steps that require a browser is Internet Explorer 7.

If you are using this book on Windows XP, please see the "Important Notes for Windows XP Users" on the next page. If you are using this book on Windows Vista, please see the appendix at the end of this book.

Do I need to be connected to the Internet to complete the steps and exercises in this book?

Some of the exercises in this book assume that your computer is connected to the Internet. If you are not connected to the Internet, see your instructor for information on how to complete the exercises.

What do I do if my screen is different from the figures shown in this book?

This book was written and tested on computers with monitors set at a resolution of 1024 × 768. If your screen shows more or less information than the figures in the book, your monitor is probably set at a higher or lower resolution. If you don't see something on your screen, you might have to scroll down or up to see the object identified in the figures.

The Ribbon (the blue area at the top of the screen) in Microsoft Office 2007 adapts to different resolutions. If your monitor is set at a lower resolution than 1024 × 768, you might not see all of the buttons shown in the figures. The groups of buttons will always appear, but the entire group might be condensed into a single button that you need to click to access the buttons described in the instructions. For example, the figures and steps in this book assume that the Editing group on the Home tab in Word looks like the following:

If your resolution is set to 800 × 600, the Ribbon in Word will look like the following figure, and you will need to click the Editing button to access the buttons that are visible in the Editing group.

1024 × 768 Editing Group

Editing Group on the
Home Tab of the
Ribbon at 1024 × 768

800 × 600 Editing Group

Editing Group
on the Home Tab of the
Ribbon at 800 × 600

800 × 600 Editing Group Clicked

Editing Group on the Home Tab of the Ribbon at
800 × 600 is selected to show available buttons

Important Notes for Windows XP Users

The screen shots in this book show Microsoft Office 2007 running on Windows Vista. However, if you are using Microsoft Windows XP, you can still use this book because Office 2007 runs virtually the same on both platforms. There are a few differences that you will encounter if you are using Windows XP. Read this section to understand the differences.

Dialog boxes

If you are a Windows XP user, dialog boxes shown in this book will look slightly different than what you see on your screen. Dialog boxes for Windows XP have a blue title bar, instead of a gray title bar. However, beyond this difference in appearance, the options in the dialog boxes across platforms are the same. For instance, the screen shots below show the Font dialog box running on Windows XP and the Font dialog box running on Windows Vista.

FIGURE 1: Dialog box in Windows XP

FIGURE 2: Dialog box in Windows Vista

Alternate Steps for Windows XP Users

Nearly all of the steps in this book work exactly the same for Windows XP users. However, there are a few tasks that will require you to complete slightly different steps. This section provides alternate steps for a few specific skills.

Starting a program

1. Click the **Start button** on the taskbar
2. Point to **All Programs**, point to **Microsoft Office**, then click the application you want to use

FIGURE 3: Starting a program

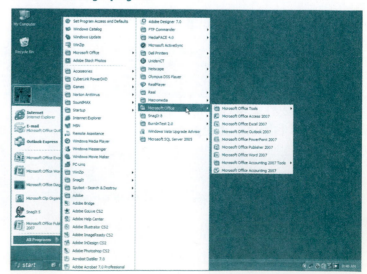

Saving a file for the first time

1. Click the **Office button**, then click **Save As**
2. Type a name for your file in the File name text box
3. Click the **Save in list arrow**, then navigate to the drive and folder where you store your Data Files
4. Click **Save**

FIGURE 4: Save As dialog box

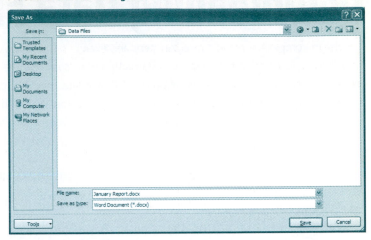

Opening a file

1. Click the **Office button**, then click **Open**
2. Click the **Look in list arrow**, then navigate to the drive and folder where you store your Data Files
3. Click the file you want to open
4. Click **Open**

FIGURE 5: Open dialog box

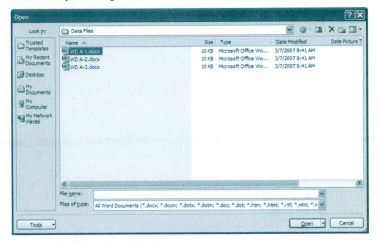

Downloading Data Files for This Book

In order to complete some of the lesson steps and exercises in this book, you are asked to open and save Data Files. A **Data File** is a partially completed file that you use as a starting point to complete the steps in the units and exercises. The benefit of using a Data File is that it saves you the time and effort needed to create a file; you can simply open a Data File, save it with a new name (so the original file remains intact), then make changes to it to complete lesson steps or an exercise. Your instructor will provide the Data Files to you or direct you to a location on a network drive from which you can download them. Alternatively, you can follow the instructions in this lesson to download the Data Files from this book's Web page.

1. Start Internet Explorer, type **www.course.com** in the address bar, then press **[Enter]**

2. When the Course.com Web site opens, click the **Student Downloads link**

3. On the Student Downloads page, click in the **Search text box**, type this book's ISBN, **9781423905462**, then click **Go**

4. When the page opens for this textbook, in the left navigation bar, click the **Download Student Files link**, then, on the Student Downloads page, click the **Data Files link**

5. If the File Download – Security Warning dialog box opens, click **Save**. (If no dialog box appears, skip this step and go to Step 6)

6. If the Save As dialog box opens, click the **Save in list arrow** at the top of the dialog box, select a folder on your USB drive or hard disk to download the file to, then click **Save**

7. Close Internet Explorer and then open My Computer or Windows Explorer and display the contents of the drive and folder to which you downloaded the file

8. Double-click the file **905462.exe** in the drive or folder, then, if the Open File – Security Warning dialog box opens, click **Run**

9. In the WinZip Self-Extractor window, navigate to the drive and folder where you want to unzip the files to, then click **Unzip**

10. When the WinZip Self-Extractor displays a dialog box listing the number of files that have unzipped successfully, click **OK**, click **Close** in the WinZip Self-Extractor dialog box, then close Windows Explorer or My Computer

    You are now ready to open the required files.

Hint

You can also click Student Downloads on the right side of the product page.

Trouble

If a dialog box opens telling you that the download is complete, click Close.

Hint

By default, the files will extract to C:\CourseTechnology\905462

Microsoft
► **Word**
Projects

Unit **A**

Word Projects I

In This Unit You Will Create the Following:

 **Trip Schedule**

 **Newsletter**

 **Business Card**

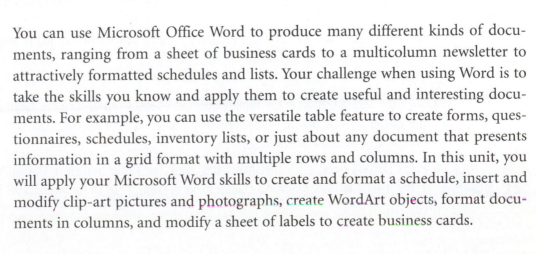

You can use Microsoft Office Word to produce many different kinds of documents, ranging from a sheet of business cards to a multicolumn newsletter to attractively formatted schedules and lists. Your challenge when using Word is to take the skills you know and apply them to create useful and interesting documents. For example, you can use the versatile table feature to create forms, questionnaires, schedules, inventory lists, or just about any document that presents information in a grid format with multiple rows and columns. In this unit, you will apply your Microsoft Word skills to create and format a schedule, insert and modify clip-art pictures and photographs, create WordArt objects, format documents in columns, and modify a sheet of labels to create business cards.

Schedule for Pinnacle Hiking Club

The Pinnacle Hiking Club in North Vancouver, British Columbia, provides its members with walking and hiking tours in three categories: Strolls, Day Hikes, and Backcountry Adventures. Club members are busy people who want an easy-to-read schedule that shows the monthly tours. As the office manager, you need to create the schedule for August. You will **Create Tables**, **Merge Cells and Add Shading**, and **Add and Modify a Graphic**. The completed schedule appears in Figure A-6 on page 7.

Activity:

Create Tables

You need to set up the document in landscape format so that the completed schedule is 9" wide. Then you need to create a small table for the legend and a large table with 7 columns and 15 rows.

Steps:

Trouble

This unit assumes Show/Hide ¶ is on. Click the Show/Hide ¶ button in the Paragraph group.

Trouble

If Tahoma is not available, select Arial.

1. Open a blank document in Word, click the **Page Layout tab**, click the **Orientation button** in the Page Setup group, click **Landscape**, click the **Margins button** in the Page Setup group, click **Custom Margins**, set a top margin of **.8**, then set a bottom margin of **.5** as shown in Figure A-1

2. Click **OK**, save the document as **Pinnacle Hiking Club Schedule** in the location where you store your Data Files, click the **View tab**, then click the **Page Width button** in the Zoom group

3. Click the **Home tab**, click the **Font list arrow** [Calibri (Body)] in the Font group, scroll to and click **Tahoma**, type **Pinnacle Hiking Club August Trip Schedule**, then press **[Enter]** twice

   All the text you enter for the schedule will be formatted in the Tahoma font.

4. Click the **Insert tab**, click the **Table button** in the Tables group, drag to create a table that is **2** columns wide and **3** rows high, then enter text as shown in Figure A-2

5. Click **cell 1** (which contains "Stroll"), click the **Table Tools Layout tab**, click **Properties** in the Table group, click the **Column tab**, select the contents of the Preferred width text box, type **2**, click **Next Column**, select the contents of the Preferred width text box for column 2, then type **.6**

   In the Table Properties dialog box, you can make changes to all components of a table including rows, columns, cells, and the table itself.

6. Click the **Table tab** in the Table Properties dialog box, click the **Right alignment symbol** in the Alignment section, then click **OK**

   The width of the two columns is modified, and the entire table is right aligned.

7. Click the **Select button** in the Table group, click **Select Table**, click the **Table Tools Design tab**, click the **Borders list arrow** in the Table Styles group, click **No Border**, then press **[→]** once

   The table borders are removed.

8. Press **[Enter]** once, click the **Insert tab**, click the **Table button** in the Tables group, click **Insert Table**, type **7** for the number of columns, press **[Tab]**, type **15** for the number of rows, then clic k **OK**

9. Enter the text for row 1 of the new table as shown in Figure A-3, then save the document

Trouble

If your legend table does not have light blue gridlines, click in the table, then click the View Gridlines button in the Table group.

FIGURE A-1: Page Setup dialog box

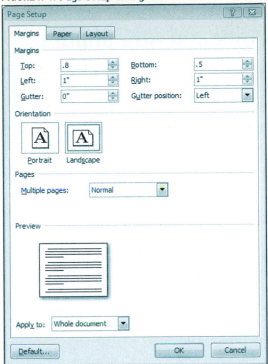

FIGURE A-2: Text for the legend

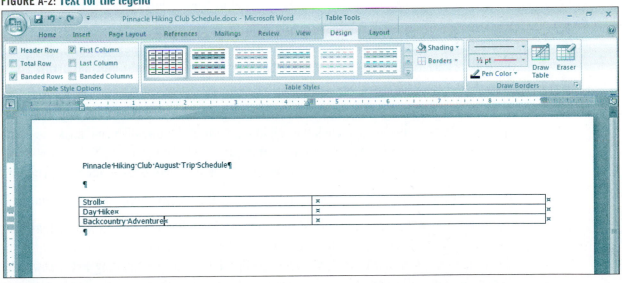

FIGURE A-3: Text for row 1

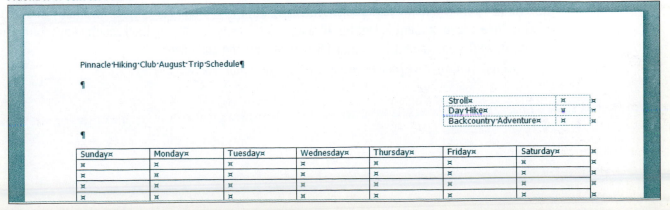

Activity:

Merge Cells and Add Shading

In the completed schedule, two or more cells are merged so that the text for the Backcountry Adventure tours—each of which lasts for more than one day—spans the merged cells. In addition, different levels of shading indicate the different trip categories. You need to enter text into the schedule and then use the Table Tools Design and Layout tabs and the Mini toolbar so you can quickly merge selected cells and add shading where required.

Steps:

1. Click the cell below Tuesday, type **1**, press **[Tab]**, type **2**, press **[Tab]**, then continue to enter the date for each day in the first week of August (ending with a 5 for Saturday)

2. Select **cells 1** to **4** at the beginning of the next row (Sunday to Wednesday), click the **Table Tools Layout tab**, then click **Merge Cells** in the Merge group to merge the four cells as shown in Figure A-4

3. Type **Skyline Trail to Manning Park**, press **[Tab]** two times, type **Deep Cove** for Friday, press **[Tab]**, then type **Helm Lake** for Saturday

You've entered three of the hikes being held during the first week in August.

Hint

Make sure you include the date for each day and all the hikes.

4. Refer to Figure A-5 to enter the remaining text for the table and merge cells where needed

At this point, just enter the text and merge cells. You will add shading in later steps.

5. Click to the left of row 1 (contains the days of the week) to select the entire row, click the **Table Tools Design tab**, click the **Shading list arrow** in the Table Styles group, click **Olive Green, Accent 3, Darker 50%**, right-click the selected cells, click the **Font Color list arrow** [A▾] on the Mini toolbar, then click the **White, Background 1**

6. Click the cell to the right of the Stroll cell in the legend table, click the **Shading button** [⬚] to fill the cell with dark olive green, click the cell to the right of the Day Hike cell, click the **Shading list arrow**, click the **Olive Green, Accent 3, Lighter 40%**, click the cell to the right of the Backcountry Adventure cell, click the **Shading list arrow**, then click the **Olive Green, Accent 3, Lighter 80%**

7. Format the text in column 1 of the legend table with **Bold**, then change the alignment to **Right**

8. Place the pointer over the left side of the cell containing Deep Cove in row 3 so that the pointer becomes ➜, click once, press and hold **[Ctrl]**, select only the cells that are filled with dark olive green in Figure A-5, click the **Table Tools Design tab**, click the **Shading list arrow**, click **Olive Green, Accent 3, Darker 50%**, right-click any selected cell, then click the **Font Color button** [A] on the Mini toolbar

9. Refer to Figure A-5 to fill all the cells containing Day Hikes (Helm Lake, Black Mountain, and so on) with **Olive Green, Accent 3, Lighter 40%** and all the cells containing Backcountry Adventure hikes with **Olive Green, Accent 3, Lighter 80%**, then save the document

Remember you can save time by using [Ctrl] to select multiple cells at once.

FIGURE A-4: Merging cells

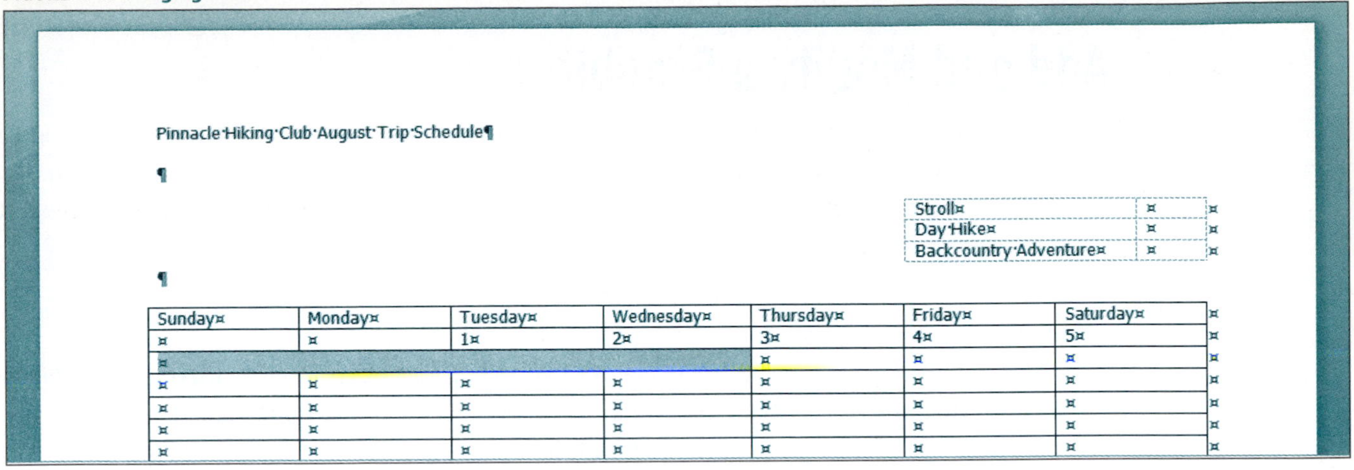

Pinnacle·Hiking·Club·August·Trip·Schedule¶

¶

Stroll¤	¤	¤
Day·Hike¤	¤	¤
Backcountry·Adventure¤	¤	¤

¶

Sunday¤	Monday¤	Tuesday¤	Wednesday¤	Thursday¤	Friday¤	Saturday¤	¤
¤	¤	1¤	2¤	3¤	4¤	5¤	¤
¤				¤	¤	¤	¤
¤	¤	¤	¤	¤	¤	¤	¤
¤	¤	¤	¤	¤	¤	¤	¤
¤	¤	¤	¤	¤	¤	¤	¤
¤	¤	¤	¤	¤	¤	¤	¤

FIGURE A-5: Text for Pinnacle Hiking Club schedule

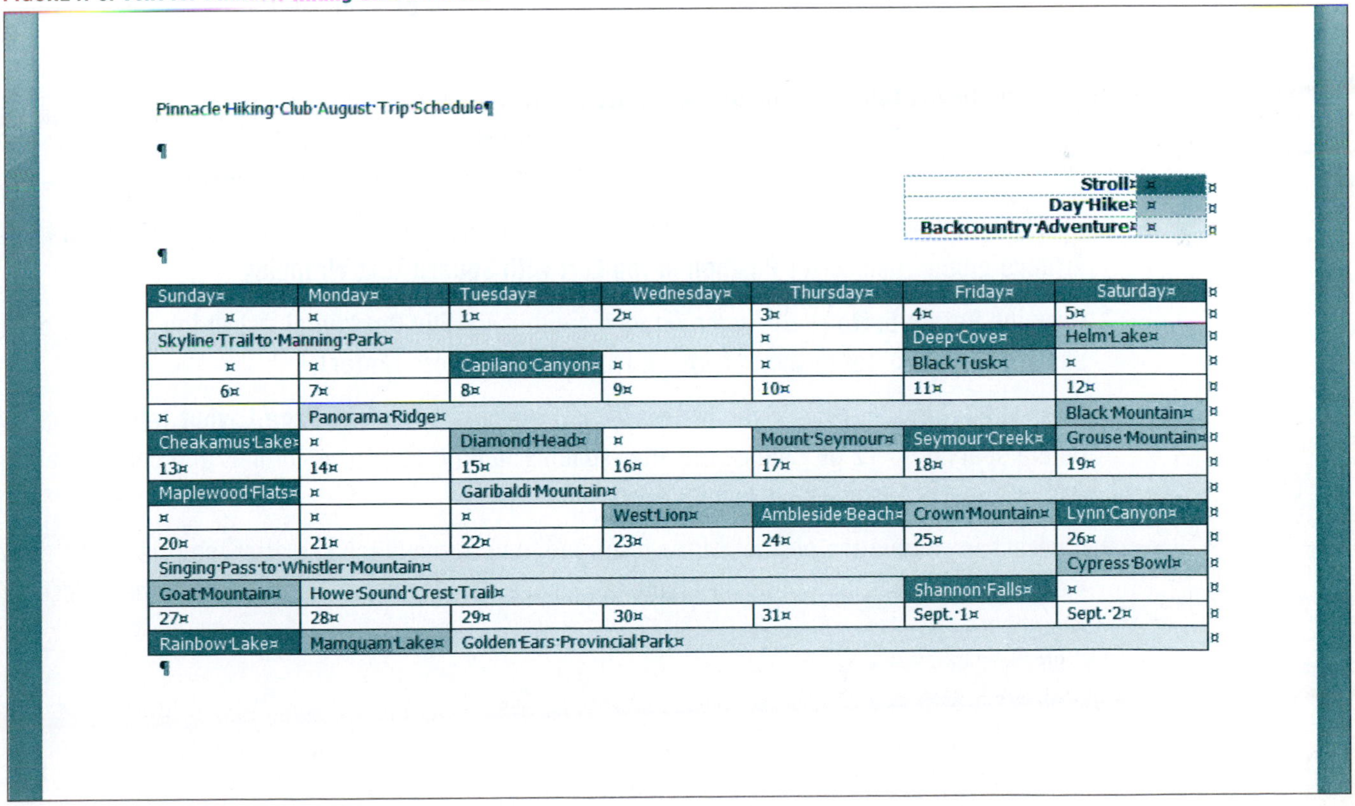

Pinnacle·Hiking·Club·August·Trip·Schedule¶

¶

Stroll¤	¤	¤
Day·Hike¤	¤	¤
Backcountry·Adventure¤	¤	¤

¶

Sunday¤	Monday¤	Tuesday¤	Wednesday¤	Thursday¤	Friday¤	Saturday¤	¤
¤	¤	1¤	2¤	3¤	4¤	5¤	¤
Skyline·Trail·to·Manning·Park¤				¤	Deep·Cove¤	Helm·Lake¤	¤
¤	¤	Capilano·Canyon¤	¤	¤	Black·Tusk¤	¤	¤
6¤	7¤	8¤	9¤	10¤	11¤	12¤	¤
¤	Panorama·Ridge¤					Black·Mountain¤	¤
Cheakamus·Lake¤	¤	Diamond·Head¤	¤	Mount·Seymour¤	Seymour·Creek¤	Grouse·Mountain¤	¤
13¤	14¤	15¤	16¤	17¤	18¤	19¤	¤
Maplewood·Flats¤	¤	Garibaldi·Mountain¤					¤
¤	¤	¤	West·Lion¤	Ambleside·Beach¤	Crown·Mountain¤	Lynn·Canyon¤	¤
20¤	21¤	22¤	23¤	24¤	25¤	26¤	¤
Singing·Pass·to·Whistler·Mountain¤						Cypress·Bowl¤	¤
Goat·Mountain¤	Howe·Sound·Crest·Trail¤				Shannon·Falls¤	¤	¤
27¤	28¤	29¤	30¤	31¤	Sept.·1¤	Sept.·2¤	¤
Rainbow·Lake¤	Mamquam·Lake¤	Golden·Ears·Provincial·Park¤					¤

¶

Activity:

Add and Modify a Graphic

After adjusting row heights and text alignment, you enhance the completed schedule with a clip-art picture that you will modify. In the original clip art, the image of the hiker faces to the left. You need to "flip" the image so that it faces right. Finally, you need to enter the address of the club at the bottom of the page. The completed schedule is shown in Figure A-6.

Steps:

1. Click to the left of row 1 of the schedule table to select it, press and hold **[Ctrl]**, select *only* the rows containing hikes (*not* the rows containing the dates), click the **Table Tools Layout tab**, click **Properties** in the Table group, click the **Row tab** if necessary, click the **Specify height check box**, press **[Tab]**, type **.4**, then click **OK**

2. Click anywhere in the table, click **Select** in the Table group, click **Select Table**, click the **Align Center button**  in the Alignment group, click the **Home tab**, then click the **Bold button** **B** in the Font group

3. Press **[Ctrl][Home]** to move the insertion point to the top of the document, select **Pinnacle Hiking Club August Trip Schedule**, then format it with **22 pt**, **Bold**, **Italic**, and **Right alignment**

4. Click the **Page Layout tab**, change the After Spacing to **0 pt**, then click to the left of the title to deselect it

5. Click the **Insert tab**, click the **Clip Art button** in the Illustrations group, select the contents of the Search for text box in the Clip Art task pane, type **hiker**, click **Go**, then scroll down to find the clip-art picture shown in Figure A-6 (except the hiker will face in the opposite direction)

6. Click the **picture** to place it in your document, close the Clip Art task pane, click **Position** in the Arrange group, then select **Position in Top Left with Square Text Wrapping**

7. Click the **Rotate button** in the Arrange group, click **Flip Horizontal**, select the contents of the Shape Height text box in the Size group, type **1.6**, then press **[Enter]**

8. Press **[Ctrl][End]** to move to the bottom of the document, click the **Page Layout tab**, change the Before spacing to **12 pt**, change the After spacing to **0 pt**, then type, format, and center the contact information as shown in Figure A-6

9. If necessary, adjust the position of the hiker and remove the blank line after the title so the document fits the page as shown in Figure A-6, save the document, print a copy, then close the document

Pinnacle Hiking Club August Trip Schedule

Legend:
- Stroll
- Day Hike
- Backcountry Adventure

Sunday	Monday	Tuesday	Wednesday	Thursday	Friday	Saturday
	Skyline Trail to Manning Park	1 — Capilano Canyon	2	3	4 — Deep Cove	5 — Helm Lake
6	7	8	9 — Panorama Ridge	10	11 — Black Tusk	12 — Black Mountain
13 — Cheakamus Lake	14	15 — Diamond Head	16 — Garibaldi Mountain	17 — Mount Seymour	18 — Seymour Creek	19 — Grouse Mountain
20 — Maplewood Flats	21	22 — Singing Pass to Whistler Mountain	23 — West Lion	24 — Ambleside Beach	25 — Crown Mountain	26 — Lynn Canyon
27 — Rainbow Lake / Goat Mountain	28 — Mamquam Lake	29 — Howe Sound Crest Trail	30	31 — Golden Ears Provincial Park	Sept. 1 — Shannon Falls	Sept. 2 — Cypress Bowl

Your Name, *Pinnacle Hiking Club*, 1090 Mountain Road, North Vancouver, BC V7H 1A9; Phone: (604) 555-3344

Newsletter for Savannah Arts Association

The Savannah Arts Association supports local artists and sponsors art exhibitions each year. As publicist for the association, you are in charge of creating and distributing a newsletter four times a year. To create the newsletter for Spring 2010, you need to **Create the Heading**, **Enter and Format the Text**, and **Format Columns**. The completed newsletter appears in Figure A-12 on page 13.

Activity:

Create the Heading

You need to create a heading for the newsletter that includes a picture and two WordArt objects.

Steps:

1. Open a blank Word document, click the **Page Layout tab**, click the **Margins button** in the Page Setup group, click **Narrow**, then save the document as **Newsletter for Savannah Arts Association** in the location where you store your Data Files

2. Click the **Insert tab**, click **Picture** in the Illustrations group, navigate to the location where you store your Data Files, then double-click **BlueCascade.jpg**

3. Click the **Size dialog box launcher** 🖾, change the Height to **2.73**, click the **Lock aspect ratio check box** to deselect it, change the Width to **7.6**, click **Close**, click **Text Wrapping** in the Arrange group, then click **Behind Text**

   With the layout changed to Behind Text, you can now overlay two WordArt objects and some text.

4. Click the **Insert tab**, click the **WordArt button** in the Text group, click the **upper-left selection**, type **2010**, then click **OK**

5. Click the **Shape Fill list arrow** 🗏 ▾ in the WordArt Styles group, click **Orange, Accent 6, Lighter 80%**, click the **Shape Outline list arrow** 🖉 ▾ in the WordArt Styles group, then click **No Outline**

6. Click **Text Wrapping** in the Arrange group, click **In Front of Text**, then drag the WordArt object to position it as shown in Figure A-7

   By selecting the In Front of Text layout, you convert the WordArt object from an inline graphic to a floating graphic that you can position easily.

7. Create another WordArt object with the text **Spring** using the same WordArt style but leaving the text outline and white fill, change the Text Wrapping to **In Front of Text**, then drag the object to position it as shown in Figure A-8

8. Press **[Ctrl][Home]**, type **Savannah Arts Association**, select the text, change the font to **Arial**, change the font size to **36**, then change the Before spacing to **12 pt**

9. Right-click the selected text, click the **Font Color list arrow** 🅰 ▾ on the Mini toolbar, click **White, Background 1**, apply **Bold** and **Italic,** press **[→]** once to deselect the text, save the document, then compare the completed heading to Figure A-9

Hint

Click the Page Layout tab to change the Before spacing.

FIGURE A-7: 2010 WordArt object positioned

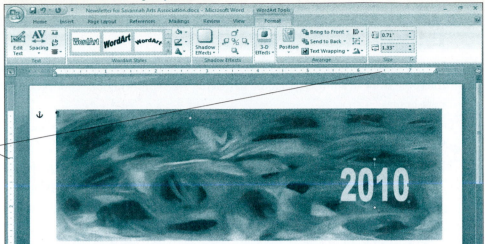

Position the WordArt object relative to 5.5 on the horizontal ruler bar and 1 on the vertical ruler bar

FIGURE A-8: Spring WordArt object positioned

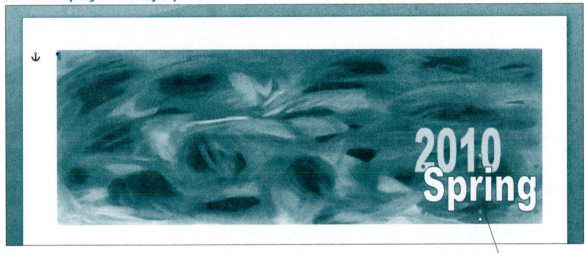

Use arrow keys to position the WordArt object precisely

FIGURE A-9: Completed newsletter heading

Activity:

Enter and Format the Text

The newsletter consists of three stories. First, you need to create a style that you can apply to each of the three story headings so that the newsletter has a unified look. Then, you need to enter text for the newsletter.

Steps:

1. Double-click in the left margin about **.5"** below the picture, click the **Home tab**, click the **Clear Formatting button in the Font group**, then, if necessary, press **[Enter]** once or twice more to move the insertion point down so it appears approximately **.5"** below the picture

2. Click the **Styles dialog box launcher** 🔲 in the Styles group to open the Styles task pane, click the **New Style button** 🔄 at the bottom of the Styles task pane, type **Newsletter Story** as the style name, click the **Style for following paragraph list arrow**, click **Normal**, select the **Arial Black font**, then select the **14-pt font size**

3. Click **Format** in the Create New Style from Formatting dialog box, click **Border**, then click the **Borders tab** if necessary

4. Click the **Width list arrow**, click **6 pt**, click the **Top Border button** 🔲 in the Preview area, click **OK**, then click **OK**

   The Newsletter Story style includes a solid line above the text.

5. Type **Upcoming Exhibitions**, then press **[Enter]**

   Note that the Normal style is automatically applied to the new paragraph because you selected Normal as the Style for following paragraph when you created the Newsletter Story style.

6. Close the Styles task pane, then type the text of the first story in the newsletter as shown in Figure A-10

7. Press **[Enter]** following "village," right-click at the insertion point location, click the **Change Styles button** 🔲 on the Mini toolbar, click **Newsletter Story**, type **Volunteer of the Season**, then press **[Enter]**

8. Type the text for the Volunteer story and the Featured Work heading and story as shown in Figure A-11

   Remember to format the Featured Work heading with the Newsletter Story style as shown in Figure A-11.

9. Click the **Review tab**, click the **Spelling & Grammar button** in the Proofing group, make any necessary corrections, then save the document

FIGURE A-10: **Text for the "Upcoming Exhibitions" story**

Upcoming·Exhibitions¶

Spring·2010·will·be·our·best·exhibition·season·ever!·The·Savannah·Arts·Association·is·proud·to·host·exhibitions·by·three· internationally·acclaimed·artists·who·all·call·Savannah·home.·First·up·on·April·2·is·Maria·Simpson·with·her·*Landscape· Rhythm*·exhibition.·This·intriguing·series·of·works·is·based·on·video·studies·of·the·unusual·and·historic·landscapes·that· Simpson·often·visited·in·France.·Simpson's·exhibition·runs·to·April·28.¶

Peter·Moore's·surreal·paintings·take·center·stage·in·the·gallery·from·May·1·to·May·25.·The·paintings·are·inspired·by·the· works·of·the·Italian·Metaphysical·painters·of·the·early·20th·century,·such·as·Giorgio·de·Chirico·and·Carlo·Carra.·Moore's· work·has·attracted·notice·throughout·the·United·States.·In·September,·his·work·will·be·featured·in·two·solo·exhibitions· in·New·York.¶

On·June·2,·photographer·Jay·Singh·presents·*My·Home·Town*,·an·exhibition·of·black-and-white·photographs·of·the·village· in·India·where·Singh·grew·up·before·immigrating·to·America·at·the·age·of·25.·The·haunting·photographs·take·the·viewer· into·the·very·soul·of·the·village.¶

FIGURE A-11: **Text for the "Volunteer" and "Featured work" stories**

Volunteer·of·the·Season¶

Janice·Brown·is·our·Volunteer·of·the·Season—the·Spring·Season·in·this·case!·On·more·than·one·occasion,·Janice·has· gone·above·and·beyond·the·call·of·duty·in·her·tireless·efforts·to·communicate·the·activities·of·the·Savannah·Arts· Association·to·the·public.·We·honor·her·this·season·because·of·her·incredible·contribution·to·our·recent·fund-raising· event.·Thanks·to·Janice,·the·Savannah·Arts·Association·raised·a·staggering·$50,000—that's·40%·higher·than·last·year's· total!·Janice·continues·to·inspire·all·of·us·with·her·entrepreneurial·spirit·and·her·enthusiasm·for·art.¶

Featured·Work¶

Each·season,·the·Savannah·Arts·Association·selects·the·painting·that·will·represent·the·association·in·all·its·advertising.· Shown·at·the·right·is·the·image·that·will·be·used·as·the·cover·photo·for·our·spring·ads·in·*Savannah·Arts,·Arts·Alive,*·and· *Art,·etc.*·Entitled·*Cote·de·Granite·Rose*,·this·luscious·canvas·is·the·work·of·Maria·Simpson.·Her·April·exhibition,·*Landscape· Rhythm*,·is·sure·to·be·a·big·hit·with·Savannah·art·lovers.·At·her·last·exhibition·with·the·association,·Maria·sold·every· single·canvas!¶

Activity:

Format Columns

You can achieve some interesting effects by using a variety of column styles to display text in a newsletter as shown in the completed newsletter (see Figure A-12). The "Upcoming Exhibitions" and "Volunteer of the Season" stories appear in two columns of equal width and the "Featured Work" story appears in one column at the bottom of the page. In addition, a picture is inserted into the "Featured Work" story.

Steps:

1. Press **[Ctrl][Home]** to move to the top of the newsletter, click to the left of the Upcoming Exhibitions heading (but don't select the heading), click the **Page Layout Tab**, click **Columns** in the Page Setup group, click **More Columns**, then click **Two**

2. Click the **Apply to list arrow**, click **This point forward**, then click **OK**
   By selecting This point forward, you set columns only from the current position of your insertion point to the end of the document.

3. Click at the beginning of paragraph 3 in the Upcoming Exhibitions story (begins with the text On June 2…), click **Breaks** in the Page Setup group, then click **Column**

4. Click to the left of the Featured Work heading to position the insertion point, click **Columns** in the Page Setup group, click **More Columns**, click **One**, click the **Apply to list arrow**, click **This point forward**, then click **OK**
   You have made the last story in the newsletter span one column.

5. Click the **Insert tab**, click **Picture**, navigate to the location where you store your Data Files, then double-click **GraniteRose.jpg**

6. Click **Picture Effects** in the Picture Styles group, point to **Bevel**, then select the **Angle Bevel style** (2nd row, far-left style)

7. Select the **contents of the Shape Height text box** in the Size group, type **1.3**, press **[Enter]**, click **Text Wrapping** in the Arrange group, click **Square**, then drag the picture to position it as shown in Figure A-12

8. Click the **Insert tab**, click the **Footer button** in the Header & Footer group, click **Blank**, press **[Delete]** twice to remove the placeholder and the extra paragraph mark, type and center the contact text as shown in Figure A-12, then exit the footer

9. Save the file, preview the completed newsletter, print a copy, then close the document

Additional Practice

For additional practice with the skills presented in this project, complete Independent Challenge 2.

Savannah Arts Association
2010 Spring

Upcoming Exhibitions

Spring 2010 will be our best exhibition season ever! The Savannah Arts Association is proud to host exhibitions by three internationally acclaimed artists who all call Savannah home. First up on April 2 is Maria Simpson with her *Landscape Rhythm* exhibition. This intriguing series of works is based on video studies of the unusual and historic landscapes that Simpson often visited in France. Simpson's exhibition runs to April 28.

Peter Moore's surreal paintings take center stage in the gallery from May 1 to May 25. The paintings are inspired by the works of the Italian Metaphysical painters of the early 20th century, such as Giorgio de Chirico and Carlo Carra. Moore's work has attracted notice throughout the United States. In September, his work will be featured in two solo exhibitions in New York.

On June 2, photographer Jay Singh presents *My Home Town*, an exhibition of black and white photographs of the village in India where Singh grew up before immigrating to America at the age of 25. The haunting photographs take the viewer into the very soul of the village.

Volunteer of the Season

Janice Brown is our Volunteer of the Season—the Spring Season in this case! On more than one occasion, Janice has gone above and beyond the call of duty in her tireless efforts to communicate the activities of the Savannah Arts Association to the public. We honor her this season because of her incredible contribution to our recent fund-raising event. Thanks to Janice, the Savannah Arts Association raised a staggering $50,000—that's 40% higher than last year's total! Janice continues to inspire all of us with her entrepreneurial spirit and her enthusiasm for art.

Featured Work

Each season, the Savannah Arts Association selects the painting that will represent the association in all its advertising. Shown at the right is the image that will be used as the cover photo for our spring ads in *Savannah Arts, Arts Alive,* and *Art, etc.* Entitled *Cote de Granite Rose*, this luscious canvas is the work of Maria Simpson. Her April exhibition, *Landscape Rhythm*, is sure to be a big hit with Savannah art lovers. At her last exhibition with the association, Maria sold every single canvas!

Your Name, Editor, Maple Building, 2000 Confederate Way, Savannah, GA, 30349; Phone: (770) 550-1889

Business Cards for José Alvarez

José Alvarez, a freelance writer from New York, has asked you to create his business cards. He wants you to combine text and graphics to make his business cards eye-catching. To create José's business cards, you need to **Create Labels and Enter Text**, **Add a WordArt Logo**, and **Add an Object and Print the Label Sheet**. The completed sheet of business cards is shown in Figure A-20 on page 19.

Activity:

Create Labels and Enter Text

You use a label sheet selected in the Labels Options dialog box as the basis for José's business cards.

Steps:

1. Open a blank Word document, click the **Mailings tab**, then click **Labels** in the Create group
   On the Labels tab of the Envelopes and Labels dialog box, you can select the size and type of label you need to create a sheet of business cards.

2. Click **Options**, click the **Label vendors list arrow**, then scroll to and click **Avery US Letter**

3. In the **Product number list box**, scroll to and click **5371**, click **Details**, verify that the Label height is **2"** and the Label width is **3.5"**, click **OK**, then click **OK**

4. Click **New Document**
   You click New Document because you want to show the label sheet as a table in which you can include the text and a WordArt object for the business card.

5. Type **Jos**
   You'll add the é next.

6. Click the **Insert tab**, click **Symbol** in the Symbols group, click **More Symbols**, select **(normal text)** as the Font type if necessary, scroll to the **é** as shown in Figure A-13, click **é**, click **Insert**, then click **Close**

7. Press **[Spacebar]** once, type **Alvarez**, save the document as **Business Cards for Jose Alvarez** in the location where you store your Data Files, press **[Enter]** once, then type the remaining text for the business card as shown in Figure A-14

8. Click in the first line, click the **Page Layout tab**, change the Before spacing to **36 pt**, select the six lines of text, click the **Home tab**, click the **Align Text Right button** ▤ in the Paragraph group, enhance **José Alvarez** with **Bold** and a font size of **14 pt**, change the font size of the remaining text to **10 pt**, then enhance **Freelance Writer** with **Italic**

9. Select all six lines of text, click the **Page Layout tab**, change the Right indent to **0.4"**, deselect the text, save the document, then compare the business card to Figure A-15

FIGURE A-13: Symbol dialog box

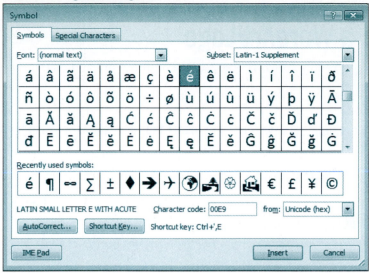

FIGURE A-14 : Text for buisness card

FIGURE A-15: Business card text formatted

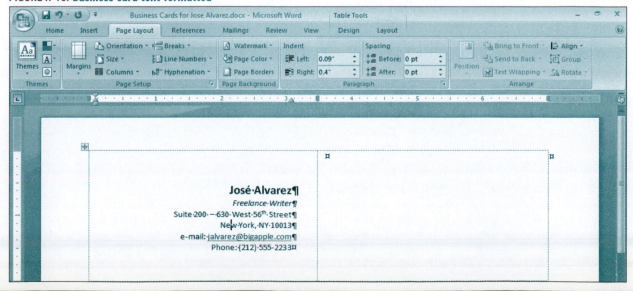

Activity:

Add a WordArt Logo

You need to add a WordArt object to the business card and then modify it.

Steps:

1. Click to the left of José, click the **Insert tab**, then click the **WordArt button** in the Text group
   The WordArt Gallery opens.

2. Select **WordArt style 14** (third row, second column) as shown in Figure A-16

3. In the Edit WordArt Text dialog box, type **JA**, change the font to **Comic Sans MS** and apply **Bold**, then click **OK**
   Black sizing handles appear around the WordArt object to indicate it is selected, and the WordArt Tools Format tab appears.

4. Click the **Change WordArt Shape button** ▲ in the WordArt Styles group to show the WordArt Shape Gallery, then click the **Slant Up** shape as shown in Figure A-17

5. Select the contents of the Height text box in the Size group, type **.5**, press **[Enter]**, change the Width to **.5**, click the **Text Wrapping button** in the Arrange group, click **More Layout Options**, click **Square**, click the **Right only option button**, then click **OK**
   By selecting the Square layout, you convert the WordArt object from an inline graphic to a floating graphic that you can position easily on the business card.

6. With the WordArt object still selected, click the **Shadow Effects button** in the Shadow Effects group, then under Additional Shadow Styles, select **Shadow Style 14**
   The WordArt object is complete.

7. Click next to the J in José, click the **Page Layout tab**, then change the Before Spacing to **48 pt**

8. Drag the **WordArt object** to the upper-left corner of the first business card as shown in Figure A-18

9. Click away from the WordArt object, then save the document

Clues to Use

Editing a WordArt object

You can modify a WordArt object in many ways by selecting different shapes, experimenting with different fill and line color options, and applying various shadow and 3D styles. To modify an existing WordArt object, double-click it to show the WordArt Tools Format tab, then select the tools you require. You can apply one of the preset WordArt styles by clicking the More button in the WordArt Styles group and selecting another style from the WordArt Gallery, then you can modify the style by selecting new options from the Shadow Effects group. You use the tools in the Text group to modify text spacing and alignment of the text within the WordArt object.

FIGURE A-16: WordArt Gallery

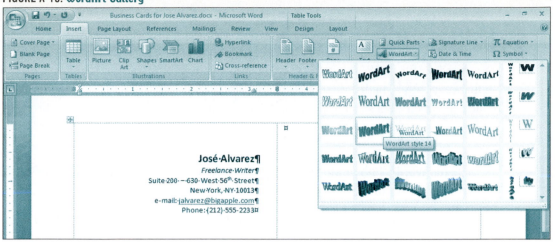

FIGURE A-17: Slant Up shape selected

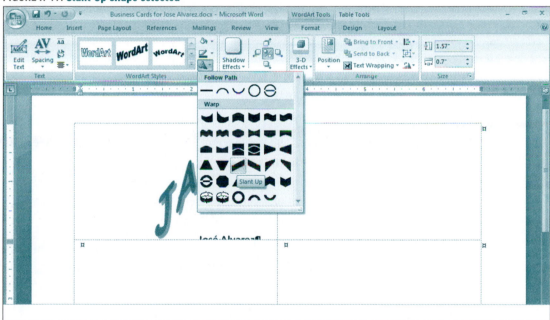

FIGURE A-18: Completed WordArt object

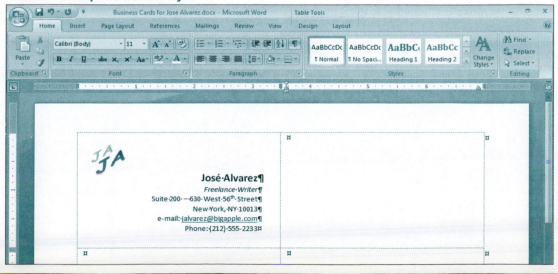

Activity:

Add an Object and Print the Label Sheet

You need to fill the WordArt with a new shaded fill, add a triangle shape to José's business card, enhance it with a shaded fill, then print the label sheet, which is actually structured as a Word table. The completed label sheet is shown in Figure A-20.

Steps:

1. Click the **WordArt object** to select it, click the **WordArt Tools Format tab**, click the **Shape Fill list arrow** in the WordArt Styles group, then select **Purple, Accent 4, Darker 25%**

2. Click the **Insert tab**, click **Shapes** in the Illustrations group, then click the **Right Triangle shape** in the top row of the Basic Shapes section

3. Point to the lower-left corner of the business card, then click and drag to draw a triangle (any size)

4. Change the height of the triangle to **1.2"** and the Width to **1.6"**, then use your mouse and arrow keys to position the triangle so the left and bottom edges are even with the left and bottom edges of the business card as shown in Figure A-19

5. With the object selected, click the **More button** ⬇ in the Shape Styles group, select **Diagonal Gradient - Accent 4** (sixth row, fifth from left), click the **Shape Outline list arrow** in the Shape Styles group, then click **No Outline**

6. Click away from the triangle to deselect it, click the **Home tab**, click the **Change Styles button** in the Styles group, point to **Colors**, move your mouse over each color set to see the effect on the business card, then select the **Urban color set**

   The business card you have created includes two graphics: the WordArt object and the triangle. As a result, you cannot use the Envelopes and Labels dialog box to print the label. Instead, you need to copy and paste the label with its objects to the other table cells and use the standard Print command.

7. With the insertion point in the upper-left table cell, click the **Table Tools Layout tab**, click **Select** in the Table group, click **Select Cell**, click the **Home tab**, click the **Copy button** 📋 in the Clipboard group, click in the upper-right table cell, then click the **Paste button** in the Clipboard group

8. Click each blank table cell and use the Paste button to paste the card in each of the other cells, click after the telephone number on the lower-right card, press **[Enter]**, change the font to **8 pt**, then type your name

9. Save the document, preview it, print a copy, then close it

   A complete sheet of cards is printed as shown in Figure A-20. If José were really printing his business cards, he would insert several sheets of the perforated cards he purchased into his printer before he clicked the Print button.

Additional Practice

For additional practice with the skills presented in this project, complete Independent Challenge 3.

FIGURE A-19: Triangle drawn, sized, and positioned

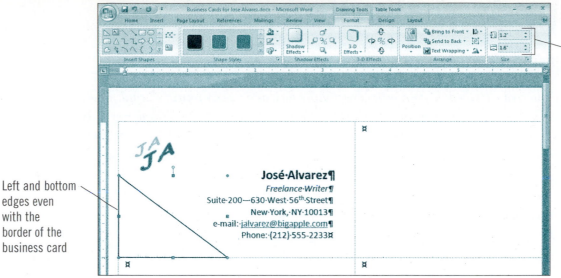

Height and width measurements

Left and bottom edges even with the border of the business card

FIGURE A-20: Completed sheet of business cards

Independent Challenges

INDEPENDENT CHALLENGE 1

Use the Table feature to create a schedule for a series of activities such as a weekly course schedule or a monthly calendar of events. For example, you could create a schedule that displays all the concerts or plays offered over a six-month period at a local theater, or you could create your personal weekly schedule that includes all your work, school, and leisure activities. To help you determine the information required for your schedule, follow the directions provided below.

1. Determine the purpose of your schedule. Do you want to keep track of your courses each week, or create your personal fitness schedule, or perhaps create a calendar of events for a local community group? Enter the purpose of your schedule in the box below:

   Schedule Purpose:_____

2. Determine the column and row labels required for your schedule. If you are creating a weekly schedule, your column labels will be the days of the week; if you are creating a monthly schedule, your column labels will be the months of the year. List the column and row labels required for your schedule in the box below.

   Column Labels: _____

   Row Labels: _____

3. Calculate the total number of rows and columns required to complete your schedule. For example, if you are creating a weekly schedule, you will need to create a table consisting of eight columns. Column 1 will contain the time increments (e.g., 8:00 to 9:00) and columns 2 through 8 will contain the days of the week.

4. Set up your document so that it prints in landscape orientation. Change the margins, if you wish.

5. Save the document as **My Schedule** to the location where you are storing the files for this book.

6. Create the table. Note that you can add new rows to the table by clicking in the last cell of the last row, then pressing [Tab]. You can add columns to the table by selecting a column, clicking the Table Tools Layout tab, then selecting the appropriate option from the Rows and Columns group.

7. Enter the information required for your schedule. Use the Copy and Paste features to minimize repetitive typing.

8. Shade selected cells with one or more shading colors. Use varying shades of the same Accent color. Remember that you can use the [Ctrl] key to select and then fill nonadjacent cells with the same shading color.

9. Create an attractive heading for your schedule, using text that describes the content of the schedule (such as "My Fitness Schedule" or "Monthly Events Calendar").

10. Include a clip-art picture that you have modified in some way. For example, you could flip the picture horizontally.

11. Size and position the clip-art picture in an attractive location (use a text-wrapping option).

12. Enter your name at the bottom of the document, check the spelling and grammar, then print a copy.

INDEPENDENT CHALLENGE 2

Adapt the newsletter you created in Project 2 to present interesting stories about an organization or company of your choice. For example, you could choose to describe the latest activities of a club you're involved in or you could develop a newsletter for customers of a company. Here are some directions for creating your newsletter:

1. Determine the name of your company or organization and the types of activities you'd like to write about.
2. Develop copy for two or three stories that would be of interest to the people who would read your newsletter. For example, if you've created a newsletter for a performing arts group such as a community choir, you could include stories such as "Fundraising News," "Special Event Concert," and "Guest Conductor Profile."
3. Set up your document with .5" margins on all four sides.
4. Create an attractive heading for your newsletter. The heading should include the name of the company or organization and the date of the newsletter publication. You may wish to adapt the heading you created for the Savannah Arts Association's newsletter. If you wish, include a WordArt object and a graphic in the heading. You can choose to include a photograph or a clip-art image.
5. Following the heading, enter text for the two or three stories you have written.
6. Create a new style for the story headings. If you wish, include a border line and shading.
7. Format the stories in columns. You can choose to format the entire newsletter in two or three columns, or you can format two of the stories in two columns and one story in one column as you did with the Savannah Arts Association's newsletter. Experiment with various combinations until you are satisfied with the overall appearance of your newsletter.
8. Include one or two pictures in the body of your newsletter. Enhance pictures with one of the preset Picture Styles, or apply a Picture Effect such as a Bevel or Glow effect.
9. Include your name as the editor of the newsletter somewhere on the document, then check the spelling and grammar.
10. Preview the newsletter and fit it to one page as necessary, save the newsletter as **My Newsletter** in the location where you store your Data Files, then print the completed newsletter.

INDEPENDENT CHALLENGE 3

Use a business card label product, such as the Avery 5371 label, available in the Envelopes and Labels dialog box, to create a sheet of business cards for yourself. Follow the directions to create your business cards:

1. Draw a business card-sized rectangle on a piece of paper, and then spend some time experimenting with different designs for your business card. For example, you could right-align your name and address and include a WordArt logo of your initials in the upper-left corner of the business card, or you could center your name and address on only two lines along the bottom of the business card, then insert the logo centered in the middle of the business card. Draw several versions of your business card until you find the one that looks right.

2. From the Mailings tab, open the Envelopes and Labels dialog box, select one of the Business Card products from the list of available label products in the Label Options dialog box, click OK, verify that the labels will print on a full sheet, then click New Document.

3. Enter your name, your title if you have one, and address on the business card. Apply formatting to selected text. For example, you may want your name to appear in a larger font and in bold.

4. Create an attractive WordArt logo based on your initials. Experiment with some of the many options available for formatting a WordArt object. For example, you can modify the shading and line color, add or remove a shadow, or add a 3D effect.

5. Format the WordArt object so that the text wrapping is Square.

6. Reduce the size of the logo and position it attractively on the business card.

7. From the Page Layout tab, modify the Before or After Paragraph spacing of the text, depending on where you've inserted the WordArt logo. You may need to experiment to find the best way to position the text in relation to the WordArt logo.

8. Draw a shape on the business card, then fill it with a shape style of your choice.

9. Change the color scheme for the business cards, copy the text and graphics to all the other labels on the page, save the document as **My Business Cards** to the location where you are storing the files for this book.

10. Print your sheet of business cards. If possible, print the cards on a sheet of perforated business card stock. +

INDEPENDENT CHALLENGE 4

Type the text for the confirmation letter shown in Figure A-21, then enhance the letter as directed. Note that the purpose of a confirmation letter is to confirm arrangements related to a specific event or agreement made between two companies or organizations. In the confirmation letter below, Midlands Communications, a company based in the United Kingdom, confirms a seminar they are hosting for employees of the Thames Bank.

1. Type the text as shown in Figure A-21. Note that you will find the £ symbol in the (normal text) font in the Symbol dialog box.

2. Replace the text "Midlands Communications, Inc." at the top of the document with a WordArt object. Change the fill color or texture of the WordArt object and modify the 3D or shadow settings. Your goal is to make the WordArt object different from the preset style you selected.

3. Use your own judgment to enhance the letter attractively, then check spelling and grammar.

4. View the letter in the Print Preview screen, then fit the letter on one page.

5. Save the letter as **Confirmation Letter** to the location where you are storing the files for this book, then print a copy.

Midlands Communications

1603 Woodley Road, Reading, Berkshire, RG22 2RP, England
www.midlandscommunications.co.uk

Current Date

Gary McGraw
Personnel Manager
Thames Bank: Basingstoke Branch
24 London Road
Reading, Berkshire RG30 1TN

Dear Mr. McGraw,

Thank you for your letter of [specify a date one week prior to the current date] confirming a one-day communications seminar at the Basingstoke Branch of the Thames Bank. My colleague, Mr. Darryl Shaw, will be conducting the seminar and supplying all the materials the participants will require.

Here again are the seminar details:

Date:	[specify a date one month after the current date]
Time:	0900 to 1700
Location:	2nd Floor, Administration Building, Reading University, Whiteknights Campus
Cost:	£3000 for 20 participants.

As we discussed, the communications seminar will include the following activities:

1. Warm-up exercises to stimulate a relaxed atmosphere and to determine the general level of communication skills among the participants.
2. Analysis of various communications situations to assess writing strengths and weaknesses.
3. Intensive "hands-on" practice in the communication of clear and effective sales, training, and informational presentations.

I'm very much looking forward to an exciting seminar. Thank you again, Ms. Shaw, for your interest in Midlands Communications, Inc. If you have any further questions, please call me at 0118 555 2222.

Sincerely,

Your Name
President

Visual Workshop

Create the letterhead shown in Figure A-22 in a new document. Save the document as **Ocean Adventures Letterhead** to the location where you store your Data Files for this book. Reduce the size of the WordArt object to .7" high and 4" wide, then change the layout to match the figure. Enhance the WordArt object by experimenting with texture, shadows, and character spacing. (*Hint*: To change the texture field of the object, click the Shape Fill list arrow in the WordArt Styles group, point to Texture, then select the appropriate texture.) Find the clip-art picture by searching the Clip Organizer. If you can't find the picture shown, choose a similar picture. Change the text wrapping of the clip-art picture to Square and left-aligned, then flip the picture horizontally. Reduce the height of the drawing canvas containing the dolphin so that it appears as shown in Figure A-22. Print a copy, save the document, then close the document and exit Word.

FIGURE A-22: Completed letterhead

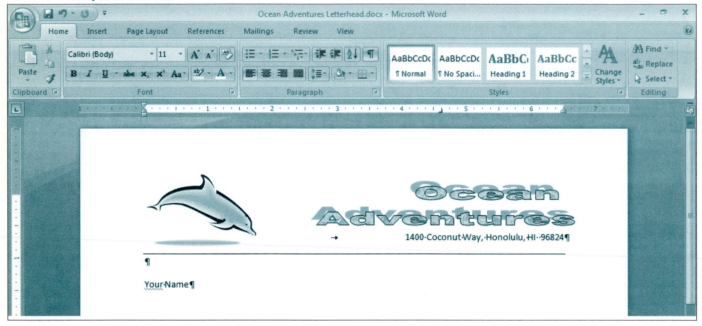

Microsoft
► Word
Projects

Unit **B**

Word Projects II

In This Unit You Will Create the Following:

 ► **Five-Page Proposal**

 ► **Six-Panel Brochure**

 ► **One-Page Resume**

With Microsoft Word, you can design multiple-page documents such as proposals and reports that include page numbers, headers and footers, charts and diagrams, and an automatically generated table of contents. You can also use Word to create multipanel brochures containing text formatted in columns, and you can insert a variety of graphics, including clip-art pictures, drawn shapes, and SmartArt graphics. In this unit, you will apply your Microsoft Word skills to modify styles, generate a table of contents, add section breaks, insert a footnote, format text in columns, create a SmartArt diagram, and modify clip-art pictures.

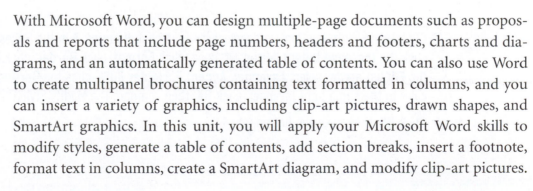

Five-Page Proposal for Marina College

The dean of Marina College in Seattle has asked the Business Department to submit a proposal to request approval for a new program to train office administrators. You will **Set up the Document**, **Create Page 1**, **Create Page 2**, **Create Pages 3 and 4**, and **Create the Table of Contents and Cover Page**. Figures B-3 through B-7 on pages 29 through 35 show the five pages of the completed proposal.

Activity:

Set Up the Document

You need to insert a header and a footer, and then modify styles in the Modern Quick Style set.

Steps:

Trouble

Click the Show/Hide ¶ button ▛ to show the paragraph marks if necessary, and click the View Ruler button ▣ if necessary to show the ruler.

1. Start Word, click the **Insert tab**, click the **Header button** in the Header & Footer group, click the **Blank style**, type **Executive Assistant Program Proposal**, press **[Tab]** twice, click the **Date & Time button** in the Insert group, click the style that corresponds to April 20, 2010, then click **OK**

2. Click the **Go To Footer button** in the Navigation group, type your name, then press **[Tab]** twice

3. Click the **Page Number button** in the Header & Footer group, point to **Current Position**, select the **Plain Number style**, click the **Close Header and Footer button** in the Close group, then save the document as **Marina College Proposal** in the location where you store your Data Files

4. Click the **Change Styles button** in the Styles group, point to **Style Set**, then click **Modern**

5. Click the **Heading 1** style in the Styles gallery, type **Introduction**, press **[Enter]**, click the **Change Styles button** in the Styles group, point to **Colors**, then click **Paper**

6. Select **Introduction**, change the font size to **14 pt**, click the **Shading list arrow** in the Paragraph group, click **Lavender, Accent 5, Darker 50%**, click the **Borders list arrow** in the Paragraph group, click **Borders and Shading**, click the **Color list arrow**, select the same lavender color, then click **OK**

Hint

The method you used in Step 7 to update the Heading 1 style is a shortcut method that works well when you need to make several changes at once to the formatting associated with a style.

7. Right-click **Introduction**, point to **Styles**, then click **Update Heading 1 to Match Selection** as shown in Figure B-1

8. Click below "Introduction" to deselect it, right-click **Heading 2** in the Styles gallery, click **Modify**, click the **Increase Indent button** ▤ once, click **Format**, click **Border**, click the **Shading tab**, click the **Fill list arrow**, select **Lavender, Accent 5, Lighter 80%**, click the **Borders tab**, change the line color to the same light lavender, click **OK**, then compare the Modify Style dialog box to Figure B-2

9. Click **OK**, then save the document

FIGURE B-1: Updating the Heading 1 style

Paragraph formatted with a new shading style and border color

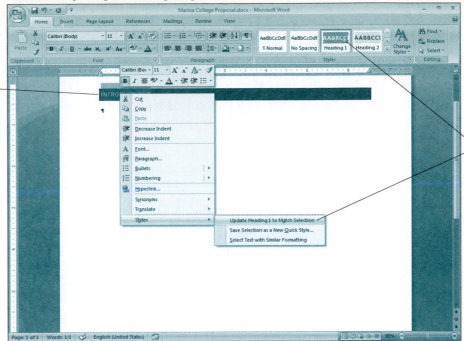

Heading 1 is updated when you click Update Heading 1 to Match Selection

FIGURE B-2: Heading 2 style modified

Click Format to access a wide range of formatting options

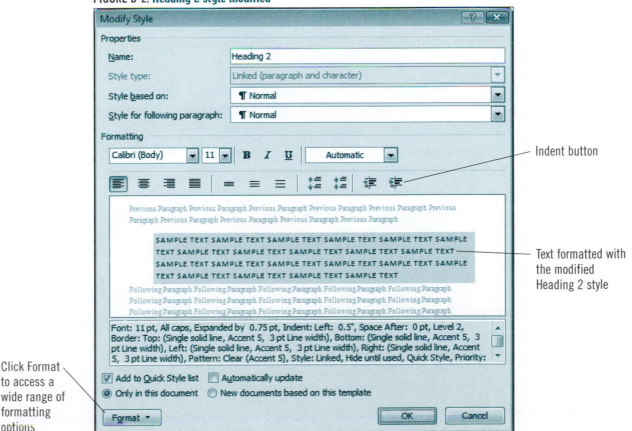

Indent button

Text formatted with the modified Heading 2 style

Activity:

Create Page 1

First, you need to create a new style to format the proposal text. The new style, which you name Proposal Text, changes the text indent to .5, the line spacing to 1.5, and the before paragraph spacing to 12 pt. Then, you need to enter the text required for page 1 and create a citation. The completed page 1 is shown in Figure B-3.

Steps:

1. Click the **Styles dialog box launcher** , click the **New Style button** at the bottom of the task pane, then type **Proposal Text** as the style name

2. Select the **11 pt** font size, click the **1.5 Space button** , click the **Increase Paragraph Spacing button** once, click the **Increase Indent button** , then click **OK**

   All text formatted with the new Proposal Text style will have 1.5 spacing between lines, 12-pt spacing between paragraphs, and be indented .5".

3. Close the Styles task pane, then type the introductory paragraph as shown in Figure B-3

4. Press **[Enter]**, click **Heading 1** in the Styles gallery, type **Scope of the Program**, press **[Enter]**, click **Proposal Text** in the Styles gallery, then type the next paragraph as shown in Figure B-3

5. Press **[Enter]**, select the **Heading 2** style from the Styles gallery, type **Description of Need**, then press **[Enter]**

6. Select the **Proposal Text style**, then type the next two paragraphs as shown in Figure B-3

7. Click the **References tab**, click the **Insert Footnote button** in the Footnotes group, then type the footnote text as shown in Figure B-3

8. Click the **Home tab**, click the **Styles dialog box launcher** , click the **Style Inspector button** at the bottom of the Styles task pane, then click the **Reveal Formatting button** in the Style Inspector task pane

   When text is formatted with a style that is not included in the Styles gallery, you can determine and then modify the formats in the Reveal Formatting task pane.

9. Click **Paragraph Style** in the Paragraph section of the Reveal Formatting task pane, click **Modify**, click the **Increase Indent button** , change the font size to **11 pt**, click **OK**, click **Apply**, close all open task panes, click anywhere in the text to exit the footnote area, then save the document

Trouble

If Heading 2 is not visible in the Styles gallery, click the Gallery's down scroll arrow or the More button.

Word

Executive Assistant Program Proposal   Current Date

INTRODUCTION

This proposal presents a request to develop the Executive Assistant program to train students for employment as Administrative and Executive Assistants, Office Managers, and Office Administrators. Included in the proposal is a discussion of three factors related to the development of the program: Scope of the Program, Proposed Courses, and Funding Requirements. If approved, the Coordinator of the Business Department will develop course outlines and begin to recruit students for entry into the program in September 2010.

SCOPE OF THE PROGRAM

The proposed program will provide students with extensive training in computer applications and business-related skills. The goal of the program is to train students for employment. The program will run for nine months from September to May and include a two-week work practicum. Students who graduate from the program will be prepared to enter the workforce.

DESCRIPTION OF NEED

At present, none of the local community colleges offers an Executive Assistant program. Westview College, the closest competitor to Marina College, offers an Administrative Assistant program that primarily attracts students who have just graduated from high school. The proposed Executive Assistant program will target candidates who have either several years of college or considerable work experience. These candidates require practical skills that will help them gain employment in an office environment.

The marketing survey conducted by Martha Wise, Coordinator of the Business Department, is attached to this proposal.[1]

---

[1] Personnel agencies, human resources professionals, and businesspeople responded to the survey. The results show a need for candidates with the skills offered by the Executive Assistant program.

Your Name   1

Activity:

Create Page 2

You need to insert a page break so that the text and headings you enter next appear on page 2. When you have finished entering the text and headings, you insert the table for the list of courses and enclose it in a rounded rectangle. The completed page 2 is shown in Figure B-4.

Steps:

1. Click at the **end of the last paragraph** on page 1 after the footnote reference number, click the **Page Layout tab**, click **Breaks** in the Page Setup group, click **Page**, click the **Home tab**, select the **Heading 1** style, type **Proposed Courses**, then press **[Enter]**

2. Select the **Proposal Text style**, then enter and format the text required for the rest of page 2, except the table in the Course Descriptions section as shown in Figure B-4

   Remember to format the two subheadings with the Heading 2 style and the paragraphs of text with the Proposal Text style.

3. Press **[Enter]** following "Executive Assistant program.", click the **Insert tab**, click the **Table button** in the Tables group, click **Insert Table**, type **2**, press **[Tab]**, type **9**, click **OK**, then enter the text for the table as shown in Figure B-4

   The text will wrap to page 4. You'll fix this problem in the next step.

4. Scroll up to the top of the table, move the pointer over the **upper-left corner** of the table to display the **table move handle** ⊞, then click ⊞ to select the entire table

5. Drag the **left edge** of the table to the right to reduce the width of column 1 to approximately **1.5"**, double-click the **right edge** of the table to increase the width of column 2 so none of the lines wrap, click the **More button** ▾ in the Table Styles group to show the selection of table styles, then click **Medium Shading 1 - Accent 5** (fourth row, lavender)

6. With the table still selected, click the **Page Layout tab**, reduce both the Before and After Paragraph Spacing in the Paragraph group to **0**, click the **Home tab**, then click the **Center button** ▤ in the Paragraph group

7. Click above the table to deselect it, click the **View tab**, click the **Zoom button** in the Zoom group, click the **75% option button**, then click **OK**

   In 75 percent view, you can easily see the entire table.

8. Click the **Insert tab**, click the **Shapes button** in the Illustrations group, then click the **Rounded Rectangle button** (top row in the Basic Shapes section)

9. Drag the mouse to draw a rounded rectangle (any size), click the **Shape Fill list arrow** ▨ ▾ in the Shape Styles group, click **No Fill**, use your mouse to adjust the size and position of the rounded rectangle so that it encloses the table like a border as shown in Figure B-4, then save the document

Hint

You can use your arrow keys to position the rectangle precisely.

Executive Assistant Program Proposal   Current Date

PROPOSED COURSES

Mark Trent, an instructor in the Business Department, developed eight new courses for the proposed Executive Assistant program. He was assisted by Dr. Wendy Knutson, a Management Consultant and former faculty member at Marina College.

COURSE OVERVIEW

Students in the proposed Executive Assistant program will take eight courses over two terms: September to December and January to May. The courses are evenly divided between theory-based and application-based courses. During the program, students become proficient in several software applications. In addition, students improve their written and oral communication skills, develop project management skills, and learn how to plan and run special events.

COURSE DESCRIPTIONS

The following table lists the eight courses offered to students in the proposed Executive Assistant program.

Course	Description
Basic Business Skills	Learn the fundamentals of business
Document Design	Develop expert-level skills in Microsoft Word
Project Management	Learn the fundamentals of project management
Budgeting & Analysis	Develop spreadsheet skills using Microsoft Excel
Web Page Design	Use HTML to design Web pages
Event Planning	Organize special events
Data Management	Develop database skills using Microsoft Access
Communications	Develop written and oral communication skills

Your Name   2

Activity:

Create Pages 3 and 4

You need to include a radial diagram that illustrates the various sources of revenue required to run the Executive Assistant program. In addition, you need to include information about estimated expenses and a conclusion. The completed page 3 is shown in Figure B-5.

Steps:

1. Change the zoom to 100%, add a page break at the bottom of page 2, click at the top of page 3, click the **Home tab**, select the **Heading 1** style, type **Funding Requirements**, then enter the headings and text required for the Estimated Costs and Estimated Revenue sections as shown in Figure B-5
   Remember to format the two subheadings with the Heading 2 style and the paragraphs of text with the Proposal Text style.

2. Press **[Enter]**, click the **Insert tab**, click the **SmartArt button** in the Illustrations group, then click **Cycle**

3. Click the **Basic Radial diagram** (third row, second column), then click **OK**
   A diagram with five circles is inserted, and the SmartArt Tools Design and Format tabs appear, with the Design tab selected.

4. Click in the **middle circle**, type **Funding Sources**, click the **Add Shape button** in the Create Graphic group to insert a new circle, then enter text in the five perimeter circles as shown in Figure B-5

5. Click the **SmartArt Styles More button** ⯆ in the SmartArt Styles group, click the **Polished style** in the 3-D section, click the **Change Colors button** in the SmartArt Styles group, then click **Colorful - Accent Colors** (the leftmost style in the Colorful group)

6. Click the **SmartArt Tools Format tab**, click the **Size button**, set the height at **3.2"**, then press **[Enter]**

7. Click the **Home tab**, click a white area of the diagram, then click the **Bold button** **B** in the Font group
   All the text in the SmartArt diagram is formatted with bold.

8. Close the SmartArt task pane if necessary, double-click at the left margin below the diagram, type **Conclusion** and apply the **Heading 1** style, enter the concluding paragraph in the Proposal Text style as shown in Figure B-5, then save the document

Executive Assistant Program Proposal   Current Date

FUNDING REQUIREMENTS

ESTIMATED COSTS

The total estimated cost for the proposed program is $138,000 broken down as follows: $80,000 for faulty (based on a $10,000 cost per course), $35,000 for administrative support, $10,000 for advertising, and $13,000 for new software.

ESTIMATED REVENUE

The radial diagram shown below displays the various funding sources available.

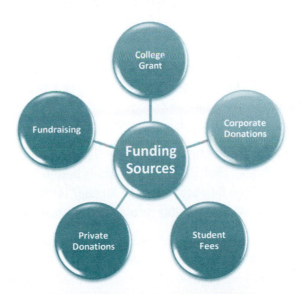

CONCLUSION

The Executive Assistant program will enroll 36 students at a cost of $3,000 per student for total fees of $108,000. The remaining funding should break down as follows: College Grant; $15,000, Corporate and Private Donations: $10,000, and Fundraising: $5,000.

Your Name   3

Activity:

Create the Table of Contents and Cover Page

You need to insert a section break above the first page of the proposal text, generate a table of contents, and create a cover page.

Steps:

Hint

The table of contents is automatically generated based on the styles you applied to the various headings.

Hint

By deselecting the Link to Previous button in section 3, you ensure that any changes you make to the header and footer in section 2 will not affect the header and footer in section 3.

Additional Practice

For additional practice with the skills presented in this project, complete Independent Challenge 1.

1. Press **[Ctrl][Home]**, click the **Page Layout tab**, click **Breaks**, click **Next Page**, press **[Ctrl][Home]**, click the **Home tab**, then click the **Clear Formatting button** in the Font group

2. Type **Table of Contents**, press **[Enter]** four times, then enhance the Table of Contents title with **Bold**, a font size of **16 pt**, and **Center alignment**

3. Click at the second paragraph mark below "Table of Contents," click the **References tab**, click the **Table of Contents button** in the Table of Contents group, click **Insert Table of Contents**, click the **Formats list arrow**, click **Formal**, then click **OK**

4. Press **[Ctrl][Home]**, insert another **Next Page section break**, move to the top of the document again, click the **Insert tab**, click the **Header button**, click **Edit Header**, then click the **Different First Page check box** in the Options group to select it
   This step returns the header and footer on the first page to blank.

5. Click the **Next Section button** twice in the Navigation group to move to the header for section 3 (which contains the proposal text), click the **Link to Previous button** in the Navigation group to deselect it, click the **Go to Footer button**, click the **Link to Previous button** to deselect it, click the **Page Number button** in the Header & Footer group, click **Format Page Numbers**, click the **Start at option button**, verify that "1" appears in the Start at text box, then click **OK**

6. Click the **Previous Section button** in the Navigation group to move to the footer for section 2 (the table of contents), click the **Link to Previous button** to deselect it, click the **Page Number button**, click **Format Page Numbers**, click the **Number format list arrow**, click the **i, ii, iii** number format, click the **Start at option button**, verify that "i" appears, then click **OK**

7. Go to the header, click to the left of the header text to select it, press **[Delete]**, then click the **Close Header and Footer button** in the Close group
   The table of contents page appears in its own section. You can delete the header text without deleting it from the rest of the proposal text because you deselected Link to Previous in section 3.

8. Scroll to and then right-click the **table of contents**, click **Update Field**, click the **Update entire table option button**, click **OK**, deselect the table of contents, then compare it to Figure B-6

9. Scroll the document, verify that "i" appears in the footer on the Table of Contents page and "1" appears in the footer on the first page of the text, press **[Ctrl][Home]**, click the **Insert tab**, click **Cover Page** in the Pages group, select the **Pinstripes** style, enter text in the content controls as shown in Figure B-7, save the document, print a copy, then close the document

FIGURE B-6: Completed table of contents

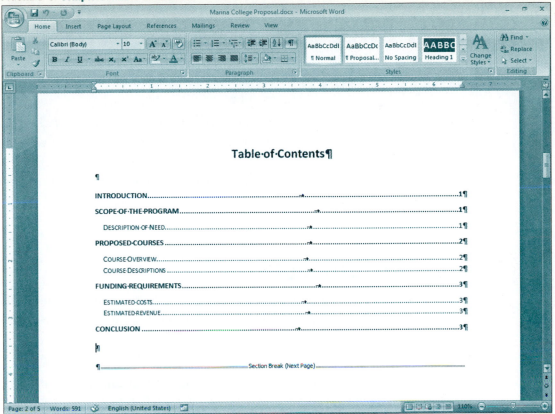

FIGURE B-7: Completed title page with the Pinstripes style

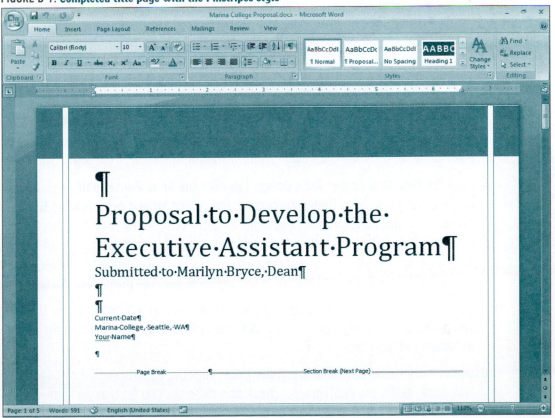

Six-Panel Brochure for British Castle Tours

You need to create a six-panel brochure on tours of the United Kingdom. Page 1 of the document consists of the inside three panels of the brochure (panels 1, 2, and 3), and page 2 consists of the folded-over panel, the back panel, and the front panel (panels 4, 5, and 6). To create the brochure for British Castle Tours, you need to **Set Up the Brochure**, **Create Page 1**, and then **Create Page 2**. The completed brochure is shown in Figure B-10 and Figure B-11 on pages 39 and 41.

Activity:

Set Up the Brochure

You need to set up the brochure in landscape orientation, create a header and footer that appear only on the first page of the brochure, and then insert and modify a clip-art picture in the footer.

Steps:

1. Open a new blank document in Word, click the **Page Layout tab**, select **Landscape orientation**, select the **Narrow** margin setting (all four margins at 0.5''), then save the document as **British Castle Tours Brochure** in the location where you store your Data Files

2. Click the **Home tab**, right-click **Normal** in the Styles gallery, modify the Normal style so that the font is **Arial**, then modify the Heading 1 style so the font is **Arial** and the font size is **16 pt**

3. Switch to **Page Width** view, insert a header using the Blank style, then click the **Different First Page check box** in the Options group to select it

4. Click the **Insert tab**, click the **Shapes button** in the Illustrations group, click the **Line button** ⬈, hold down **[Shift]**, then draw a **straight line** in the header to the right margin as shown in Figure B-8

5. With the line still selected, click the **Shape Outline list arrow** ✎▾, click **Blue, Accent 1, Darker 50%**, click ✎▾ again, click **Pattern**, select the **Light upward diagonal pattern** (second row of the third column), click **OK**, click ✎▾, point to **Weight**, then select the **6 pt** style

6. Click the **Header & Footer Tools Design tab**, click the **Go to Footer button**, click the **Clip Art button** in the Insert group, type **United Kingdom** in the Search for text box, click the **Results should be list arrow**, click the **Photographs check box** to deselect it, verify that All collections appears in the Search in text box, click **Go**, then find and insert the picture of the map shown in Figure B-9

   You will need to scroll down to find the picture, which shows the United Kingdom map filled with green shading. When you insert the picture, it will appear larger than the picture shown in Figure B-9.

7. Select the contents of the **Height text box** in the Size group, enter **1''** as the height, click **Text Wrapping** in the Arrange group, click **In Front of Text**, then drag the clip-art picture to position it as shown in Figure B-9

8. Double-click in the document to exit the footer, click the **Results should be list arrow** in the Clip Art task pane, select the **Photographs check box**, close the Clip Art task pane, then save the document

FIGURE B-8: Drawing a line

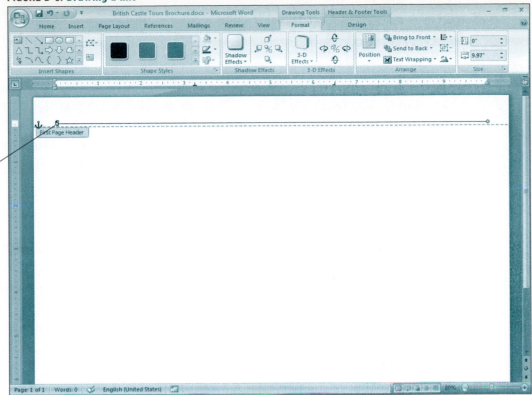

Start drawing
the line here

FIGURE B-9: First page footer

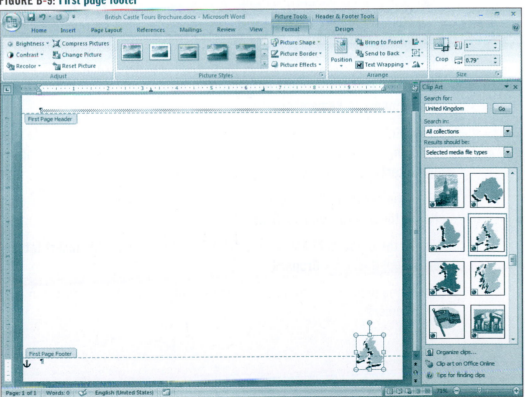

Activity:

Create Page 1

Although many brochures display all information in a three-column format, you decide to create a more interesting effect by formatting the text in two columns of uneven width. Page 1 of the British Castle Tours brochure appears in Figure B-10. As you can see, the text appears in two columns of uneven width. Column 1 is about 3" wide, and column 2 is a little more than double that width. You need to format the columns, then enter the text for columns 1 and 2. After you create the text for column 1, you need to insert and modify a clip-art picture, and after you create the text for column 2, you need to insert drop caps to spell "Castle."

Steps:

1. With the insertion point positioned at the top of the document, click the **Page Layout tab**, click **Columns** in the Page Setup group, then click the **Left** column type

   The Left column type formats the document in two uneven columns, with the narrower column to the left.

2. Switch to 100% view, click the **Home tab**, click **Heading 1** in the Styles group, type **Tour Description**, press **[Enter]**, then type the first four paragraphs of text (through "bacon, eggs, and fried bread.") shown in Figure B-10

   The text will flow to column 2 as you type. You will adjust how the text wraps between columns in Step 4.

3. Click at the **beginning of paragraph 3** (which starts "Sharon McCarthy..."), click the **Insert tab**, click the **Clip Art button** in the Illustrations group, enter **Windsor Castle** in the Search for text box, insert the clip-art picture shown in Figure B-10, right-click the picture, point to **Text Wrapping**, click **Square**, set the Height at **1.3"** in the Size group, then use your mouse and arrow keys to position the picture in column 1 as shown in Figure B-10

4. Close the Clip Art task pane, click at the **beginning of paragraph 4** ("After a day..."), press **[Enter]**, click at the **end of the fourth paragraph** ("...fried bread."), press **[Enter]**, apply **Heading 1**, then type **Moments to Remember**

5. Press **[Enter]**, type the paragraph that begins "Here are just...", press **[Enter]**, then type the remaining six paragraphs of text, typing the letters that appear as drop caps normally, and pressing **[Enter]** once between each paragraph

6. Select the text from "Chart a course" to "homes and palaces," click the **Page Layout tab**, then change the After spacing to **24 pt**

7. Click in the paragraph that begins "Chart a course...", click the **Insert tab**, click **Drop Cap** in the Text group, then click **Dropped**

8. Repeat the process to add drop caps to each of the paragraphs shown in Figure B-10, then save the document

FIGURE B-10: Page 1 complete

Tour Description

British Castle Tours, Inc., is proud to offer two-week tours of the great castles and stately homes of England, Scotland, and Wales. These tours will appeal to you if you are longing to experience the United Kingdom and its wealth of history, but you *don't* want to worry about arranging transportation and accommodations, and you *don't* want to spend your vacation on a crowded tour bus.

Each British Castle Tour is limited to 20 people. To keep costs down and make your travel experience as authentic as possible, you travel on local buses and trains and stay in comfortable one- and two-star bed and breakfasts.

Sharon McCarthy, our experienced guide and historian, takes care of all the travel details as she escorts you through the great houses and castles of the United Kingdom. Our tour takes you from Windsor Castle, home of the Queen, north through the heartland of England to mystical Edinburgh Castle in Scotland and from there to the castle strongholds of Northern Wales.

After a day touring the stately homes and castles of Britain, you can relax with a pint of best bitter in a charming pub and then take a stroll down winding country lanes. Sleep comfortably in cozy bed and breakfasts and awake each morning to the legendary full English breakfast complete with bacon, eggs, and fried bread.

Moments to Remember

Here are just some of the moments you will share with other history lovers on our British Castle Tour:

C hart a course through British history as you wander the crumbling hallways of castles that were new a thousand years ago.

A ppreciate firsthand the warm hospitality of your British hosts at family-run bed and breakfasts where the beds are comfortable and the company is cheerful.

S ettle down with a good book by a roaring fire in an Elizabethan inn, then sleep in a four-poster bed straight out of a Jane Austen novel.

T ake time out to enjoy an English cream tea with strawberries and clotted cream, then feast on the best salmon in the world—caught fresh from a Scottish mountain stream.

L inger atop the battlements of Carnarvon Castle and imagine ancient sieges as the sun dips below the Welsh hills.

E njoy touring sumptuous gardens and marveling at the wealth of art treasures in stately homes and palaces.

Activity:

Create Page 2

Page 2 of the British Castle Tours brochure is shown in Figure B-11. You need to select the three-column format, then insert a table, a WordArt object, and a photograph.

Steps:

1. Click at the **end of the final paragraph** on page 1, click the **Page Layout tab**, click **Breaks** in the Page Setup group, click **Column**, click **Columns** in the Page Setup group, click **More Columns**, click **Three**, click the **Apply to list arrow**, click **This point forward**, then click **OK**

2. Click the **Home tab**, select the **Heading 1** style, type **Tour Itinerary**, press **[Enter]**, then type the first two paragraphs of text as shown in Figure B-11

3. Press **[Enter]** after the second paragraph, insert a table with **3 columns** and **17 rows**, select the table, change the font size of the text to **9 pt** and the line spacing to **1.5**, enter the text shown in Figure B-11, select the table, apply the **Medium Shading 1 - Accent 5** table design (turquoise), then use the pointer to modify the column sizes so the table appears as shown in Figure B-11

4. Click below the table, insert a **column break**, type and center the text as shown in the box at the top of column 2 in Figure B-11, press **[Enter]** twice, select all the text from **Tour Cost** through **"...meals are not included."**, click the **Page Layout tab**, click **Page Borders** in the Page Background group, click the **Borders tab**, click **Box**, click **Options**, set the From text Top and Bottom settings to **4 pt**, then click **OK** twice

5. Click the **last paragraph mark** in column 2, press **[Enter]** three times, then enter the remaining text for column 2 as shown in Figure B-11, pressing **[Shift][Enter]** after each line to insert manual line breaks, and including your name where indicated

6. Insert a column break following your name, click the **Insert tab**, click the **WordArt button** in the Text group, select the style in column 1, row 5 (the last row), type **British Castle Tours** on three lines, select the **Arial Black font**, then click **OK**

7. Set the Height of the WordArt object at **3"**, set the Width at **2.4"**, click the **Shape Fill list arrow** , point to **Gradient**, click **More Gradients**, click the **Preset colors list arrow**, select **Gold**, then click **OK**

8. Click to the right of the WordArt object to deselect it, press **[Enter]**, click the **Insert tab**, click the **Picture button** in the Illustrations group, navigate to the location where you store your Data Files, double-click **Tower.jpg**, set the height of the picture at **2.7"**, then center it

9. Right-click the picture, click **Insert Caption**, click **New Label**, type **Tower of London**, click **OK**, verify that the Exclude label from the Caption checkbox is not selected, click **OK**, then press **[Backspace]** three times to remove the "1" and the extra spaces

10. Compare page 2 to Figure B-11, make any spacing adjustments required, check the spelling, save and print a copy, then close the document

    If possible, print the brochure on two sides of the same sheet of paper. If you cannot do so, place the two printed pages back to back, staple them, then fold them so that "British Castle Tours" appears on the front panel and the contact information appears on the back panel.

Hint

By inserting manual line breaks, you keep all the lines single-spaced with no Before or After spacing.

Trouble

To center the picture, click the Home tab, then click the Center button in the Paragraph group.

Additional Practice

For additional practice with the skills presented in this project, complete Independent Challenge 2.

British Castle Tours

Tower of London

Tour Cost: $4,400 per person

Cost includes travel insurance, accommodations, transportation, museum entrance fees, and six full-course dinners. Airfare to London and all additional meals are not included.

Call (415) 555-1223 to book your British Castle Tour

British Castle Tours, Inc.
Dundas Street West
Toronto, ON M5W 1E7
www.britishcastletours.ca
Your Name

Tour Itinerary

You can choose from four tour dates: May 16 to May 31, June 15 to June 30, July 16 to July 31, or September 15 to September 30.

The tour starts and ends in London. The following itinerary lists only those activities in which your guide accompanies you. You will also have plenty of time to explore on your own.

Day	Overnight	Sites
Day 1	London	Tower of London
Day 2	London	Westminster Abbey
Day 3	Arundel	Arundel Castle
Day 4	Maidstone	Leeds Castle
Day 5	Windsor	Windsor Castle
Day 6	Oxford	Blenheim Palace
Day 7	Stratford	Warwick Castle
Day 8	Northumbria	Bamburgh Castle
Day 9	Edinburgh	Edinburgh Castle
Day 10	Aberdeen	Craigievar Castle
Day 11	Stirling	Stirling Castle
Day 12	Carnarvon	Carnarvon Castle
Day 13	Conwy	Conwy Castle
Day 14	Harlech	Harlech Castle
Day 15	Cardiff	Cardiff Castle
Day 16	London	Farewell Banquet

One-Page Resume for Jan Gazdov

Jan Gazdov earned an Office Management certificate from North Shore College in Sydney, Australia. Now, he needs to create a one-page resume to include with his job applications. For this project, you will **Create and Enhance the Resume**. The completed resume is shown in Figure B-12.

Activity:

Create and Enhance the Resume

You need to set up the resume heading, modify styles, and then create a table to contain the resume text. Finally, you need to enter and format the text.

Hint

Jan's name is enhanced with 18 pt and bold.

Hint

In the Modify Style dialog box, click Format, then click Paragraph to modify the Before and After spacing.

Steps:

1. Open a new blank document in Word, change the left and right margins to **1.2"**, type and center the name and address as shown in Figure B-12 (press **[Shift][Enter]** between each line), press **[Enter]** following the e-mail address, click the **Align Text Left button** in the Paragraph group, type **Objective**, press **[Enter]**, type the objective text shown in Figure B-12, press **[Enter]**, then save the resume as **Jan Gazdov Resume** in the location where you store your Data Files

2. Select the **Distinctive style set**, modify the **Heading 1** style so that it formats text with **16 pt**, **Bold**, and **Italic**, and includes a bottom border line with a width of **1½ pt**, change the Before Spacing to **12 pt** and the After Spacing to **3 pt**, then apply the **Heading 1** style to **Objective**

3. Click the **paragraph mark** below the text, then insert a table consisting of **two columns** and **nine rows**

4. With the column 1 selected, click the **Table Tools Layout tab**, click **Properties** in the Table group, click the **Column tab**, enter **1.5** as the preferred width of column 1, click the **Next Column button**, enter **4.76** as the preferred width of column 2, then click **OK**

5. Select the **cells in the first row** of the table, then click the **Merge Cells button** in the Merge group

6. Select the **entire table**, click the **Table Tools Design tab**, click the **Borders list arrow** in the Table Styles group, then click **No Border**

7. Using Figure B-12 as your guide, type **Education** in the merged row, apply the **Heading 1** style, press **[Tab]**, type **2008-2009** in column 1 of the new row, press **[Tab]**, type **North Shore College, Sydney, NSW** in column 2, press **[Enter]**, then type and format the text that appears under North Shore College

8. Complete the resume as shown in Figure B-12

   Remember to merge the rows that contain headings (e.g., "Work Experience"), to apply the Heading 1 style to the headings, and to apply bold, italic, and bullets where required.

9. Adjust spacing where necessary, print a copy of the resume, then save and close it

Additional Practice

For additional practice with the skills presented in this project, complete Independent Challenge 3.

Jan Gazdov

1200 Shore Road
NSW 2042, Sydney, Australia
Phone/Fax: 0440 555 544
E-mail: jangaz@webplace.au

OBJECTIVE

An office manager in a fast-paced environment where I can apply my excellent computer skills to streamline office systems

EDUCATION

2008-2009	**North Shore College**, Sydney, NSW
	Office Management Certificate

- Computer skills: Microsoft Office 2007: Word, Excel, Access, PowerPoint, Project, and Publisher
- Business Communications and Organizational Behaviour
- Accounting and Bookkeeping
- Project Management
- Supervisory Skills

2008	**Allenham High School**
	School Leaving Certificate

WORK EXPERIENCE

2009-Date	**Branson's Bookkeeping**, 3100 Walloonga Street, Sydney
	Office Assistant (part time)
	Responsibilities include:

- Maintain company records
- Format documents in Word 2007
- Organize company database with Access 2007

2007-2009	**Camp Koala**, Hart Valley, Queensland
	Camp Counselor (summers)
	Responsibilities included:

- Supervised groups of 10 campers aged 9 to 11
- Organized crafts and sports activities
- Assisted with general office duties

2007-2008	**Mario's Pizza Palace**, Sydney
	Pizza cook and cashier (part time)

VOLUNTEER EXPERIENCE

2008-2009	**North College Applied Business Technology Department**
	Student Activities Coordinator
2006-2008	**Food Bank**, South Sydney

Independent Challenges

INDEPENDENT CHALLENGE 1

Write a multiple-page proposal that requests a significant change in a course, program, or company procedure. For example, you could request more hours of computer training as part of a college course or propose the setting up of a day care facility at your company. Alternatively, you could write a proposal to purchase new computer equipment or to establish a more equitable procedure for allocating holiday time. If you are a student, you may want to request that more classroom time be allocated to a specific topic such as the Internet or computerized accounting. If you are in the workplace, you could propose a new marketing strategy for a particular product or you could request new computer software (such as the latest Office upgrade). The possibilities are endless! Fill in the boxes provided below with information about your proposal, and then follow the steps to create and format the proposal, a title page, and a table of contents page. The completed proposal should consist of approximately three pages of text (excluding the title page and table of contents).

1. Determine the subject of your proposal. To help you focus on a subject, ask yourself what changes you would like to see happen in your own workplace or at college. Write the principal request that your proposal will make in the box below:

> **Proposal request:**

2. Determine the three or four principal sections of your proposal in addition to the introduction and conclusion. These sections will form the basis of your outline. For example, suppose you decide to write a proposal that requests changes to a college course on computer applications that you have just taken. You could organize your proposal into the following three sections:

   I.   Recommended Software
   II.   Laboratory Hours
   III.   Learning Materials

   Under each of these headings, you would describe the current situation in the course and then offer your recommendations for improvement. Write the three principal sections of your proposal in the box below:

> I. _____
>
> II. _____
>
> III. _____

3. After each of the principal topics you listed above, add subheadings and even sub-subheadings that will further organize your proposal. Limit the number of additional headings to one or two for each section.
4. Start a new document in Word, then create a header that includes the name of the proposal at the left margin and the current date aligned at the right margin.
5. Create a footer that includes your name at the left margin and the page number at the right margin.
6. Save the proposal as **My Proposal** to the location where you are storing the files for this book.

7. Select the Style Set you prefer, then modify the Heading 1 and Heading 2 styles. You choose the settings you prefer.

8. Create a new style called Proposal Text that is based on the Normal style and will format the proposal text with 1.5 spacing, a left indent of .5", and 12-pt After paragraph spacing and 0-pt Before paragraph spacing.

9. Type **Introduction**, apply the Heading 1 style, press [Enter], apply the new Proposal Text style you created, then type the text for your introduction.

10. Enter headings and write the text required for your proposal. As you write, try to visualize your reader. What information does your reader need to make an informed decision concerning your request? How will your request directly affect your reader? What benefits will your reader gain by granting your request? What benefits will other people gain? All of these questions will help you to focus on communicating the information your reader needs in order to respond positively to the principal request your proposal makes.

11. Insert up to two footnotes in appropriate places in your proposal. Remember that a footnote is used to reference any books, periodicals, or Web sites you mention in your proposal or to add additional information.

12. Include a SmartArt diagram or chart in an appropriate section of your proposal. For example, you could include a Target diagram that shows the steps toward a specific goal related to your proposal, or you could include a chart that shows statistical information.

13. Insert a Next Page section break above page 1 of your proposal, clear formatting, enter and format **Table of Contents**, then generate a table of contents.

14. Double-click in the header area to show the Header & Footer Tools Design tab, move to the footer for the first page of the proposal (starts with "Introduction"), deselect the Same as Previous button, then start the page numbering at 1.

15. Show the footer for the Table of Contents page, then change the page numbering style on the Table of Contents page to lowercase Roman numerals that start at "i".

16. Add a Next Page section break above the Table of Contents page, then create an attractive cover page for your proposal. Use one of the built-in cover pages.

17. Double-click in the header area, then click the Different first page check box so that no text appears in the header and footer on the title page of your proposal.

18. View the proposal in Two Pages view, make any spacing adjustments required, check spelling and grammar, then save the document and print a copy.

INDEPENDENT CHALLENGE 2

Create a two-page, six-panel brochure that advertises the products or services sold by a fictitious company of your choice. For example, you could create a brochure to advertise the programs offered by a public television station or to present the products sold by Quick Buzz, a company that sells high-energy snack foods. If you are involved in sports, your brochure could describe the sports training programs offered by a company called Fitness Forever, or if you are interested in art, your brochure could list the products sold by an art supply store called Painting Plus. For ideas, check out the pictures in the Clip Art task pane. A particular clip-art picture may provide you with just the subject you require.

1. Determine the name of your company and the products or services that it sells. Think of your own interests, and then create a company that reflects these interests.

2. Select two or three products or services that your brochure will highlight. For example, a brochure for a landscaping company called Greenscapes could present information about bedding plant sales, landscaping design, and garden maintenance services.

3. Allocate one of the three inside panels (1, 2, and 3) for each of the products or services you have selected. For example, if you wish to create a brochure for the Painting Plus art supply store, you could devote one panel to each of the three main types of products sold: Painting Supplies, Papers and Canvases, and Drawing Supplies. Alternatively, you could include two sections in panels 1, 2, and 3 of a brochure that advertises the sports training programs offered by Fitness Forever. Panel 1 could describe the sports facilities, and the weekly program schedule could be spread over panels 2 and 3.

4. Determine the information required for page 2 of the brochure. This page includes panel 4 (usually a continuation of the information on page 1 of the brochure), panel 5 (the back panel), and panel 6 (the front panel). For example, you could include a price list on panel 4, contact information on panel 5, and just the company name and one or two enhancements on panel 6. Note that the readers of your brochure see panel 6 first. Therefore, you want to make it as attractive as possible to encourage readers to open the brochure and read the contents.

5. Before you start creating the brochure in Word, sketch the brochure layout on two blank pieces of paper. Put the sketch back to back and fold the brochure so that you can see how it will appear to readers. The more time you spend planning your brochure, the fewer problems you will encounter when you start creating your brochure in Word.

6. Refer to the brochure you created in Project 2. If you wish, you can adapt this brochure to advertise a tour that would interest you.

7. In Word, start a new document, select Landscape orientation and set the four margins to .5, create an attractive header and /or footer that appears only on page 1 of the brochure, then save the brochure as **My Brochure** in the location where you store the files for this book.

8. Set the number of columns for page 1, then enter the text and enhancements for panels 1, 2, and 3. Include attractively formatted section headings and use drop caps to emphasize the first letter of several paragraphs. Alternatively, you can use drop caps to spell a word and then add appropriate text next to each letter. For ideas, refer to the "Moments to Remember" section of the brochure you created for Project 2.

9. Insert a section break at the end of page 1, then format the columns for page 2 of the brochure. Note that page 2 must display the information in three columns of equal width because readers will usually see only one panel at a time.

10. Enter the text and enhancements for page 2 of the brochure.

11. Add at least one piece of clip art and one piece of WordArt. You can add more pictures if you want, but be careful not to enhance your brochure with too many graphics. You want the finished brochure to have a clean, easy-to-read look.

12. View the brochure in Two Pages view, check the spelling and grammar, make any spacing adjustments required, save the brochure, then print a copy and close the document.

INDEPENDENT CHALLENGE 3

Create or modify your own resume. To help you determine the information required for your resume, fill in the boxes below and then create the resume in Word as directed.

1. Determine your objective. What kinds of positions are you looking for that will match your qualifications and experience? How will your skills help the company that employs you? Refer to the objective you typed in Project 3, then enter your objective in the box below:

Resume Objective:

_____

_____

2. In the table below, list the components related to your educational background, starting with your most recent school or college. Note the name of the institution, the certificate or degree you received, and a selection of the courses relevant to the type of work you are seeking.

Year(s):	Institution:	Certificate/Degree:	Courses:

3. In the table below, list the details related to your work experience. Use parallel structure when listing your responsibilities; that is, make sure that each element uses the same grammatical structure. For example, you can start each point with a verb, such as "maintain," "manage," or "use," and then follow it with the relevant object, for example, "maintain company records" and "use Microsoft Word 2007 to create promotional materials." Make sure you use the appropriate tense: present tense for your current position and past tense for former positions.

Year(s):	Company or Institution:	Responsibilities:

4. In the table below, describe any volunteer experience you have, awards you have received and, if you wish, your hobbies and interests:

Year(s)	Focus of Additional Information	Examples
	Volunteer Experience	
	Awards	
	Hobbies/Interests	

5. Set up your resume in Word as follows:

    a. Type your name and format it attractively, then enter and enhance the appropriate contact information. Don't forget to include your e-mail address and your Web site address, if you have them.

    b. Save the resume as **My Resume** to the location where you are storing the files for this book.

    c. Create a new style called Resume Heading Style based on the Normal style with formatting you choose.

    d. Enter **Objective** formatted with the new Resume Heading Style, then type your objective.

    e. Create a table consisting of two columns, then enter the headings and text required for your resume. Refer to Project 3 for ideas.

    f. Fit the resume to one page, check spelling and grammar, print a copy, then save and close the document.

INDEPENDENT CHALLENGE 4

You have been asked to create a six-panel brochure to advertise a two-year intensive training program in drama and theatrical production offered by the Denver School of Drama. The information you need to include in the brochure is provided in a Word document. The completed brochure is shown in Figure B-13. Following are the directions required to complete the brochure:

1. Open Denver Brochure.docx from the location where you store the files for this book, then save it as **Denver School of Drama Brochure** to the same location.

2. Change the orientation of the document to landscape orientation with .5" margins.

3. Create a header on the first page only that contains a 6-pt, green line filled with the Wide upward diagonal pattern.

4. Format the text in three evenly spaced columns.

5. Change the Color Scheme to Module, then modify the Heading 1 style so that it enhances text with a 16-pt, green font.

6. Apply the Heading 1 style and format the text as shown in Figure B-13. Note that you will need to add a column break at the bottom of column 1, press [Enter] at the top of column 2, then add a column break at the bottom of column 2. At the top of column 3, press [Enter], then change the Before spacing of "Program Content" to 0. These steps ensure that the tops of the three columns start at the same place.

7. Format the table in panel 3 attractively as shown in Figure B-13, then center the table.

8. Create a new style called **Course** that applies bold and italics and changes the After spacing to 0. Apply the Course style to all the course names and the faculty names as shown in Figure B-13.

9. On panel 6, create a WordArt object using "Denver School of Drama," change the fill color to one of the green Accent shades, then insert an appropriate clip-art picture. (*Hint:* Search for "drama" or "theater" in the Clip Art task pane.)

10. View the brochure over two pages, adjust the formatting where required, check the spelling and grammar, type your name at the bottom of panel 5, print a copy, then save and close the brochure.

Program Objectives

The Denver School of Drama offers students a wide range of courses in acting, directing, and stagecraft.

This two-year intensive program provides students with the training required to develop professional-level skills in all areas of theatrical production.

Upon successful completion of the Denver School of Drama program, graduates receive a certificate recognized as equivalent to 36 credits at the university level. Students may then enter university in the Junior year where they can fulfill the requirements for a Bachelor of Fine Arts in Drama.

Admission Procedures

Auditions for the Denver School of Drama are held at the school in January and February of each year for admission to the school in September. Candidates may apply for an audition by calling the School Registrar at (918) 555-3321.

The following materials must be provided to the Audition Committee six months prior to the audition date:

- Resume detailing performance experience and drama-theater education
- Transcript from the last educational institution attended
- Reference letter from two or more instructors (one of which should be a drama instructor)
- Video of a recent performance (acting students only)
- Directing script of a recent production (directing students only)
- Costume, lighting, or set designs of a recent production (stagecraft students only)

The audition will consist of the following elements:

- Sight analysis of a selection from a contemporary play chosen by the audition committee.
- Thirty-minute interview

In addition, acting students must present two prepared speeches and perform one sight reading of a role chosen by the audition committee.

Program Content

The Denver School of Drama program is divided into two 8-month terms.

Year 1:	
DRA 100	History of Theater 1
DRA 101	Dramatic Theory 1
DRA 102	Elective 1
DRA 103	Elective 2
DRA 104	Year 1 Production
Year 2:	
DRA 200	History of Theater 2
DRA 201	Dramatic Theory 2
DRA 202	Elective 3
DRA 203	Career Choices
DRA 204	Year 2 Production

Course Descriptions

DRA 100: History of Theater 1
Evolution of theater from the Greeks to the English Restoration. Special emphasis on Shakespearean drama.

DRA 101: Dramatic Theory 1
The fundamentals of dramatic theory, including techniques for dramatic criticism.

DRA 102: Elective 1
Choice of Acting 1, Directing 1, or Stagecraft 1.

DRA 103: Elective 2
Choice of Improvisation 1, Production 1, or Graphic Design 1

DRA 104: Year 1 Production
Participation in a full-length production of a play selected by the students

DRA 200: History of Theater 2
Development of the theater from the 19th century in England and the United States with special emphasis on contemporary US playwrights

DRA 201: Dramatic Theory 2
In-depth analysis of selected plays from a variety of genres and historical periods.

DRA 202: Elective 3
Choice of Acting 2, Directing 2, or Stagecraft 2

DRA 203: Career Choices
Development of job search skills to obtain employment in theater or film.

DRA 204: Year 2 Production
Participation in a full-length production of a musical selected by the students.

Faculty

All the instructors at the Denver School of Drama continue to work professionally in theaters throughout North America. In addition to our regular faculty, we are proud to welcome the following artists-in-residence for the 2007 program:

Merilee Montcalm: Acting
Ms. Montcalm has won acclaim for her performances on and off Broadway. Her most recent triumph was playing Lady Macbeth in the recent production staged by the New York Theater.

Mark Levine: Directing
In 2010, Mr. Levine won the coveted Players Trophy for his production of A Streetcar Named Desire at the Old Vic Theater in London, England.

Rachel Goldblum: Stagecraft
Ms. Goldblum has won numerous awards for her costumer and set designs. Recently, she designed the costumes for the Oscar-winning film adaptation of Wuthering Heights.

Denver School of Drama
180 Mountain Road
Denver, CO 80220
Phone: (303) 555-3321
www.DenverDrama.com

Your Name

Visual Workshop

As part of a report you've prepared for Sage Designs about the development of their new e-business initiative, you need to create the Target SmartArt diagram shown in Figure B-14. Match the diagram by experimenting with inserting shapes and applying SmartArt styles. Apply the Fancy Style Set and change the color scheme to Apex. Format the title with the Title style and the subtitle with the Subtitle style. Save the diagram as **Sage Designs Web Site Target Diagram** to the location where you are storing the files for this book, print a copy, then close the document.

FIGURE B-14: Target diagram

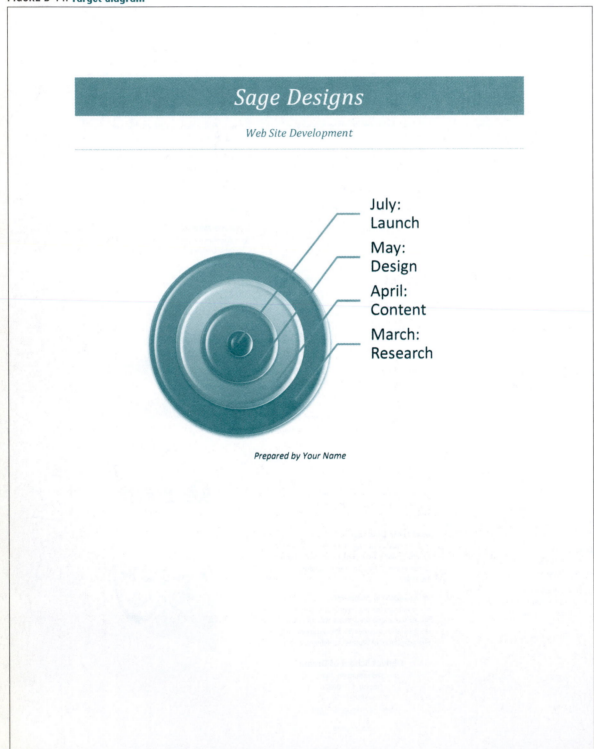

Microsoft
► # Excel
Projects

Unit C

Excel Projects I

In This Unit You Will Create the Following:

► **Projected Budget**

► **Expense Report**

► **Trip Planning Budget**

Microsoft Excel provides the tools you need to make effective planning decisions. For example, suppose you plan to take a two-week vacation to Cancun and you have allocated $2,500 to cover all trip expenses. To find out if you have allocated enough money to cover expenses, you can set up a simple worksheet that lists anticipated expenses for airfare, accommodations, food, and entertainment. Once you total the expenses, you may find that they exceed the budgeted amount of $2,500. Rather than cancel your trip, you can try to determine which expenses you can decrease. For example, you could decide to decrease the cost of accommodations by staying at a less expensive hotel or you could allocate a reduced amount for shopping. In this unit, you will create and format two budgets and an expense report, build formulas, use functions, and ask relevant "What if?" questions.

Projected Budget for Eagle Lake Camp

Eagle Lake Camp in Banff, Alberta, hosts rock climbing, and mountain biking camps for teens. As the camp's office assistant, you need to create the Eagle Lake Camp's budget for the 2010 summer season, and then ask "What if?" questions to determine goals. To create the budget, you **Enter and Enhance Labels**, **Calculate Totals**, **Ask "What if?" Questions**, and **Format and Print the Budget**. The completed budget appears in Figure C-8 on page 59.

Activity:

Enter and Enhance Labels

You need to enter and enhance the worksheet labels.

Trouble

The Select All button is located to the left of the "A" at the upper-left corner of the worksheet frame.

Hint

Although the text extends into columns B and C, you need to select only cells A4 and A5—the place where the text originated.

Steps:

1. Start Excel and open a new blank workbook, click the **Select All button** to select the entire worksheet, click the **Font Size list arrow** 11 in the Font group, then click **12**

2. Click cell **A1**, type **Eagle Lake Summer Camp**, press [Enter], type the remaining labels as shown in Figure C-1, then save the workbook as **Projected Budget for Eagle Lake Summer Camp** in the location where you store your Data Files

3. Click cell **A1**, click the **Page Layout tab**, click **Themes** in the Themes group, click **Aspect**, click the **Home tab**, change the font size to **20**, then click the **Bold button** B in the Font group

4. Select cells **A4** and **A5**, then change the font size to **16**

5. Select cells **A1:G5**, right-click the selection, click **Format Cells**, click the **Alignment tab**, click the **Horizontal list arrow**, click **Center Across Selection**, then click **OK**

6. Select cells **A4:G5**, click the **Fill Color list arrow** in the Font group, select **Dark Green, Accent 4, Darker 25%**, click the **Font Color list arrow** A in the Font group, then select **White, Background 1**

7. Click cell **B7**, type **May**, then click the **Enter button** on the formula bar

8. Position the pointer over the lower-right corner of cell B7 to show the **Fill Handle pointer** +, drag the + pointer to cell **F7**, then click the **Center button** in the Alignment group

9. Click cell **G7**, enter **Totals** and center it, click cell **A8**, enter the labels required for cells **A8:A23** as shown in Figure C-2, click the **Review tab**, click the **Spelling button** in the Proofing group, correct any spelling errors, then save the workbook

FIGURE C-1: Labels for cells A1 to A5

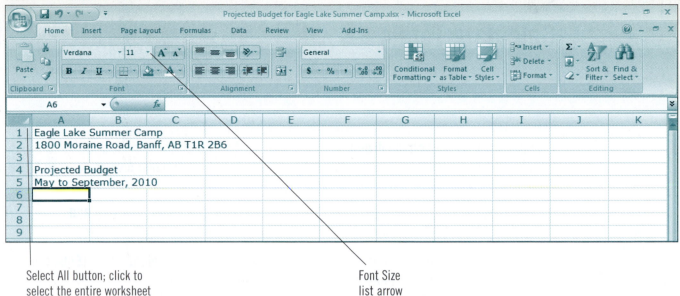

Select All button; click to select the entire worksheet

Font Size list arrow

FIGURE C-2: Labels for budget categories

	A	B	C	D	E	F	G	H	I
7		May	June	July	August	September	Totals		
8	Income								
9	Camp fees								
10	Grants								
11	Donations								
12	Total Income								
13									
14	Expenses								
15	Food								
16	Instructors								
17	Camp Supplies								
18	Administration								
19	Maintenance								
20	Advertising								
21	Total Expenses								
22									
23	Profit/Loss								
24									
25									
26									

Labels for cells A8 through A23

Enter "Totals" in cell G7

Clues to Use

Merging Cells

A merged cell is created by combining two or more cells into a single cell. The cell reference for the merged cell is the upper-left cell of the originally selected range. When you merge a range of cells containing data, only the data in the upper-left cell of the range is included in the merged cell. If you want to merge cells in a single row quickly, use the Merge and Center button in the Alignment group on the Home tab and then adjust the alignment as needed. If you want to merge cells in several consecutive rows, use the Alignment tab in the Format Cells dialog box.

Activity:

Calculate Totals

You need to enter the income and expenses that Eagle Lake Camp anticipates in 2010. Then, you need to calculate the camp fees and the total income and expenses.

Steps:

1. Double-click on the **column divider** between columns **A** and **B** on the worksheet frame to increase the width of column A to fit all the labels, then double-click the **column divider** between **F** and **G** on the worksheet frame to fit September in cell F7

2. Click cell **B10**, enter the values for May as shown in Figure C-3, select cells **B10:B20**, position the pointer over the lower-right corner of cell **B20**, then drag the ✛ pointer to cell **F20**

3. Double-click the **Sheet1 tab** at the bottom of the worksheet, type **Budget**, press **[Enter]**, double-click the **Sheet2 tab**, type **Fees**, then press **[Enter]**

   In the previous year (2009), you know that approximately 100 teens attended camp each month in three payment categories: one-week, two-week, and three-week. You use this data as the basis for your calculations for the 2010 budget.

4. Enter and format the labels and values in the Fees worksheet as shown in Figure C-4

   Double-click or drag the column divider to widen column A so that the labels are clearly visible, and then center and bold the labels in cells A1:D1.

5. Click cell **D2**, type the formula **=B2*C2**, then press **[Enter]**

   You should see 45000 in cell D2. If not, check your formula and try again.

6. Click cell **D2** again, drag the ✛ pointer down to cell **D4** to copy the formula into the next two cells, click cell **D5**, then double-click the **Sum button** Σ in the Editing group

   The camp fees collected should be 149000.

7. Click the **Budget sheet tab**, click cell **B9**, type **=**, click the **Fees sheet tab**, click cell **D5**, press **[Enter]**, click cell **B9** again, then drag the pointer across to cell **F9** to copy the formula to the other months

   Oooops! Cells C9 through F9 contain zeroes. Why? Excel changed the copied formula because it uses relative references by default. However, you need to enter a formula that designates cell D5 in the Fees worksheet as an absolute value to ensure that the formula always contains a reference to cell D5, no matter where in the workbook the formula is copied.

8. Click cell **B9**, select **D5** in the formula bar, press **[F4]** to insert dollar ($) signs to make it an absolute reference, press **[Enter]**, click cell **B9** again, then drag the ✛ pointer to fill cells **C9:F9** with the new formula

9. Select cells **B9:G12**, click Σ, select cells **B15:G21**, click Σ again, click cell **G22**, then save the workbook

   The total income displayed is 782500, and the total for expenses shown is 523500, as shown in Figure C-5.

Hint

You use a new worksheet to avoid cluttering the first worksheet with data that will not be printed.

Hint

The exclamation mark (!) following Fees indicates that the formula comes from a worksheet other than the active worksheet.

FIGURE C-3: Values for cells B10 to B20

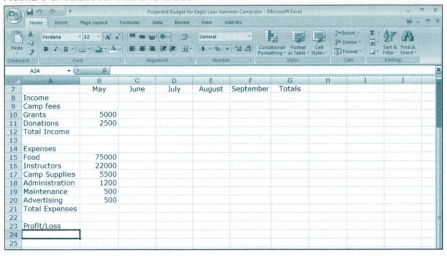

	A	B	C	D	E	F	G	H
7		May	June	July	August	September	Totals	
8	Income							
9	Camp fees							
10	Grants	5000						
11	Donations	2500						
12	Total Income							
13								
14	Expenses							
15	Food	75000						
16	Instructors	22000						
17	Camp Supplies	5500						
18	Administration	1200						
19	Maintenance	500						
20	Advertising	500						
21	Total Expenses							
22								
23	Profit/Loss							
24								
25								

FIGURE C-4: Fees sheet labels and values

	A	B	C	D
1	**Category**	**Campers**	**Cost**	**Total Fees**
2	One-Week	50	900	
3	Two-Week	30	1800	
4	Three-Week	20	2500	
5				
6				

FIGURE C-5: Worksheet completed with totals

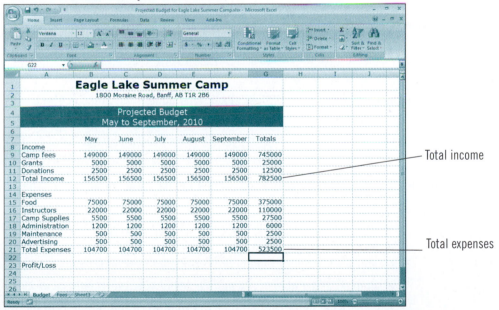

Total income

Total expenses

Clues to Use

Understanding Relative and Absolute References

By default, Microsoft Office Excel considers all values entered in formulas as relative values. That is, Excel automatically changes all cell addresses in a formula when you copy the formula to a new location. If you do not want Excel to change the cell address of a value when you copy it, you must make the value absolute. To do this, you enter a dollar sign ($) before both the column and the row designation in the address. You can also press [F4] to insert the $ symbol. For example, $C$26 tells Excel that the reference to cell C26 must not change, even if you copy the formula to a new location in the worksheet.

Activity:

Ask "What if?" Questions

You need to calculate the profit you expect to make in each of the five months of the 2010 season, and then perform the calculations required to answer several "What if?" questions.

Steps:

1. Click cell **B23**, enter the formula **=B12-B21**, press **[Enter]**, copy the formula across to cell **G23**, then click cell **G23** to deselect the range

   The total projected profit for the 2010 camp season is 259000. The first "What if?" question is: "What if you raise the one-week course fee to $1,000?"

2. Click the **Fees sheet tab**, click cell **C2**, type **1000**, press **[Enter]**, then click the **Budget sheet tab**

   By changing the value in C2, you answer the "What if?" question and see that your total profit in cell G23 increases to 284000. Next, you want to know, "What if an increase in the one-week camp fee results in a 30-percent drop in the number of campers you can expect in 2010?"

3. Click the **Fees sheet tab**, click cell **B2**, replace 50 with the formula **=50-(50*.3)** as shown in Figure C-6, press **[Enter]**, then click the **Budget tab**

   The formula you entered in the Fees sheet subtracts 30 percent of 50 from the number of teens expected to take a one-week course (50). The new profit in cell G23 is 209000—quite a reduction from 284000! Perhaps you shouldn't raise the one-week camp fee to $1,000.

4. Return to the **Fees sheet**, change the cost of the one-week camp fee in cell **C2** to **900** and the number of campers in cell **B2** to **50**, then return to the Budget sheet

   The value in cell G23 is again 259000. Next, you want to know, "What if you launch a $5,000 advertising campaign in May?"

5. Click cell **B20** in the Budget sheet, type **5000**, then press **[Enter]**

   If you increase your advertising cost, you reduce your total profit for the summer season to 254500. Next, you want to know, "What if the May advertising campaign leads to a 30-percent increase in revenue from camp fees in August and September?" You edit the formula in cells E9 and F9 to show the increase.

Trouble

If a green triangle appears in cell E9, move the pointer over the triangle to read the comment. When you copy the formula, the triangle disappears.

6. Click cell **E9**, click at the end of the formula in the formula bar, type ***1.3**, press **[Enter]**, then copy the formula to cell **F9**

   The new total profit shown in cell G23 is 343900, a significant increase. As a result, you decide to keep the advertising campaign in place. Finally, you want to know, "What if you hire a full-time executive assistant for $22,000?" You divide this amount by 5 to determine the monthly rate for the five months the camp is open and then you add the total to the values entered in the Administration row.

7. Click cell **B18**, enter the formula **=(22000/5)+1200**, press **[Enter]**, then copy the formula across to cell **F18**

   Based on this "What if?" analysis, your total profit as shown in cell G23 is now 321900.

8. Click cell **A24**, compare your worksheet to Figure C-7, then save the workbook

FIGURE C-6: Decreasing the number of campers by 30%

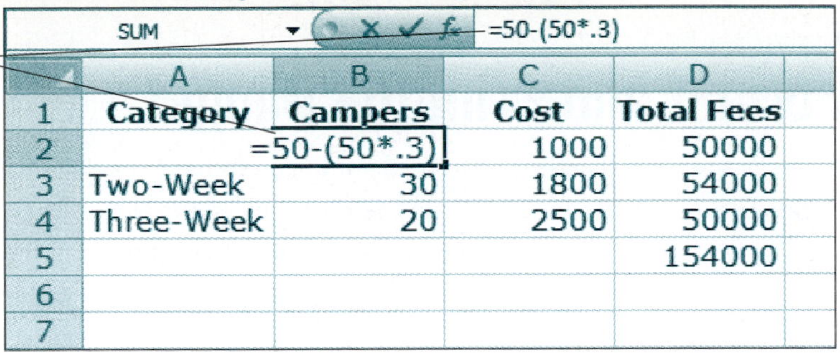

Formula in cell B2

	SUM		X ✓ ƒₓ	=50-(50*.3)
	A	**B**	**C**	**D**
1	**Category**	**Campers**	**Cost**	**Total Fees**
2		=50-(50*.3)	1000	50000
3	Two-Week	30	1800	54000
4	Three-Week	20	2500	50000
5				154000
6				
7				

FIGURE C-7: Worksheet with completed budget

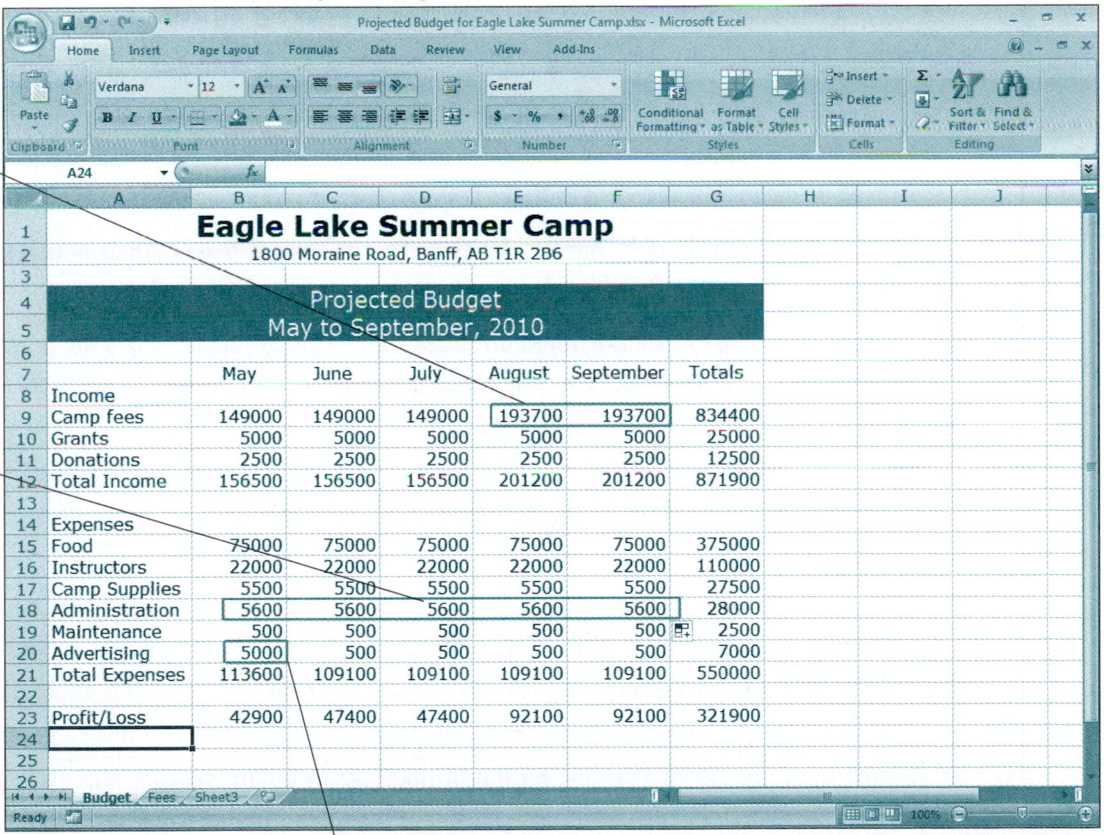

Increases in the August and September fee income result from the ad campaign

Administration includes new Executive Assistant position

Projected Budget for Eagle Lake Summer Camp.xlsx - Microsoft Excel

Home | Insert | Page Layout | Formulas | Data | Review | View | Add-Ins

A24

Eagle Lake Summer Camp
1800 Moraine Road, Banff, AB T1R 2B6

Projected Budget
May to September, 2010

	A	B	C	D	E	F	G
7		May	June	July	August	September	Totals
8	Income						
9	Camp fees	149000	149000	149000	193700	193700	834400
10	Grants	5000	5000	5000	5000	5000	25000
11	Donations	2500	2500	2500	2500	2500	12500
12	Total Income	156500	156500	156500	201200	201200	871900
13							
14	Expenses						
15	Food	75000	75000	75000	75000	75000	375000
16	Instructors	22000	22000	22000	22000	22000	110000
17	Camp Supplies	5500	5500	5500	5500	5500	27500
18	Administration	5600	5600	5600	5600	5600	28000
19	Maintenance	500	500	500	500	500	2500
20	Advertising	5000	500	500	500	500	7000
21	Total Expenses	113600	109100	109100	109100	109100	550000
22							
23	Profit/Loss	42900	47400	47400	92100	92100	321900
24							
25							
26							

Budget Fees Sheet3

Advertising expense increased in May

Activity:

Format and Print the Budget

To make the worksheet easier to read, you need to format values in the Accounting Number Format or the Comma Style (depending on their location in the worksheet), add border lines to selected cells, and use a variety of Page Setup features. Then you need to print a copy of your budget.

Steps:

1. Select cells **B9:G9**, click the **Accounting Number Format button** $ in the Number group, then click the **Decrease Decimal button** in the Number group two times

   The widths of columns B through G automatically increase to make room for the formatting.

2. Select cells **B12:G12**, press and hold **[Ctrl]**, select cells **B15:G15**, cells **B21:G21**, and cells **B23:G23**, click $, click twice, then click cell **A24** to deselect the cells

   You use the [Ctrl] key to select a series of nonadjacent cells.

3. Use **[Ctrl]** to select cells **B10:G11** and cells **B16:G20**, click the **Comma Style button** in the Number group, click twice, then click cell **A24** to deselect the cells

   Refer to Figure C-8 as you work.

4. Select cells **B12:G12**, click the **Borders list arrow** in the Font group, select the **Top and Double Bottom Border** style, then click outside the selected cells to see the change

   A single line appears above cells B12 through G12 and a double line appears below them.

5. Add the **Top and Double Bottom Border** style to cells **B21:G21**, then add the **Bottom Double Border** style to cells **B23:G23**

6. Select cells **B7:G7**, click the **Bold button** B in the Font group, click cell **A8**, press and hold **[Ctrl]**, select cells **A12**, **A14**, **A21**, and **A23:G23**, click B to format all the cells at once, then widen column A

7. Click the **Office button**, point to **Print**, click **Print Preview**, click the **Page Setup button** in the Print group, click the **Landscape option button**, then click the **Fit to option button**

   The default setting will fit the worksheet to one-page wide by one-page tall.

Trouble

If all the values are not visible, return to the workbook, adjust the column widths, then view them in Print Preview.

8. Click the **Margins tab**, click to select the **Horizontally** and **Vertically check boxes**, click the **Header/Footer tab**, click **Custom Header**, type **Eagle Lake Camp Budget** in the left section, press **[Tab]** twice, type your name in the right section, click **OK**, then click **OK** again

   To fit the budget attractively on the page in landscape orientation, you specify column widths.

9. Click the **Close Print Preview button** in the Preview group, select columns **B** through **G,** right-click the selection, click **Column Width**, type **12**, press **[Enter]**, then view the workbook in Print Preview

Additional Practice

For additional practice with the skills presented in this project, complete Independent Challenge 1.

10. Verify that all the values are visible, click **Print**, click **Close** to return to the workbook, then save and close the workbook

    The printed budget for Eagle Lake Camp is shown in Figure C-8.

FIGURE C-8: Completed budget

Your Name

Eagle Lake Camp Budget

Eagle Lake Summer Camp
1800 Moraine Road, Banff, AB T1R 2B6

Projected Budget
May to September, 2010

	May	June	July	August	September	Totals
Income						
Camp fees	$ 149,000	$ 149,000	$ 149,000	$ 193,700	$ 193,700	$ 834,400
Grants	5,000	5,000	5,000	5,000	5,000	25,000
Donations	2,500	2,500	2,500	2,500	2,500	12,500
Total Income	$ 156,500	$ 156,500	$ 156,500	$ 201,200	$ 201,200	$ 871,900
Expenses						
Food	$ 75,000	$ 75,000	$ 75,000	$ 75,000	$ 75,000	$ 375,000
Instructors	22,000	22,000	22,000	22,000	22,000	110,000
Camp Supplies	5,500	5,500	5,500	5,500	5,500	27,500
Administration	5,600	5,600	5,600	5,600	5,600	28,000
Maintenance	500	500	500	500	500	2,500
Advertising	5,000	500	500	500	500	7,000
Total Expenses	$ 113,600	$ 109,100	$ 109,100	$ 109,100	$ 109,100	$ 550,000
Profit/Loss	$ 42,900	$ 47,400	$ 47,400	$ 92,100	$ 92,100	$ 321,900

Travel Expense Report for Web Learning Associates

The three sales representatives at Web Learning Associates, a company that develops online course materials, have each submitted travel expenses for June. As the office manager, you record the expenses and prepare an expense report that summarizes all June travel expenses. To create the travel expense report, you **Create the Expenses Form**, **Calculate Expenses**, and **Prepare the Expense Report**. The completed report is shown in Figure C-16 on page 65.

Activity:

Create the Expenses Form

You need to create the expenses form shown in Figure C-11.

Steps:

Trouble

To apply the Technic theme, click the Page Layout tab, then click Themes in the Themes group.

1. Open a new workbook in Excel, apply the **Technic** theme, enter and format the labels as shown in Figure C-9, then save the workbook as **Expense Statements for Web Learning Associates** in the location where you store your Data Files

   Note the formatting directions in Figure C-9. If you do not have the Aharoni font, choose a different font.

2. Fill cell **A1** with **Gold, Accent 2, Lighter 60%**, click cell **A30**, type **Note that the current mileage reimbursement rate is $.25 per mile.**, then press **[Enter]**

3. Click cell **H12**, click the **Formulas tab**, click the **AutoSum button** in the Function Library group, select cells **B12:G12**, press **[Enter]**, copy the formula down through cell **H25**, click cell **B26**, click the **AutoSum button** in the Function Library group, select cells **B12:B25**, press **[Enter]**, then copy the formula across through cell **H26**

   Zeroes appear in the cells that contain formulas.

4. Click cell **H27**, enter the formula **=SUM(H12:H25)**, press **[Enter]**, click cell **H29**, enter the formula **=H27-H28**, press **[Enter]**, select cells **B12:H29**, click the **Home tab**, then click the **Accounting Number Format button** $ in the Number group

   You have entered a formula to add the total expenses incurred by Adam Grant and then you entered a formula that subtracted the total expenses from any advance Adam may have received.

5. Select rows **6**, **7**, and **8**, click the **Format button** in the Cells group, click **Row Height**, type **20**, click **OK**, select columns **B** through **H**, click the **Format button** in the Cells group, click **Column Width**, type **12**, click **OK**, then increase the width of column A to **18**

6. Select cells **B6:G6**, click the **Borders list arrow** in the Font group, click **Bottom Border**, then add a bottom border to cells **B7:G7**, cells **C8:D8**, and cells **F8:G8**

7. Select cells **A11:H26**, click the **Borders list arrow** in the Font group, click **All Borders**, then enter and format text and add borders to cells **G27:H29** as shown in Figure C-10

8. Double-click the **Sheet1 tab**, type **Grant**, press **[Enter]**, name the Sheet2 tab **Lee**, name the Sheet3 tab **Sanchez**, go to the **Grant sheet**, select the worksheet, click the **Copy button**, show the **Lee worksheet**, click the **Paste button**, paste the worksheet in the Sanchez worksheet, then save the workbook

   The Sanchez worksheet appears as shown in Figure C-11.

FIGURE C-9: Labels entered and enhanced

Aharoni font, 22-pt, centered across cells A1:H1

Italic, centered across cells A2:H2

20-pt, bold, merged, centered across cells A4:H4

Bold all labels

Center labels in cells A11 to H11

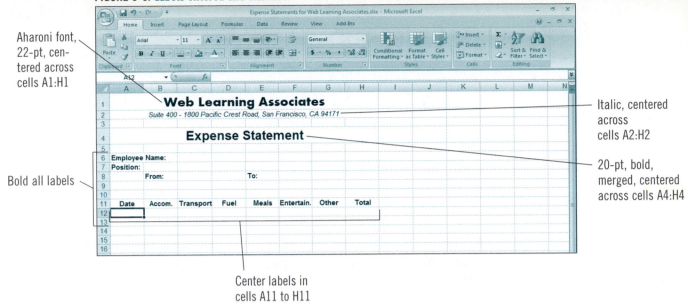

FIGURE C-10: Formatting for cells G27 to H29

Bold and right-align cells G27, G28, and G29

Apply borders to cells H27, H28, and H29

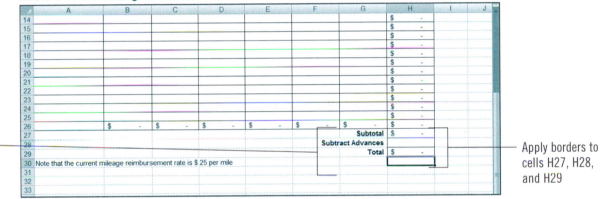

FIGURE C-11: Formatted form

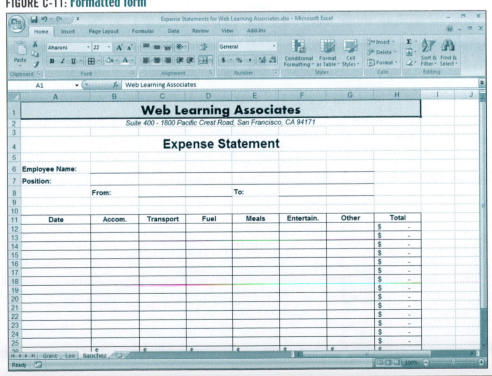

Activity:

Calculate Expenses

The three sales representatives have provided you with receipts from the various business trips they took in April. You need to enter these expenses in the expense form.

Steps:

1. Click the **Grant sheet tab**, click cell **B6**, type **Adam Grant**, press **[Enter]**, then type **Sales Representative**

2. Click cell **C8**, type **June 2, 2010**, press **[Tab]** three times, type **June 5, 2010**, then press **[Enter]**
   When you enter the dates, Excel automatically changes the format to 2-Jun-10.

3. Click cell **C8**, press and hold **[Ctrl]**, click cell **F8**, click the **Number Format list arrow** in the Number group, click **More Number Formats**, click **Date** in the Category list, select the date format **March 14, 2001** (you'll need to scroll down) in the Type list, then click **OK**

4. Click cell **A12**, type **June 2**, press **[Tab]**, type **=420/3**, press **[Tab]**, type **=194*1.09**, press **[Tab]**, type **=12*0.25**, press **[Tab]**, type **=12.5+45**, then press **[Enter]**
   *You've entered the expenses that Adam incurred on June 2. He stayed one of three nights in Dallas ($420/3), he flew to Dallas ($194 + 9 percent tax), he drove 12 miles to the airport (12*$0.25), and he bought lunch and dinner ($12.50 + $45.00). The total in cell H12 should be $411.96.*

5. Enter the remaining expenses for Adam Grant according to the following information:
   On June 3 and 4, Adam stayed two more nights at the Dallas Hilton Hotel at the same rate he paid on June 2. From June 3 to 4, he rented a car @ $32.50/day + $4.30/day for insurance. On June 3, he drove 25 miles; he spent $10 on breakfast, $25 on lunch, and $50 on dinner; in the evening he spent $72 on a theater ticket. On June 4, he drove 35 miles, he spent $105 on meals, and he spent $12 on other expenses. On June 5, he paid $15 for breakfast, he drove 12 miles from the airport back to his home, and he spent $13 on other expenses.

6. Check your work against Figure C-12 to verify that the total in cell H29 is **$1,085.56**

7. Click the **Lee sheet tab**, then refer to Figure C-13 to enter the information and expenses for Jason Lee

8. Verify that Jason's total expenses (less his advance) are **$530.36** in cell H29

9. Click the **Sanchez tab**, refer to Figure C-13 to enter the information and expenses for Maria Sanchez, verify that Maria's total expenses (less her advance) are **$628.25** in cell H29, then save the workbook

Hint

Remember to format the dates in cells C8 and F8 in the same way you did in Step 3.

FIGURE C-12: Expenses for Adam Grant

	A	B	C	D	E	F	G	H	I	J
6	**Employee Name:**	Adam Grant								
7	**Position:**	Sales Representative								
8		From:	June 2, 2010		To:	June 5, 2010				
9										
10										
11	**Date**	**Accom.**	**Transport**	**Fuel**	**Meals**	**Entertain.**	**Other**	**Total**		
12	2-Jun	$ 140.00	$ 211.46	$ 3.00	$ 57.50			$ 411.96		
13	3-Jun	$ 140.00	$ 36.80	$ 6.25	$ 85.00	$ 72.00		$ 340.05		
14	4-Jun	$ 140.00	$ 36.80	$ 8.75	$ 105.00		$ 12.00	$ 302.55		
15	5-Jun			$ 3.00	$ 15.00		$ 13.00	$ 31.00		
16								$ -		
17								$ -		
18								$ -		
19								$ -		
20								$ -		
21								$ -		
22								$ -		
23								$ -		
24								$ -		
25								$ -		
26		$ 420.00	$ 285.06	$ 21.00	$ 262.50	$ 72.00	$ 25.00	$ 1,085.56		
27							**Subtotal**	$ 1,085.56		
28							**Subtract Advances**			
29							**Total**	$ 1,085.56		
30	Note that the current mileage reimbursement rate is $.25 per mile									
31										
32										

Grant / Lee / Sanchez

FIGURE C-13: Expenses for Jason and Maria

JASON LEE

Jason Lee, Sales Representative, incurred his expenses from June 8 to June 16, 2010, and has already been advanced $150. On June 8, Jason drove 30 miles, flew to Seattle for $90 + 9% tax, stayed overnight at the Baker Mountain Inn for $80 + 7% tax, and spent $52 on meals. On June 9, he took a ferry ride for $60, drove 30 miles, spent $45 on meals, and $22 on other expenses. On June 15, he drove 30 miles, flew to Phoenix for $110 + 9% tax, stayed overnight at the Sagebrush Motel for $72 + 8% tax, and spent $40 on meals. On June 16, he drove 30 miles, spent $35 on meals, and $15 on other expenses.

MARIA SANCHEZ

Maria Sanchez, Sales Representative, incurred her expenses from June 5 to June 11, 2010 and has already been advanced $200. On June 5, Maria drove 28 miles and spent $55 on meals. On June 9, she flew to Chicago for $225.00 + 9% tax, spent $72 on meals, and drove 18 miles. On June 9 and June 10, she stayed at the Lakeside Hotel for $125/night + 11% tax. On June 10, she spent $88 on meals, and $42.50 on other expenses. On June 11, she drove 18 miles and spent $32 on meals.

Activity:

Prepare the Expense Report

You need to consolidate data from the Grant, Lee, and Sanchez worksheets to create the June Expense Report. Then, you need to enhance the report attractively. The completed expense report is shown in Figure C-16.

Steps:

1. Click the **Insert list arrow** in the Cells group, click **Insert Sheet**, double-click the **Sheet4 tab**, type **Report**, press **[Enter]**, right-click the **Report tab**, click **Move or Copy**, click **(move to end)**, then click **OK**

2. Click the **Lee sheet tab**, copy cells **A1:A4**, click the **Report tab**, click the **Paste button** in the Clipboard group, click cell **A4**, then change "Expense Statement" to **June Expense Report**

3. Enter and format the labels as shown in Figure C-14

4. Click cell **B7**, type **=**, click the **Grant sheet tab**, click cell **B26**, press **[Enter]**, copy the formula through cell **G7**, click cell **B8**, type **=**, click the **Lee sheet tab**, click cell **B26**, press **[Enter]**, copy the formula through cell **G8**, then repeat the process to enter the amounts for Maria Sanchez in cells **B9:G9**

5. Select cells **B7:H9**, click the **Sum button** Σ in the Editing group, click cell **H10**, double-click Σ, click cell **H11**, type **=**, click the **Grant sheet tab**, click cell **H28**, type **+**, repeat the process to add cell H28 from the Lee sheet to cell H28 from the Sanchez sheet, then press **[Enter]**

   The total advances in cell H10 are $350.00.

6. Click cell **H12** if necessary, calculate the total June expenses, verify that the total expenses are **$2,244.17**, click the **Grant sheet tab**, enter an advance of **$300**, then verify that the total expenses in the Report tab are now **$1,944.17**

7. Select cells **H7:H9**, click **Conditional Formatting** in the Styles group, point to **Icon Sets**, select the **3 Traffic Lights (Unrimmed)** icon set (second row, second column), click **Conditional Formatting**, point to **Icon Sets**, then click **More Rules**

8. Click the **Reverse Icon Order check box**, click the top **Type list arrow**, click **Number**, enter **1000** in the Value text box, complete the New Formatting Rule dialog box as shown in Figure C-15, click **OK**, then widen column H if necessary

   The conditional formatting rules highlight which sales representative has spent the most money on expenses.

9. Select rows **6 through 12**, click **Format** in the Cells group, click **Row Height**, type **20**, click **OK**, click the **Page Layout tab**, click **Margins**, click **Custom Margins**, set the top margin at **1.5**, set the left and right margins at **.45**, then click **OK**

10. Click the **Office button** 🔘, point to **Print**, click **Print Preview**, click **Page Setup**, center the worksheet horizontally, include the custom header shown in Figure C-16, save the workbook, print a copy of the report, then close the workbook

Additional Practice

For additional practice with the skills presented in this project, complete Independent Challenge 2.

FIGURE C-14: Labels for the Expense report

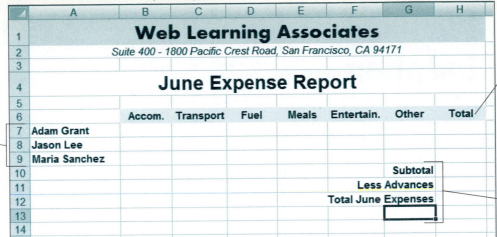

Labels in cells A7:A9 are bold; the width of column A is adjusted to fit the names

Labels in cells B6:H6 are bold, centered, and filled with Gold, Accent 2, Lighter 80%; column widths are slightly adjusted

Labels in cells G10:G12 are bold and right-aligned

FIGURE C-15: Setting conditional formatting rules

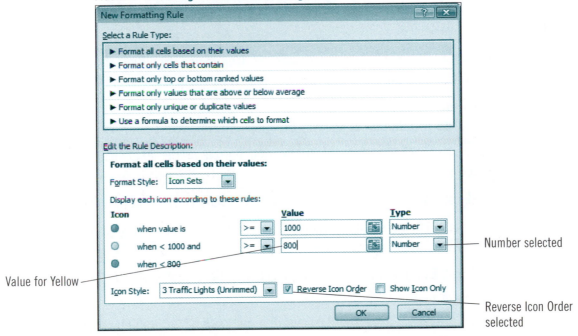

Value for Yellow

Number selected

Reverse Icon Order selected

FIGURE C-16: Completed Expense Report

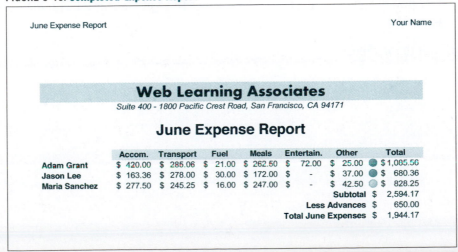

June Expense Report

Your Name

Web Learning Associates

Suite 400 - 1800 Pacific Crest Road, San Francisco, CA 94171

June Expense Report

	Accom.	Transport	Fuel	Meals	Entertain.	Other	Total
Adam Grant	$ 420.00	$ 285.06	$ 21.00	$ 262.50	$ 72.00	$ 25.00	$ 1,085.56
Jason Lee	$ 163.36	$ 278.00	$ 30.00	$ 172.00	$ -	$ 37.00	$ 680.36
Maria Sanchez	$ 277.50	$ 245.25	$ 16.00	$ 247.00	$ -	$ 42.50	$ 828.25
						Subtotal	$ 2,594.17
						Less Advances	$ 650.00
						Total June Expenses	$ 1,944.17

Planning Budget for a European Vacation

You hope to take a three-week trip to Europe with a friend. Your budget for the trip is $5,000. Before you buy your plane ticket, you need to determine how much you can spend on airfare, accommodations, food, entertainment, and transportation. You may *want* to stay in first-class hotels, but your $5,000 budget may not extend that far. What kind of trip can you really afford? For this project you need to **Set Up the Budget** and then **Calculate Options**. The completed budget appears in Figure C-19 on page 69.

Activity:

Set Up the Budget

Steps:

1. Open a blank workbook in Excel, apply the **Trek** theme, type **Budget**, press **[Enter]**, click cell **A1**, click the **Home tab**, click **Cell Styles** in the Styles group, then click **Title**

2. Enter and format the labels and values as shown in Figure C-17, then save the workbook as **European Trip Budget** in the location where you store your Data Files

3. Select cells **B3:E3**, click the **Orientation button** in the Alignment group, then click **Rotate Text Up**

4. Click cell **E4**, enter the formula **=C4*D4**, press **[Enter]**, then copy the formula through cell **E9**

5. Click cell **E10**, then double-click the **Sum button** Σ in the Editing group to calculate the subtotal
   The expense subtotal is $7,345.00.

6. Click cell **E11**, calculate a 10% contingency on the subtotal, then press **[Enter]**
   The value in the Contingency cell is $734.50.

7. Enter a formula in cell **E12** to add the **subtotal** to the **contingency** to determine your **total expenses**
   Your total expenses in cell E12 are $8,079.50. You are $3,079.50 over your budget of $5,000.

8. As shown in Figure C-18, change the font size to **14 pt** for cells **A3:E12**, then adjust column widths as needed

9. Save the workbook

Trouble

The required formula is =E10*.1.

FIGURE C-17: Worksheet setup

Merge text across A1:E1, then apply Title style

Merge text across A2:E2, then apply Heading 1 style

Bold and center labels in row 3

Apply Accounting Number Format to values in column C

Bold and right-align labels in cells D10:D12

	A	B	C	D	E	F	G	H
1			**Budget**					
2			**Three-Week Trip to Europe**					
3		**Expense**	**Unit**	**Unit Cost**	**Number**	**Total**		
4	Airfare from Seattle	Ticket	$1,100.00	1				
5	Accommodation	Night	$ 120.00	21				
6	Food	Day	$ 75.00	21				
7	Train Pass	Ticket	$1,100.00	1				
8	Sightseeing	Day	$ 30.00	21				
9	Shopping	Day	$ 20.00	21				
10				Expense Subtotal				
11				Contingency: 10%				
12				Total Expenses				
13								
14								
15								
16								
17								
18								

FIGURE C-18: Worksheet with expenses

	A	B	C	D	E	F	G	H
1			**Budget**					
2			**Three-Week Trip to Europe**					
3		**Expense**	**Unit**	**Unit Cost**	**Number**	**Total**		
4	Airfare from Seattle	Ticket	$1,100.00	1	$1,100.00			
5	Accommodation	Night	$ 120.00	21	$2,520.00			
6	Food	Day	$ 75.00	21	$1,575.00			
7	Train Pass	Ticket	$1,100.00	1	$1,100.00			
8	Sightseeing	Day	$ 30.00	21	$ 630.00			
9	Shopping	Day	$ 20.00	21	$ 420.00			
10				Expense Subtotal	$7,345.00			
11				Contingency: 10%	$ 734.50			
12				Total Expenses	$8,079.50			
13								
14								
15								
16								
17								
18								

PLANNING BUDGET FOR A EUROPEAN VACATION

Activity:

Calculate Options

You need to reduce the trip cost to $5,000. You decide to perform a variety of calculations to answer several "What if?" questions. As you enter data to answer the "What if?" questions in Steps 2 through 7, check the value in the Total Expenses cell against the total expenses value provided in the text. You will need to think carefully about the calculations required. For some steps, you need to insert new rows. The completed budget is shown in Figure C-19.

Steps:

1. Rename the Sheet1 tab **Budget 1** and rename the Sheet2 tab **Budget 2**, return to the **Budget 1** sheet, click the **Select All button** in the upper-left corner of the worksheet frame, click the **Copy button**  in the Clipboard group, click the **Budget 2 tab**, then click the **Paste button** in the Clipboard group

   Now you have two copies of the budget—your original copy and a new copy that you can modify by changing values to calculate responses to "What if?" questions.

2. Perform the calculation required to answer the question "What if you reduce your sightseeing allowance to $20 a day?"

   The total for sightseeing is $420, and the total expenses are now $7,848.50.

3. What if you do not buy a train pass, but instead lease a car for two weeks at a cost of $735 per week and share the cost of the car lease with a friend?

   Total expenses are now $7,447. Remember to divide the weekly car lease cost by two because you are sharing the expense with a friend.

4. What if you stay at youth hostels for 12 days ($30/night for one), stay in small pensions for six days ($75.00/night for one), and then stay in moderately priced hotels for the remaining three days ($200/night for two)?

   You will need to insert two new rows for the various accommodation options. See Figure C-19 for the three labels that replace the Accommodations label. You will also need to copy the formula required to calculate the Youth Hostel, Pension, and Hotel expenses. You may need to adjust the cell references in the formula used to find the expense subtotal. The total expenses are now $5,896.00. Getting there!

5. What if you buy and cook your own food on the days that you stay in youth hostels, thereby reducing your food costs on those days to $20 a day?

   The total expenses are now $5,170.00.

6. If you lease a car, you will split gas costs with your friend during the two weeks that you have the car. You plan to drive approximately 2,000 kilometers; the car you plan to rent gets 13 kilometers to the liter; gas costs approximately $1.50 a liter

   The total expenses are now $5,296.92.

7. What if you book a charter flight that costs $200 less than the current airfare?

   Total expenses are now $5,076.92. You are still $76.92 over your budget of $5,000. You decide that you can just afford to pay the shortfall, but realize that you will need to stick very carefully to your budget.

8. Click cell **A1**, fill it with **Orange, Accent 6, Lighter 40%**, then add border lines to cells as shown in Figure C-19

9. View the worksheet in Print Preview, center it **horizontally** (click the Margins tab in the Page Setup dialog box), add the **header text** shown in Figure C-19, save the workbook, print a copy, then close the workbook

FIGURE C-19: Completed European Trip Budget

European Trip Budget   Your Name

Budget
Three-Week Trip to Europe

Expense	Unit	Unit Cost	Number	Total
Airfare from Seattle	Ticket	$ 900.00	1	$ 900.00
Accommodation: Youth Hostels	Night	$ 30.00	12	$ 360.00
Accommodation: Pensions	Night	$ 75.00	6	$ 450.00
Accommodation: Hotels	Night	$ 100.00	3	$ 300.00
Food	Day	$ 75.00	9	$ 675.00
Food: Hostels	Day	$ 20.00	12	$ 240.00
Car Lease	Week	$ 367.50	2	$ 735.00
Gas	Kilometer	$ 1.50	$ 76.92	$ 115.38
Sightseeing	Day	$ 20.00	21	$ 420.00
Shopping	Day	$ 20.00	21	$ 420.00
			Expense Subtotal	$ 4,615.38
			Contingency: 10%	$ 461.54
			Total Expenses	$ 5,076.92

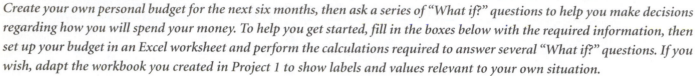

Independent Challenges

INDEPENDENT CHALLENGE 1

Create your own personal budget for the next six months, then ask a series of "What if?" questions to help you make decisions regarding how you will spend your money. To help you get started, fill in the boxes below with the required information, then set up your budget in an Excel worksheet and perform the calculations required to answer several "What if?" questions. If you wish, adapt the workbook you created in Project 1 to show labels and values relevant to your own situation.

1. You need to determine the goal of your budget. Even a personal budget should be created for a specific purpose. For example, you may wish to save for a vacation or to buy a car, or you may just want to live within a set income. Identify the goal of your budget in the box below:

   Budget goal: _____
   _____
   _____

2. Determine your sources of income. You may receive money from a paycheck, from investment dividends, or from a student loan. Each income source requires a label and a row on your budget worksheet. In the box below, list the income labels you will require:

   Income labels:

   1. _____
   2. _____
   3. _____
   4. _____
   5. _____

3. Determine your expenses. At the very least, you will probably need to list your rent, food, utilities, phone, and transportation costs such as car payments, gas, insurance, and bus fares. In addition, include labels for entertainment, clothing, incidentals, and savings. In the box below, list the expense labels you have identified:

   Expense labels:

   1. _____   6. _____
   2. _____   7. _____
   3. _____   8. _____
   4. _____   9. _____
   5. _____   10. _____

4. Create a new workbook in Excel, save it as **My Personal Budget** in the location where you store your files, then set up your budget in Excel as follows:

  a. Select a theme, then enter and enhance a title for your budget in cell A1.

  b. Enter the current date.

  c. Enter the Income and Expenses labels and appropriate subcategory labels in column A.

  d. Determine the time frame of your budget (e.g., monthly or weekly), then enter the appropriate labels starting in column B.

  e. Enter the values associated with your income and expenses categories. Adjust expenses according to the time of year. For example, your utilities costs will probably be less in the summer than in the winter, while your entertainment and travel expenses may occur mostly in the summer.

  f. Calculate your total income and expenses.

  g. Copy Sheet1 to Sheet2 of your budget, name Sheet1 **Budget** and Sheet2 **What If**, and then type at least five "What if?" questions at the bottom of the What If sheet. Try to formulate questions that will help you plan your finances to achieve the goal you set. Here are some sample "What if?" questions:

    1. What if I buy a car with payments of $250/month? (Remember to factor in costs for insurance and gas.)

    2. What if I move in March to a new apartment where my rent is 30 percent more than the current rent?

    3. What if I join a fitness club with monthly dues?

    4. What if I put 10 percent of my income in savings each month?

    5. What if I start taking violin lessons?

5. Make the necessary calculations and modifications to the copy of your budget to answer your five questions.

6. Add a row to the worksheet with a label and cells that calculate any surplus income remaining after expenses are subtracted.

7. Format and print a copy of your budget, then save and close the workbook.

INDEPENDENT CHALLENGE 2

You work for a company that requires you to travel frequently. Create expense records for three consecutive months. Then prepare an expense report that totals the expenses you incurred in each category for each month, shows the total for all expenses for each month, and calculates the total for the three-month expenses minus the advances.

1. Set up Sheet1 with a theme and an attractive heading including the name and address of the company as well as labels for dates and each expense category. Categories include: accommodations, transportation, mileage (determine the mileage rate your company will pay; e.g., $.25/mile or $.16/kilometer), meals, entertainment, and miscellaneous (or other) expenses. If you wish, adapt the expense form you created for Project 2.

2. Save the workbook as **My Travel Expenses** in the location where you store your Data Files.

3. Copy your expense form to the next two sheets and then name the sheet tabs (e.g., March, April, May).

4. Enter realistic expenses for each month. For example, a flight from New York to Los Angeles should cost more than a flight from Montreal to Toronto. Assume that each time you fly, you drive your own car to the airport from your home town. Include the mileage calculation.

5. In a new worksheet, set up an attractive expense report for the three months. Include the name of the company for which you work.

6. Enter the formulas required to calculate your total expenses for each of the three months.

7. Use conditional formatting to highlight totals that are below or above a limit you determine. Modify the formatting rules applied by the conditional formatting you selected.

8. Format the worksheet containing the expense report attractively, include your name in the header, print a copy of the report, then save and close the workbook.

INDEPENDENT CHALLENGE 3

Create a planning budget to help you determine your expenses for a vacation of your choice. Adapt the budget you created for Project 3 if you wish. The following tasks will help you get started.

1. Before you create the worksheet in Excel, answer the questions listed below:
   a. Where do you plan to go for your vacation?
   b. What is your proposed budget?
   c. How long is your planned vacation?
   d. What kind of activities do you plan to do on your vacation (e.g., sightseeing, guided tours, horseback riding, skiing, etc.)?
2. Set up your worksheet with labels for transportation costs (airfare, car rental, train fares, etc.), accommodations, food, sightseeing, shopping, and any other expense categories appropriate to the kind of vacation you plan to take. Save your vacation planning budget as **My Vacation Budget** in the location where you store your Data Files.
3. Apply styles to selected headings in the worksheet (for example, apply the Title style to "Budget" and the Heading 1 style to the location of the trip).
4. Include a contingency amount for emergency expenses that is 10 to 15 percent of your total expenses.
5. Try to make your budget as realistic as possible. You can choose to base your budget on a vacation you have already taken or on a vacation you hope to take.
6. Format the worksheet attractively, print a copy, then save and close the workbook.

INDEPENDENT CHALLENGE 4

You're planning a trip to Australia in May and decide to include your vacation budget in a personal budget for the six months from January to June. To make the budget as dynamic as possible, you include formulas that reference a Web query containing a table of currency exchange rates copied from a currency conversion Web site. You can then refresh the worksheet data periodically to see how the latest exchange rates are affecting your six-month budget.

1. Create the worksheet shown in Figure C-20, change the name of the Sheet1 tab to **Budget**, then save the workbook as **Australia Trip Budget** in the location where you store your Data Files.
2. Use the fill handle to fill in the months from February through June, then center the labels.
3. Copy the values for January through June.
4. Add a column labeled **Totals**, then calculate the row totals. Verify that all the values are formatted in the Comma Style.
5. Calculate the monthly and total income, the monthly and total expenses, and the savings. Your total income is $30,649.68, your total expenses are $11,280.00, and your total savings are $19,369.68.
6. Click the Data tab, click the From Web button in the Get External Data group, connect to the Internet if necessary, type the Web site address www.x-rates.com in the Address text box, then click Go. The x-rates.com Currency Conversion Web site opens in the New Web Query dialog box.
7. Scroll down the dialog box, then click the table select arrow next to the table shown in Figure C-21. Note that the table select arrow button turns green, and a check mark appears when you click it to indicate that the entire table has been selected.

FIGURE C-20: Australia Trip Budget

	A	B	C
1		January	
2	Income		
3	Pay Check	4,548.28	
4	Investment Dividends	560.00	
5	Total Income	5,108.28	
6			
7	Expenses		
8	Rent	700.00	
9	Food	400.00	
10	Phone	100.00	
11	Utilities	150.00	
12	Car Payment	350.00	
13	Gas	80.00	
14	Car Insurance	100.00	
15	Vacation Hotels		
16	Vacation Food		
17	Total Expenses		
18			
19	Total Savings		
20			
21			

FIGURE C-21: New Web Query dialog box

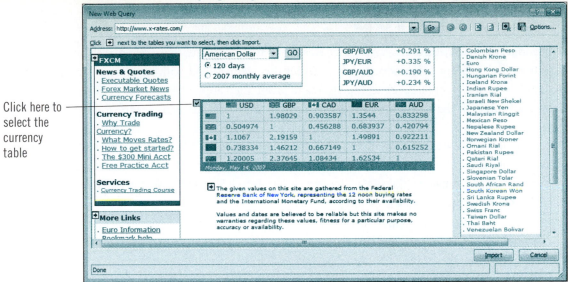

Click here to select the currency table

8. Click Import, click the New worksheet option button, then click OK if a security notice appears. The formatted data appears in a new worksheet. Note that image files are not included.

9. Rename the new worksheet **Currency**.

10. Return to the Budget worksheet, then click cell F15. You will be staying at hotels in Australia for eight days. You've checked out Australian hotels on the Internet and decided that 200 Australian dollars (AUD) per night is a reasonable amount to pay. You'd like to know what this amount converts to in U.S. dollars so you can include the hotel cost in your worksheet. You can also choose to convert the amount to euros or to another currency. However, the following steps relate to U.S. dollars.

11. In cell F15 of the Budget worksheet, enter the formula =8*200* and leave the insertion point in the cell. Switch to the Currency worksheet, click cell F2 (which contains the exchange rate for Australian dollars to U.S. dollars), then press [Enter] to add the value from cell F2 to your formula in the Budget worksheet. The value entered in cell F15 represents the cost of hotels for eight days in U.S. dollars, presuming you spend 200 AUD per night.

12. Click cell F16, enter the formula =8*100* and leave the insertion point in the cell. Switch to the Currency worksheet, click cell F2, and then press [Enter]. The amount entered in cell F16 represents the cost of food for eight days in U.S. dollars, presuming you spend 100 AUD per day. Note the total savings entered in cell H19.

13. Format the worksheet attractively with border lines in the appropriate areas, include "Australia Trip Budget" and your name in the header, print a copy of the worksheet in landscape orientation with the data centered horizontally, then save and close the workbook.

14. On another day, open the workbook, click Refresh All in the Connections group, then check if the total savings in cell H19 has changed to reflect the updated exchange rate. On the x-rates.com Web site, the exchange rates are updated every 24 hours.

Visual Workshop

Create the six-month budget shown in Figure C-22 for Net Designs, a new company that creates Web sites for small businesses. Set up the workbook in landscape orientation, apply the Apex theme, fill cell A1 with Lavender, Accent 6, Lighter 80%, enter the required formulas to calculate total revenue, expenses, and profit, then apply the Comma Style to all the values. Save the budget as **Net Designs Budget** in the location where you store your Data Files, then answer the following questions:

1. In July, you estimate that 10 new businesses will contract Net Designs to create a Web site at an average cost of $1,200 per Web site. You project that the contract revenue generated in July will increase by 5 percent in August, 10 percent in September, then 20 percent for each of the remaining months. Calculate all increases based on July revenue. What is the total revenue for Web site design contracts in cell H6? Enter the value in cell B19.

2. In July, you estimate that 15 businesses will contract Net Designs to program their Web sites with animations and other interactive elements at an average cost of $1,500 per Web site. Each month the revenue increases by 10 percent over the previous month to December. (Hint: Enter =B7*1.1 in cell C7, then copy the formula through cell G7.) What is the total revenue in cell H8? Enter the value in cell B20.

3. Make the salaries expense for both November and December $30,000. What is the total salaries expense? Enter the value in cell B21.

4. Make the equipment leases for November and December four times the current equipment leases for October (e.g., $8,000). What is the total projected profit in cell H18? Enter the value in cell B22.

5. Format the values in rows 6, 8, 11 through 16, 18, and cells B19:B22 with the Accounting Number Format style, and add border lines where appropriate.

6. Save the workbook, preview it, make sure the worksheet fits on one page in landscape orientation and is centered horizontally and vertically, add your name to the header, print a copy of the worksheet, then close the workbook and Excel.

FIGURE C-22: Net Designs worksheet

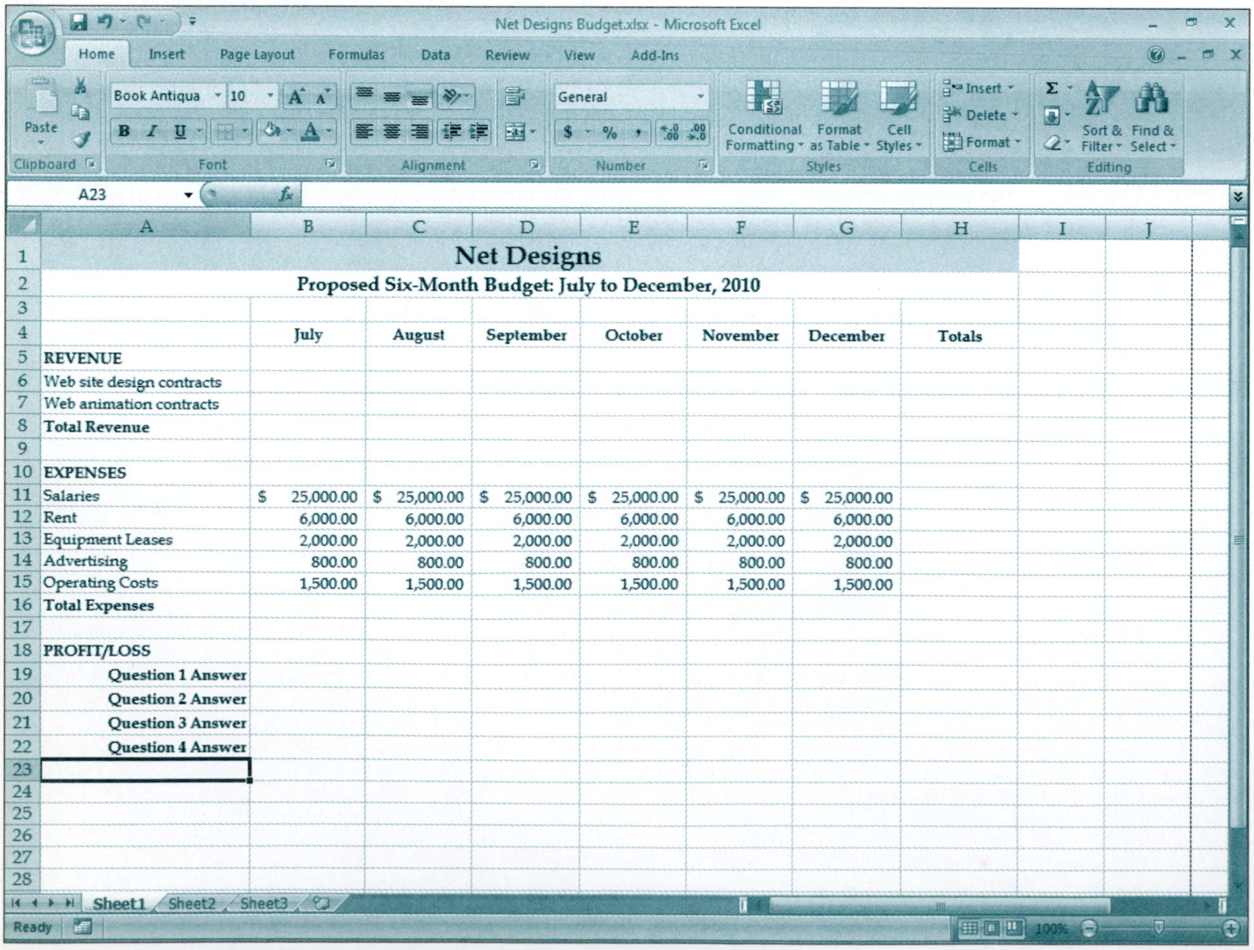

Microsoft
► # Excel
Projects

Unit D

Excel
Projects II

In This Unit You Will Create the Following:

► ## Sales Forecast

► ## Course Grades Analysis

► ## Customer Report

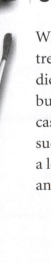

With Microsoft Excel, you can analyze numerical data and identify patterns and trends. For example, you can use the powerful Scenario Manager to make predictions based on a current set of data. You can then use these predictions to plan business and sales ventures, analyze current sales patterns, and create sales forecasts. You can also display the results of an analysis visually in the form of a chart, such as a bar chart or a pie chart. In this unit, you will create scenarios to create a lookup table and use the Lookup function, build charts, and use a PivotTable to analyze sales.

Sales Forecast for Pro-Safe

You own Pro-Safe, a small consulting firm that advises businesses about workplace safety issues and sells ergonomically correct workstations. You are considering moving from your home office to a commercial office space and hiring an executive assistant and a sales representative. To help you decide what course of action you should take, you will **Set Up the Workbook**, **Create Current Scenarios**, **Create Best and Worst Case Scenarios**, and **Format and Print the Scenarios**. The completed printouts of the Best Case and Worst Case scenarios are shown in Figures D-8 and D-9 on page 83.

Activity:

Set Up the Workbook

You need to enter the labels and values for the six-month revenue and expenses statement for Pro-Safe and calculate your total revenue, expenses, and net income.

Steps:

Hint

The result of each calculation appears in parentheses in the text.

1. Start Excel, enter data, and format the worksheet as shown in Figure D-1, then save the workbook as **Sales Forecasts for Pro-Safe** in the location where you store your Data Files

2. Click cell **B7**, enter a formula that calculates 3% of cell **B6** (450), then in cell **B8** enter a formula that subtracts cell **B7** from cell **B6** (14550)

   The formula in cell B7 calculates the value of returned products as an average of 3% of total sales. The formula in cell B8 calculates the net sales after the returns have been subtracted.

3. In cell **B9**, enter a formula that calculates 60% of cell **B8** (8730), then enter a formula in cell **B10** that subtracts cell **B9** from cell **B8** (5820)

   The formula in cell B9 calculates the cost of goods sold as 60% of the total sales. The formula in cell B10 calculates the gross profit on sales, which amounts to the cost of goods subtracted from the net sales. A green triangle appears in cell B9 because Excel has determined that the formula is inconsistent with formulas in adjacent cells. The formula in cell B9 multiplies values, while the formulas in cells B8 and B10 subtract values. You will remove the green triangle in a later step.

4. Select cells **B7:B10**, then fill cells **C7:G10** with the formulas

Trouble

Move the pointer over a green triangle to see the Trace Error Tag.

5. Select cells **B6:H10**, click the **Sum button** in the Editing group, select cells **B9:G9**, click the **Trace Error Tag** , then click **Ignore Error**

6. Select cells **B13:H17**, click Σ, click cell **B19**, then enter a formula that subtracts the total expenses in cell **B17** from the gross profit on sales in cell **B10** (920)

7. Fill cells **C19:H19** with the formula, click cell **H19**, then save the workbook

   The total net profit for sales from July to December 2010 is 11728, as shown in cell H19 in Figure D-2.

FIGURE D-1: Worksheet setup

Increase width of column A

24 pt and bold

12 pt and bold

11 pt and bold

Right-align labels

Center and bold labels; increase column widths as needed

A20			fx					

	A	B	C	D	E	F	G	H
1	**Pro-Safe**							
2	**Revenue and Expenses: July to December 2010**							
3								
4		**July**	**August**	**September**	**October**	**November**	**December**	**Totals**
5	**REVENUE**							
6	Product Sales	15000	18000	16000	22000	17000	18000	
7	Less returns							
8	**NET SALES**							
9	Less Cost of Goods Sold							
10	**GROSS PROFIT ON SALES**							
11								
12	**EXPENSES**							
13	Salaries	4000	4000	4000	4000	4000	4000	
14	Rent	500	500	500	500	500	500	
15	Advertising	200	200	200	200	200	200	
16	Operating Costs	200	200	200	200	200	200	
17	**TOTAL EXPENSES**							
18								
19	**NET PROFIT**							
20								
21								
22								
23								
24								

FIGURE D-2: Worksheet with totals calculated

H19			fx	=H10-H17				

	A	B	C	D	E	F	G	H	I
1	**Pro-Safe**								
2	**Revenue and Expenses: July to December 2010**								
3									
4		**July**	**August**	**September**	**October**	**November**	**December**	**Totals**	
5	**REVENUE**								
6	Product Sales	15000	18000	16000	22000	17000	18000	106000	
7	Less returns	450	540	480	660	510	540	3180	
8	**NET SALES**	14550	17460	15520	21340	16490	17460	102820	
9	Less Cost of Goods Sold	8730	10476	9312	12804	9894	10476	61692	
10	**GROSS PROFIT ON SALES**	5820	6984	6208	8536	6596	6984	41128	
11									
12	**EXPENSES**								
13	Salaries	4000	4000	4000	4000	4000	4000	24000	
14	Rent	500	500	500	500	500	500	3000	
15	Advertising	200	200	200	200	200	200	1200	
16	Operating Costs	200	200	200	200	200	200	1200	
17	**TOTAL EXPENSES**	4900	4900	4900	4900	4900	4900	29400	
18									
19	**NET PROFIT**	920	2084	1308	3636	1696	2084	11728	
20									
21									

Total net profit

Activity:

Create Current Scenarios

Current scenarios represent the revenue and expenses you expect to generate from July to December 2010 if you continue to manage Pro-Safe on your own from your home office. You start by highlighting the cells that contain the values you plan to change when you create various scenarios. Although highlighting the cells is not a necessary step when you create scenarios, you do so in order to quickly and easily identify which rows contain the data that will change when you change scenarios. You then use the Scenario Manager to create scenarios to represent current values for product sales and the current expenses for rent, salaries, and operating costs.

Steps:

1. Select cells **B6:H6**, press and hold **[Ctrl]**, then select cells **B13:H14** and cells **B16:H16**

2. Click the **Fill Color list arrow** in the Font group, click the **Yellow** color, format cells in the **Comma** or **Accounting** style as shown in Figure D-3, then widen the columns if necessary

   The cells to the right of Product Sales, Salaries, Rent, and Operating Costs are filled with yellow so you can easily see which values change each time you show a new scenario.

3. Select cells **B6:G6**, click the **Data tab**, click the **What-If Analysis button** in the Data Tools group, click **Scenario Manager**, then click **Add**

4. Type **Current Sales**, click **OK**, then click **OK** again to accept the values currently entered in cells **B6:G6**

   The Current Sales scenario consists of the values currently entered in cells B6:G6.

5. Click **Add**, type **Current Salaries**, click the **Collapse Dialog Box button**, select cells **B13:G13**, click the **Expand Dialog Box button**, click **OK**, then click **OK**

6. Add a scenario called **Current Rent** based on cells **B14:G14**, then add a scenario called **Current Operating Costs** based on cells **B16:G16**

7. Compare the Scenario Manager dialog box to Figure D-4

8. Click **Close** to exit the Scenario Manager dialog box, then save the workbook

FIGURE D-3: Formatted worksheet

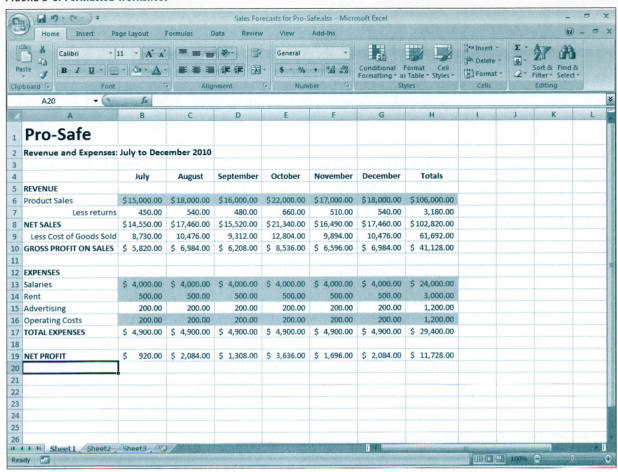

FIGURE D-4: Scenario Manager dialog box

Activity:

Create Best and Worst Case Scenarios

You need to change the values in the worksheet to reflect your Best Case projections, and then you need to change the values again to reflect your Worst Case projections.

Steps:

1. Click the **What-If Analysis button** in the Data Tools group, click **Scenario Manager**, click **Current Sales**, click **Add**, type **Best Case Sales**, then click **OK**

Trouble

Figure D-5 shows only the values required for C6:G6. The value for B6 is not shown because the dialog box shows only five items at once.

2. Type **45000**, press **[Tab]**, enter the values for cells **C6:G6** as shown in Figure D-5, then click **OK**

   These values represent the sales you hope to generate by moving to a commercial space and hiring additional help.

3. Click **Current Salaries**, click **Add**, type **Best Case Salaries**, click **OK**, type **9000**, press **[Tab]**, enter **9000** for cells **C13:G13**, then click **OK**

   You estimate that your salaries expense will more than double when you hire a new sales representative and an assistant.

4. Click **Current Rent**, add a scenario called **Best Case Rent** that changes all the values in cells **B14:G14** to **1500**, click **Current Operating Costs**, then add a scenario called **Best Case Operating Costs** that changes all the values in cells **B16:G16** to **800**

   You hope to obtain office space for $1,500 a month and generate operating costs of no more than $800 a month.

Trouble

If the correct value does not appear in cell H19, verify that all the highlighted cells contain the correct values, then edit the appropriate cells in the Scenario Manager dialog box.

5. Click **Best Case Sales**, click **Show**, click **Best Case Salaries**, click **Show**, show the remaining **Best Case scenarios**, then click **Close**

   The value in cell H19 is $72,620.00. If all goes as you have planned, your sales should increase if you move to a commercial space and hire new personnel to help you sell Pro-Safe products. But what if things don't go as planned?

6. Click the **What-If Analysis button** in the Data Tools group, click **Scenario Manager**, click **Current Sales**, click **Add**, type **Worst Case Sales**, click **OK**, type **30000**, press **[Tab]**, enter the values for cells **C6:G6** of Worst Case Sales as shown in Figure D-6, then click **OK**

7. Add the Worst Case Salaries, Worst Case Rent, and Worst Case Operating Costs scenarios based on the values displayed below:

Worst Case Salaries	10000
Worst Case Rent	4000
Worst Case Operating Costs	1000

8. Show all the Worst Case scenarios, then close the Scenario Manager dialog box

   The total net income displayed in cell H19 is now $(13,600.00) as shown in Figure D-7. If the total income is different, verify that all the highlighted cells contain the correct values.

9. Click **What-If Analysis** in the Data Tools group, click **Scenario Manager**, click **Current Sales**, click **Show**, show all the remaining Current scenarios, click **Close**, fill cell H19 with **yellow** and apply **Bold**, then verify that $11,728.00 appears in cell H19

FIGURE D-5: Best Case Sales values

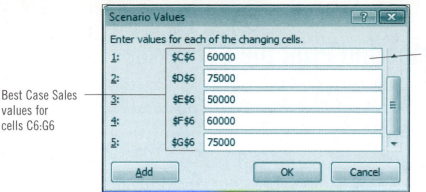

Best Case Sales values for cells C6:G6

$B$6 has scrolled up; the dialog box only displays five values at a time

FIGURE D-6: Worst Case Sales values

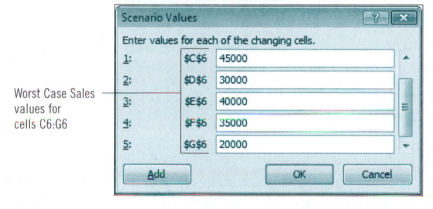

Worst Case Sales values for cells C6:G6

FIGURE D-7: Worksheet with Worst Case scenarios shown

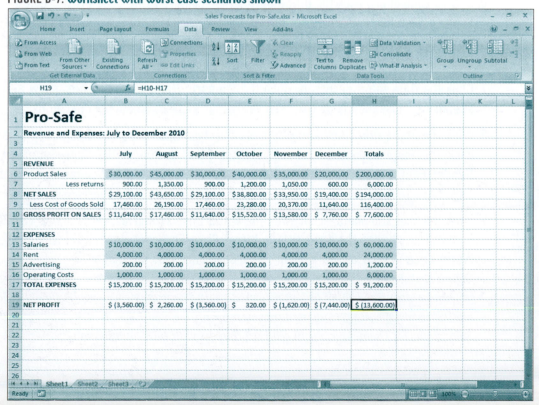

Activity:

Format and Print the Scenarios

At present, the Current scenarios are displayed. You decide to print worksheets to show the three sets of scenarios. To highlight the differences among the three sets of scenarios, you create a column chart for each set of scenarios that shows the net income generated from July to December.

Steps:

1. Select cells **B4:G4**, press and hold **[Ctrl]**, select cells **B19:G19**, click the **Insert tab**, click the **Column button** in the Charts group, click the far-left selection in the top row to insert a Clustered Column chart, click the **More button** in the Chart Styles group, then select **Style 26**

2. Click the **Chart Tools Layout tab**, click the **Chart Title button** in the Labels group, click **Above Chart**, type **Current Monthly Net Income**, press **[Enter]**, click the **Legend button** in the Labels group, then click **None**

3. Move the pointer over any white area of the chart, drag the chart down to **row 22**, then resize the chart so that it extends from halfway across cell **A22** to cell **G40**

4. Click away from the chart to deselect it, click the **Data tab**, open the **Scenario Manager dialog box**, show all the **Best Case scenarios**, close the Scenario Manager dialog box, then verify that **$20,000** appears as the top value of the value (y) axis

5. Show all the **Current scenarios** again, close the dialog box, right-click the **value axis** (containing the dollar amounts), click **Format Axis**, verify that Axis Options is active, click the **Maximum Fixed option button**, select the contents of the **Maximum text box**, type **20000**, then click **Close**

   You change the top value of the value axis to match the top value of the value axis when the Best Case scenarios are active so that the charts show a meaningful comparison among the three sets of scenarios.

6. Deselect the chart, click the **Office button** , point to **Print**, click **Print Preview**, click the **Page Setup button** in the Print group, format the worksheet so that it fits on one page, is horizontally centered, and includes a header that displays **Current Scenarios** at the left and your name at the right, click **OK**, click **OK**, click the **Print button** in the Print group, then click **OK**

7. Click the **Data tab** if necessary, open the **Scenario Manager dialog box**, show all the **Best Case scenarios**, close the dialog box, then verify that **$72,620.00** appears in cell H19

8. Click the **chart title**, click in the formula bar, type **Best Case Forecast**, click outside the chart, click the **Page Layout tab**, click the **Print Titles button** in the Page Setup group, click the **Header/Footer tab**, change the custom header text to **Best Case Scenarios**, then print a copy

   Figure D-8 shows a printout of the worksheet with the Best Case scenarios active.

9. From the Scenario Manager, show all the **Worst Case scenarios**, verify that **$(13,600.00)** appears in cell H19, change the chart title to **Worst Case Forecast**, change the custom header to show **Worst Case Scenarios**, print a copy, then save and close the workbook

   Figure D-9 shows a printout of the worksheet with the Worst Case scenarios active. You can choose to mix and match scenarios to try out new predictions. For example, you could show the Current Salaries and Current Operating Costs scenarios along with the Best Case Rent scenario and the Worst Case Sales scenario. The net income in cell H19 changes with each combination.

Hint

To use a keystroke command to show a scenario, click the scenario in the Scenario Manager, then press [Alt][S].

Additional Practice

For additional practice with the skills presented in this project, complete Independent Challenge 1.

FIGURE D-8: Best Case scenarios

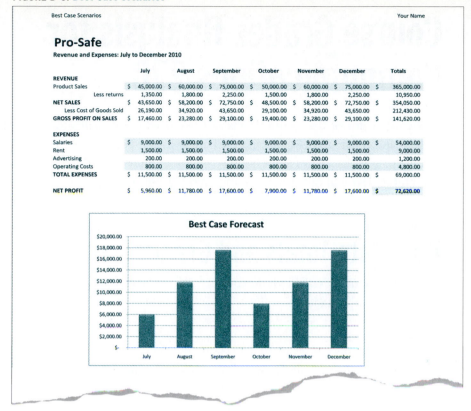

Best Case Scenarios   Your Name

Pro-Safe

Revenue and Expenses: July to December 2010

	July	August	September	October	November	December	Totals
REVENUE							
Product Sales	$ 45,000.00	$ 60,000.00	$ 75,000.00	$ 50,000.00	$ 60,000.00	$ 75,000.00	365,000.00
Less returns	1,350.00	1,800.00	2,250.00	1,500.00	1,800.00	2,250.00	10,950.00
NET SALES	$ 43,650.00	$ 58,200.00	$ 72,750.00	$ 48,500.00	$ 58,200.00	$ 72,750.00	354,050.00
Less Cost of Goods Sold	26,190.00	34,920.00	43,650.00	29,100.00	34,920.00	43,650.00	212,430.00
GROSS PROFIT ON SALES	$ 17,460.00	$ 23,280.00	$ 29,100.00	$ 19,400.00	$ 23,280.00	$ 29,100.00	141,620.00
EXPENSES							
Salaries	$ 9,000.00	$ 9,000.00	$ 9,000.00	$ 9,000.00	$ 9,000.00	$ 9,000.00	54,000.00
Rent	1,500.00	1,500.00	1,500.00	1,500.00	1,500.00	1,500.00	9,000.00
Advertising	200.00	200.00	200.00	200.00	200.00	200.00	1,200.00
Operating Costs	800.00	800.00	800.00	800.00	800.00	800.00	4,800.00
TOTAL EXPENSES	$ 11,500.00	$ 11,500.00	$ 11,500.00	$ 11,500.00	$ 11,500.00	$ 11,500.00	69,000.00
NET PROFIT	$ 5,960.00	$ 11,780.00	$ 17,600.00	$ 7,900.00	$ 11,780.00	$ 17,600.00	$ **72,620.00**

Best Case Forecast

FIGURE D-9: Worst Case scenarios

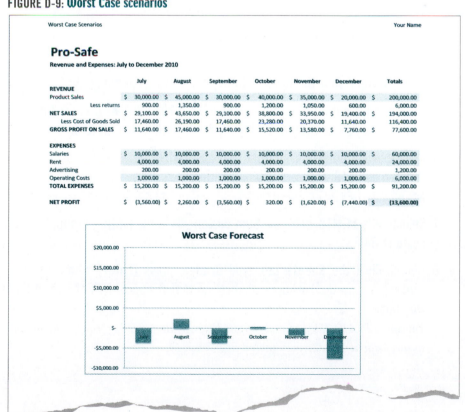

Worst Case Scenarios   Your Name

Pro-Safe

Revenue and Expenses: July to December 2010

	July	August	September	October	November	December	Totals
REVENUE							
Product Sales	$ 30,000.00	$ 45,000.00	$ 30,000.00	$ 40,000.00	$ 35,000.00	$ 20,000.00	200,000.00
Less returns	900.00	1,350.00	900.00	1,200.00	1,050.00	600.00	6,000.00
NET SALES	$ 29,100.00	$ 43,650.00	$ 29,100.00	$ 38,800.00	$ 33,950.00	$ 19,400.00	194,000.00
Less Cost of Goods Sold	17,460.00	26,190.00	17,460.00	23,280.00	20,370.00	11,640.00	116,400.00
GROSS PROFIT ON SALES	$ 11,640.00	$ 17,460.00	$ 11,640.00	$ 15,520.00	$ 13,580.00	$ 7,760.00	77,600.00
EXPENSES							
Salaries	$ 10,000.00	$ 10,000.00	$ 10,000.00	$ 10,000.00	$ 10,000.00	$ 10,000.00	60,000.00
Rent	4,000.00	4,000.00	4,000.00	4,000.00	4,000.00	4,000.00	24,000.00
Advertising	200.00	200.00	200.00	200.00	200.00	200.00	1,200.00
Operating Costs	1,000.00	1,000.00	1,000.00	1,000.00	1,000.00	1,000.00	6,000.00
TOTAL EXPENSES	$ 15,200.00	$ 15,200.00	$ 15,200.00	$ 15,200.00	$ 15,200.00	$ 15,200.00	91,200.00
NET PROFIT	$ (3,560.00)	$ 2,260.00	$ (3,560.00)	$ 320.00	$ (1,620.00)	$ (7,440.00)	$ **(13,600.00)**

Worst Case Forecast

Course Grades Analysis for Communications 220

As the instructor of Communications 220, you need to calculate a final grade for each student and then create a chart to help you analyze how well your students performed. To complete the course grades analysis shown in Figure D-15 on page 89, you need to **Calculate Totals and Grades**, **Create a Subtotals List and Chart**, and then **Format the Course Grades Analysis**.

Activity:

Calculate Totals and Grades

To calculate a student's mark for the course, you enter totals for each grade category, and then enter a formula to *weight* the grades according to type. Assignments are worth 35%, quizzes 25%, and exams 40%.

Hint

Press [Ctrl][S] frequently as you work to save.

Steps:

1. Open a new Excel workbook, save the workbook as **Course Grades Analysis** in the location where you store your Data Files, then set up and format the worksheet as shown in Figure D-10

2. Click cell **J4**, enter the formula **=(B4+C4+D4+E4)/(B20+C20+D20+E20)*J21**, press **[Enter]**, then verify that **30.625** appears in cell J4

3. Click cell **J4**, click **B20** in the formula on the formula bar, press **[F4]** to make the cell reference absolute, click **C20**, press **[F4]**, then make cells D20, E20, and J21 absolute

   You use the [F4] command to make the cells absolute so that when you copy the formula it divides the total assignment score by the value in row 21.

4. Press **[Enter]**, copy the formula through cell **J18**, then apply the Comma style

5. Click cell **K4**, enter the formula **=(F4+G4)/(F20+G20)*K21**, make the references to **F20**, **G20**, and **K21** absolute, press **[Enter]**, copy the formula through cell **K18**, then apply the Comma style

Hint

The formula required is =(H4+I4)/($H$20+$I$20)* $L$21.

6. Click cell **L4**, enter the formula that calculates the weighted score for exams, copy the formula through cell **L18**, then apply the Comma style

   Michael earned 24.00 out of 25 for quizzes and 33.60 out of 40 for exams.

7. Select cells **J4:M18**, click the **Sum button** Σ in the Editing group, then verify that Michael's total score is 88.23

Trouble

Be careful to enter "A," "B," and "C" where indicated; Excel AutoComplete adds the minus sign (-), which you will need to delete.

8. Double-click the **Sheet1 tab**, type **Grades**, press **[Enter]**, name the Sheet2 tab **Lookup**, press **[Enter]**, set up the Lookup worksheet so that it appears as shown in Figure D-11, then save the workbook

   You use a lookup table to look up the letter grade earned by each student; the letter grade corresponds to the student's total score entered in column M.

FIGURE D-10 Course Grades Analysis worksheet

Set the width of columns B to N at 6 pixels

Bold row 3

Center across columns A to N and format with bold and 20 pt

Right-align and bold labels in rows 20 and 21

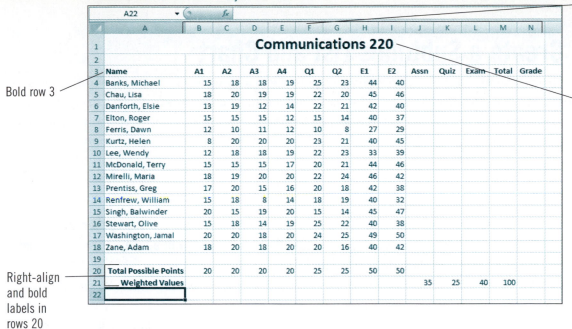

Name	A1	A2	A3	A4	Q1	Q2	E1	E2	Assn	Quiz	Exam	Total	Grade
Banks, Michael	15	18	18	19	25	23	44	40					
Chau, Lisa	18	20	19	19	22	20	45	46					
Danforth, Elsie	13	19	12	14	22	21	42	40					
Elton, Roger	15	15	15	12	15	14	40	37					
Ferris, Dawn	12	10	11	12	10	8	27	29					
Kurtz, Helen	8	20	20	20	23	21	40	45					
Lee, Wendy	12	18	18	19	22	23	33	39					
McDonald, Terry	15	15	15	17	20	21	44	46					
Mirelli, Maria	18	19	20	20	22	24	46	42					
Prentiss, Greg	17	20	15	16	20	18	42	38					
Renfrew, William	15	18	8	14	18	19	40	32					
Singh, Balwinder	20	15	19	20	15	14	45	47					
Stewart, Olive	15	18	14	19	25	22	40	38					
Washington, Jamal	20	20	18	20	24	25	49	50					
Zane, Adam	18	20	18	20	20	16	40	42					
Total Possible Points	20	20	20	20	25	25	50	50					
Weighted Values									35	25	40	100	

Communications 220

FIGURE D-11 Lookup table

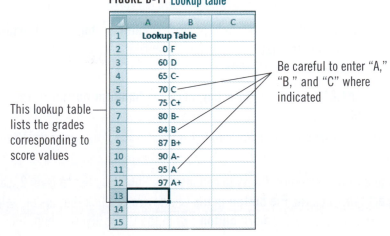

	A	B	C
1	**Lookup Table**		
2	0	F	
3	60	D	
4	65	C-	
5	70	C	
6	75	C+	
7	80	B-	
8	84	B	
9	87	B+	
10	90	A-	
11	95	A	
12	97	A+	
13			
14			
15			

This lookup table lists the grades corresponding to score values

Be careful to enter "A," "B," and "C" where indicated

Activity:

Create a Subtotals List and Chart

First you need to enter a formula that refers to the lookup table you created in the Lookup sheet. Then you need to create a Subtotals list that counts the number of times that each letter grade appears in column N of the Grades sheet. You create a Subtotals list when you want a quick way to sort, subtotal, and then total a series of values. Once you have completed the Subtotals list from the list of student grades, you need to create a pie chart that compares how many students earned each letter grade.

Steps:

1. Click the **Grades sheet tab**, click cell **N4**, click the **Formulas tab**, click the **Lookup & Reference button** in the Function Library group, click **LOOKUP**, click **lookup_value,array**, click **OK**, type **M4** in the Lookup_value text box, then press **[Tab]**

   You've entered the cell address of the value that the lookup table must use to assign a grade. This value represents Michael's total score out of 100 for the course.

2. Click the **Collapse Dialog Box button** next to Array, click the **Lookup sheet tab** to show the Lookup worksheet, select cells **A2:B12**, press **[F4]**, then click the **Expand Dialog Box button**

   The Function Arguments dialog box appears as shown in Figure D-12. Michael will earn a B+ for Communications 220.

3. Click **OK**, copy the formula in cell **N4** down through cell **N18**, select cells **N3:N18**, click the **Home tab**, click the **Copy button** in the Clipboard group, click the **Sheet3 tab**, click the **Paste list arrow** in the Clipboard group, click **Paste Values**, then change the name of the Sheet3 tab to **Subtotals**

4. Select cells **A2:A16**, click the **Sort & Filter button** in the Editing group, then click **Sort A to Z**

   Before you create a Subtotals list, you sort data so that the data you want to subtotal is arranged in groups. However, the results of the default sort are not correct. You want the grades sorted from A+ to F.

5. With cells **A2:A16** still selected, click the **Sort & Filter button**, click **Custom Sort**, click the **Order list arrow**, click **Custom List**, click in the List entries box, enter the grades in the order shown in Figure D-13, click **OK**, then click **OK**

6. Select cells **A1:A16**, click the **Data tab**, click the **Subtotal button** in the Outline group, click **OK**, then click **OK**

   The Subtotals function counts the number of times each grade appears. You can create a chart from this data.

7. Click the **2** in the Grouping frame to collapse the Subtotals list to level 2, select cells **A1:B24**, click the **Insert tab**, click the **Pie button** in the Charts group, click the far-left selection in the top row to insert a Pie chart, click the **More button** in the Chart Styles group, then select **Style 31**

8. Select **Grade A+** in the chart title, type **Breakdown of Final Grades**, click above the chart, then save the document

   The pie chart appears as shown in Figure D-14.

FIGURE D-12 Function Arguments dialog box

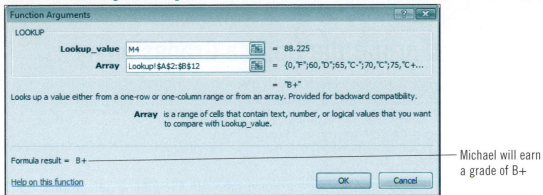

Michael will earn a grade of B+

FIGURE D-13 Creating a Custom List

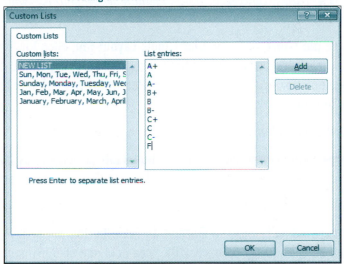

FIGURE D-14 Pie chart created

Click 2 in the Grouping pane to collapse the Subtotal list to level 2

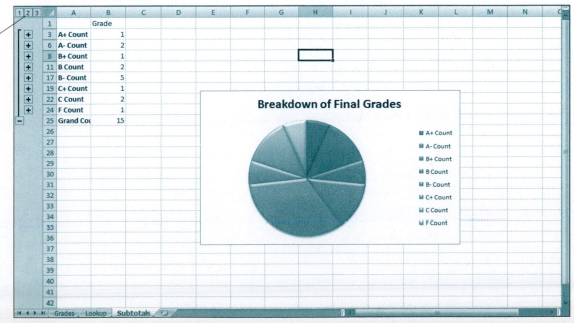

Activity:

Format the Course Grades Analysis

Now that you have created a pie chart that shows the breakdown of grades for the students in Communications 220, you need to format the chart, copy it into the Grades worksheet, and then format the worksheet for printing. Your completed course grades analysis will appear as shown in Figure D-15.

Steps:

1. Click cell **A1**, click the **Home tab**, click the **Find & Select button** in the Editing group, click **Replace**, type **Count**, press **[Tab]**, click **Replace All**, click **OK**, then click **Close**

   The "Count" label is removed from each of the entries on the worksheet and in the chart legend.

2. Click **3** in the Grouping pane, note how the pie chart data is no longer correct, then click **2**

   When you create a chart from grouped data in a Subtotals list, you need to keep the data grouped to maintain the integrity of the chart.

3. Click the **pie chart**, click the **Chart Tools Layout tab**, click the **Data Labels button** in the Labels group, click **More Data Label Options**, click the **Category Name check box** to select it, click the **Value check box** to deselect it, click the **Percentage check box** to select it, click the **Outside End option button**, then click **Close**

4. Click the **Legend button** in the Labels group, then click **None**

5. Click a white area of the chart, click the **Home tab**, click the **Copy button** ⬛ in the Clipboard group, click the **Grades sheet tab**, click cell **A24**, then click the **Paste button** in the Clipboard group

6. Drag the lower-right corner of the chart to cell N48, then click away from the chart to deselect it

7. Select cells **A3:N21**, click the **Format as Table button** in the Styles group, select the **Table Style Medium 20** (turquoise) style, click **OK**, then bold and center the grades in column N

8. Click the **Office Button** ⬤, point to **Print**, click **Print Preview**, then format the worksheet so that it fits on one page, is horizontally centered, and includes a custom header that displays **Course Grades Analysis** at the left and your name at the right

9. Print a copy of the worksheet, then save and close the workbook

   Your printed worksheet should appear similar to Figure D-15.

Additional Practice

For additional practice with the skills presented in this project, complete Independent Challenge 2.

Course Grades Analysis

Your Name

Communications 220

Name	A1	A2	A3	A4	Q1	Q2	E1	E2	Assn	Quiz	Exam	Total	Grade
Banks, Michael	15	18	18	19	25	23	44	40	30.63	24.00	33.60	88.23	B+
Chau, Lisa	18	20	19	19	22	20	45	46	33.25	21.00	36.40	90.65	A-
Danforth, Elsie	13	19	12	14	22	21	42	40	25.38	21.50	32.80	79.68	C+
Elton, Roger	15	15	15	12	15	14	40	37	24.94	14.50	30.80	70.24	C
Ferris, Dawn	12	10	11	12	10	8	27	29	19.69	9.00	22.40	51.09	F
Kurtz, Helen	8	20	20	20	23	21	40	45	29.75	22.00	34.00	85.75	B
Lee, Wendy	12	18	18	19	22	23	33	39	29.31	22.50	28.80	80.61	B-
McDonald, Terry	15	15	15	17	20	21	44	46	27.13	20.50	36.00	83.63	B-
Mirelli, Maria	18	19	20	20	22	24	46	42	33.69	23.00	35.20	91.89	A-
Prentiss, Greg	17	20	15	16	20	18	42	38	29.75	19.00	32.00	80.75	B-
Renfrew, William	15	18	8	14	18	19	40	32	24.06	18.50	28.80	71.36	C
Singh, Balwinder	20	15	19	20	15	14	45	47	32.38	14.50	36.80	83.68	B-
Stewart, Olive	15	18	14	19	25	22	40	38	28.88	23.50	31.20	83.58	B-
Washington, Jamal	20	20	18	20	24	25	49	50	34.13	24.50	39.60	98.23	A+
Zane, Adam	18	20	18	20	20	16	40	42	33.25	18.00	32.80	84.05	B
Total Possible Points	20	20	20	20	25	25	50	50					
Weighted Values									35	25	40	100	

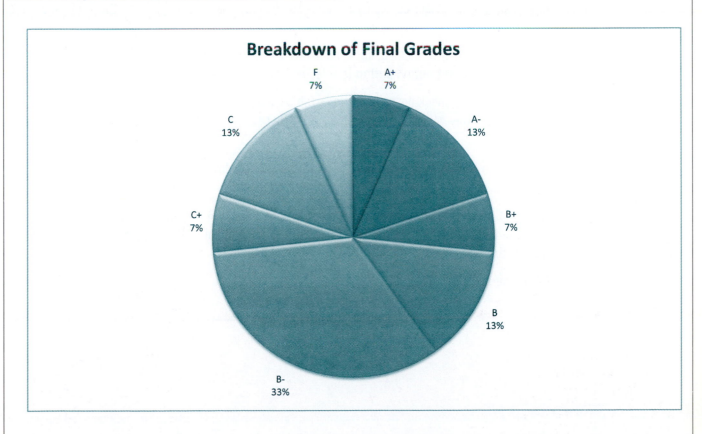

Breakdown of Final Grades

F 7% · A+ 7% · C 13% · A- 13% · C+ 7% · B+ 7% · B 13% · B- 33%

Customer Report for Fairhaven Foods

As an analyst for Fairhaven Foods, a small wholesaler of gourmet foods based in San Diego, you work with a product list already created in Excel to produce a report that analyzes sales over a four-year period. You use the PivotTable feature to create a report that includes a PivotTable and a chart. A PivotTable arranges and summarizes data so that you can make comparisons and analyze trends. To create the report, you need to **Create a PivotTable** and **Chart Results**.

Activity:

Create a PivotTable

You open the product list, then use the PivotTable function to create a PivotTable that shows yearly sales of each product category.

Steps:

1. Start Excel, open **Fairhaven Products.xlsx** from the location where you store the Data Files, save it as **Fairhaven Product Report** in the same location, double-click the **Sheet1 tab**, type **Sales Data**, then press **[Enter]**

2. Select cells **A1:F1**, click the **Bold button** B in the Font group, click the **Center button** ≣ in the Alignment group, select cells **A1:F30**, click the **Borders list arrow** ⊞ in the Font group, then click **All Borders**

3. With cells A1:F30 still selected, click the **Insert tab**, click **PivotTable** in the Tables group, verify that the **New Worksheet option button** is selected, then click **OK**

4. Click each of the check boxes in the PivotTable Field List as shown in Figure D-16
   All the data from the list is added to the PivotTable. You can choose how you want this data to be analyzed.

5. As shown in Figure D-17, click and then drag **Product** below Category in the Row Labels area
   The products are sorted by category.

6. Move the mouse just above cell **B4** to show the ↓ , click ↓ to select all the data in column B, drag the ↓ to cell **E4** to select all the values in the PivotTable, click the **Home tab**, then click the **Accounting Number Format button** $

7. Name the sheet tab **Product Sales**, then save the workbook

FIGURE D-16 Selecting fields for the PivotTable

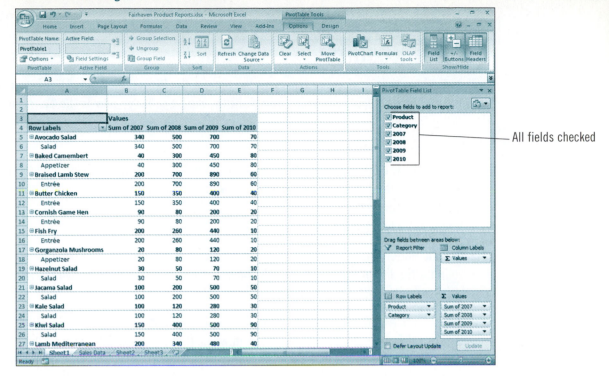

All fields checked

FIGURE D-17 Organizing row labels in the PivotTable

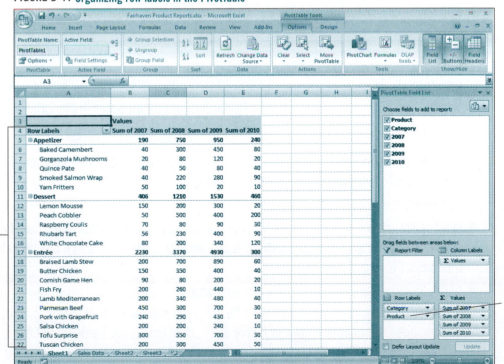

Data is sorted by Category and then Product

Drag Product below Category

Activity:

Chart Results

You need to create a chart to represent the data in the PivotTable, add callouts to the chart to highlight important data, then format and print the report so it appears as shown in Figure D-19.

Trouble

To apply a style, click the Cell Styles button in the Styles group.

Hint

In a PivotTable, cell references include the column name ("Sum of 2007"), the cell containing the upper-left corner of the PivotTable ("$B$3"), and the row name ("Category", "Entree").

Trouble

You will modify the callout text to match Figure D-19 in a later step.

Additional Practice

For additional practice with the skills presented in this project, complete Independent Challenge 3.

Steps:

1. Click cell **A1**, type **Fairhaven Foods**, press **[Enter]**, type **Category Sales**, press **[Enter]**, select cells **A1:E2**, click the **Merge & Center list arrow** in the Alignment group, click **Merge Across**, click the **Center button** ▥ in the Alignment group, then apply the **Heading 1 style** to cell **A1** and the **Heading 3 style** to cell **A2**

2. Use the button with the ▷ arrow to click the **Collapse Outline button** ⊟ to the left of **Appetizer** to collapse the list of appetizers so only the category name shows as shown in Figure D-18, then click ⊟ next to **Dessert**, **Entrée**, and **Salad**

3. Select cells **A4:E8**, click the **Insert tab**, click the **Column button** in the Charts group, click the **3-D Clustered Column** type, drag the chart down so that its upper-left corner is positioned in cell A11, resize the chart so it appears as shown in Figure D-19, click the check box next to **2008** in the PivotTable Field List to deselect it, then click the check box next to **2009** to deselect it

   Only data for 2007 and 2010 is shown. As you can see, Fairhaven Foods experienced a significant reduction in the sale of entrées between 2007 and 2010.

4. Click cell **A27**, type **=100-(**, click cell **C7**, type **/**, click cell **B7**, type *100)**, press **[Enter]**, click cell **A27**, then click the **Comma Style button** ▯ in the Number group

   The formula calculates the percentage decrease in sales of entrées from 2007 to 2010. You should see 86.55 in cell A27. Notice how the formula references the cell addresses in the formula bar.

5. Click the **Insert tab**, click **Shapes** in the Illustrations group, click the **Rectangular Callout** in the Callouts section, draw a callout box similar to the box shown in the completed report in Figure D-19, then type the text **87% Reduction in Entrée Sales from 2007 to 2010**

6. Click the **Sales Data sheet tab**, click cell **F6**, type **300**, then press **[Enter]**

7. Click the **Product Sales tab**, click cell **B5** in the PivotTable, click the **PivotTable Tools Options tab**, then click the **Refresh button** in the Data group

   The value in cell A27 changes to 74.44.

8. Select **87%** in the callout, type **74%**, click the **Drawing Tools Format tab**, click the **More button** in the Shape Styles group, click **Subtle Effect - Accent 1**, click the **Page Layout tab**, click **Themes**, then select **Metro**

9. Delete the contents of cell **A27**, select cells **A3:C9**, move the selection to the right one column so the table appears centered below the title, set up the document so that it is centered horizontally and includes the header shown in Figure D-19, then enter your name in cell A27

10. Print a copy, then save and close the workbook

FIGURE D-18 Collapsing the Appetizer group

	A	B	C	D	E
1	**Fairhaven Foods**				
2	Category Percentages				
3	Values				
4	Row Labels ▾	Sum of 2007	Sum of 2008	Sum of 2009	Sum of 2010
5	⊞ **Appetizer**	**$190.00**	**$ 750.00**	**$ 950.00**	**$ 240.00**
6	⊟ **Dessert**	**$406.00**	**$ 1,210.00**	**$ 1,530.00**	**$ 460.00**
7	Lemon Mousse	$150.00	$ 200.00	$ 300.00	$ 20.00
8	Peach Cobbler	$50.00	$ 500.00	$ 400.00	$ 200.00
9	Raspberry Coulis	$70.00	$ 80.00	$ 90.00	$ 30.00
10	Rhubarb Tart	$56.00	$ 230.00	$ 400.00	$ 90.00
11	White Chocolate Cake	$80.00	$ 200.00	$ 340.00	$ 120.00
12	⊟ **Entrée**	**$2,230.00**	**$ 3,370.00**	**$ 4,930.00**	**$ 300.00**
13	Braised Lamb Stew	$200.00	$ 700.00	$ 890.00	$ 60.00
14	Butter Chicken	$150.00	$ 350.00	$ 400.00	$ 40.00
15	Cornish Game Hen	$90.00	$ 80.00	$ 200.00	$ 20.00
16	Fish Fry	$200.00	$ 260.00	$ 440.00	$ 10.00
17	Lamb Mediterranean	$200.00	$ 340.00	$ 480.00	$ 40.00
18	Parmesan Beef	$450.00	$ 300.00	$ 700.00	$ 30.00
19	Pork with Grapefruit	$240.00	$ 290.00	$ 430.00	$ 10.00
20	Salsa Chicken	$200.00	$ 200.00	$ 240.00	$ 10.00

Heading 1 style applied to cell A1

Heading 3 style applied to cell A2

The plus sign next to the Appetizer group indicates that it is collapsed

FIGURE D-19 Completed report

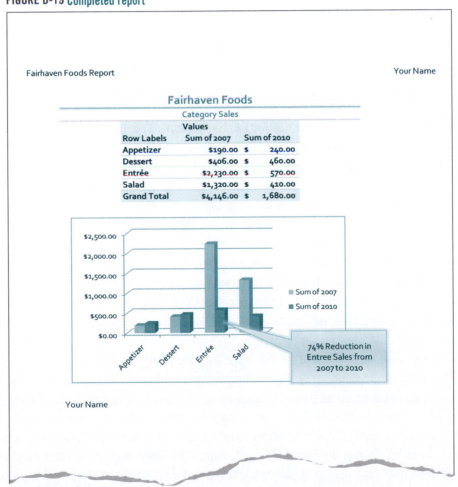

Fairhaven Foods Report   Your Name

Fairhaven Foods
Category Sales

	Values	
Row Labels	Sum of 2007	Sum of 2010
Appetizer	$190.00	$ 240.00
Dessert	$406.00	$ 460.00
Entrée	$2,230.00	$ 570.00
Salad	$1,320.00	$ 410.00
Grand Total	$4,146.00	$ 1,680.00

74% Reduction in Entree Sales from 2007 to 2010

■ Sum of 2007
■ Sum of 2010

Your Name

Independent Challenges

INDEPENDENT CHALLENGE 1

As the owner of a small business, you decide that you need to expand your operations in order to generate more income. To help you make an informed decision, you will use the Scenario Manager to see the effect of your plans on a current revenue and expenses worksheet.

1. Determine the name of your company, the type of business it conducts, and your plans for expansion. For example, you could run a home-based catering service that has grown big enough to warrant moving the business out of your home and into a commercial location. Alternatively, you could run a snow removal business from a small commercial office and decide to move into a larger office and buy several new pieces of snow removal equipment. Write the name of your company and a short description of your expansion plans in the box below:

Company Name:_____

Description of Expansion Plans:_____

2. Create a worksheet that shows your revenue and expenses over a six-month period. Include labels for each of the six months (e.g., January to June); labels for the various types of revenue you generate (e.g., Catering Sales and Consulting); and labels for your various expenses (e.g., Rent, Salaries, Advertising, Equipment, and Operating Costs). Note that returns and cost of goods sold are calculated as a percentage of your gross revenue (usually 3% for returns and 60% to 70% for cost of sales). Calculate your revenue and expenses both by month and by six-month total.

3. Format the worksheet attractively, then save the workbook as **My Predictions** to the location where you store the Data Files.

4. Create Current scenarios from the data currently entered in the worksheet. Note that you only need to create scenarios for the rows that contain the values you will change when you create a Best Case and Worst Case scenario.

5. Change values in the worksheet to reflect your best case predictions should you carry out your expansion plans. For example, if you decide to relocate, your Rent expense may increase, and if you hire an assistant, your Salaries expense will increase. Make sure you also increase your income to reflect the increased revenue you expect after expanding.

6. Create Best Case scenarios from the new values you have entered in the worksheet.

7. Change the values again to reflect your worst case predictions, should your expansion plans fail to proceed as well as you hope, then create Worst Case scenarios from the values that represent your worst case predictions.

8. Show the Best Case scenarios, create a column chart or bar chart that displays the Best Case monthly income, apply the chart style of your choice, add "Best Case Forecast" as the chart title, then format and print a copy of the worksheet. Make sure you include your name and "Best Case Forecast" in the header.

9. Note the upper limit of the value axis (x-axis) in the chart. You want the printed charts with the Current, Best, and Worst Case scenarios worksheets to display the same upper limit on the value axis so that the differences in the three charts are readily apparent.

10. Show the Current scenarios, change the title of the chart, change the upper limit on the value axis to the same upper limit displayed in the Best Case column chart, change the header to reflect the worksheet content, then print a copy.

11. Show the Worst Case scenarios, change the title of the chart, change the upper limit on the value axis to the same upper limit displayed in the Best Case chart, change the header to reflect the worksheet content, then print a copy.

12. Save and close the workbook.

INDEPENDENT CHALLENGE 2

You have been working all term as a teaching assistant for a course of your choice. The instructor you work for has given you the grade sheet she has kept by hand and has asked you to transfer it to Excel and then calculate each student's grade. Complete the steps below to create a course grades analysis for a course of your choice.

1. Determine the name of the course. For example, the course could be English 100, Psychology 210, or International Business 301.
2. Determine the grade categories and the percentage of scores allocated to each category. Allocate at least three grade categories and make sure the percentages (weighted values) you assign add up to 100%. For example, you could allocate 40% of the total grade to assignments, 30% to exams, and 30% to presentations.
3. Start Excel, set up a worksheet called **Grades** with the name of the course, a list of at least 15 students, and labels for the various assignments, exams, quizzes, and so on. Make sure you include at least two items in each of the three grade categories you have selected.
4. Save the workbook as **My Grades Analysis** in the location where you store your Data Files.
5. Determine the total scores possible for each item in each grade category and enter the totals two rows below the list of names. To check the setup of your course grades analysis, refer to the course grades analysis you created for Project 2.
6. Enter the points for each student. Make sure you refer to the totals you entered to ensure that each score you enter for each student is equal to or less than the total points possible.
7. Calculate the total points for each grade category, divide the total points by the total of the possible points, then multiply the result by the percentage you assigned to the Grade category. The formula required is: Sum of Student's Points/Sum of Total Points*Weighted Value. Make sure you use absolute references so that you can copy the formula without errors. For example, if the Assignment points are entered in cells C4, D4, and F4, the total possible points are entered in cells C25, D25, and F25, and the weighted value of Assignments is 40%, then the formula required is =(C4+D4+F4)/($C$25+$D$25+$F$25)*.4.
8. Calculate the total points out of 100 earned by the first student on your list.
9. Copy the formulas you used to calculate the first student's weighted score in each category and the total score for the remaining students.
10. Create a lookup table in a worksheet called Lookup that lists the letter grades and ranges you specify.
11. Enter the Lookup formula in the appropriate cell in the Grades worksheet, then copy the formula down for the remaining students.
12. Copy the grades to a new worksheet named Subtotals, then paste them as values.
13. Sort the grades in alphabetical order (you may need to create a custom list if your grades include grades such as A- and B+).
14. Create a Subtotals list that counts the occurrences of each grade, then collapse the Subtotals list to level 2.
15. Remove "Count" where needed, create a pie chart from the data in the Subtotals list to show the scores by letter grade, format the chart attractively with percentages and a chart style of your choice, then copy it to the Grades sheet.
16. Apply the table style of your choice to the Grades sheet, format the worksheet so that both the table and the chart fit on one page, include the name of the course and "Grades" (for example, "English 12 Grades") and your name in the header, print a copy, then save and close the workbook.

INDEPENDENT CHALLENGE 3

As the manager of a local video store, you have decided to evaluate the popularity of the videos and DVDs that your clientele rents and buys. The data you need is already included in an Excel file. You open this file and use the PivotTable feature to create a report and chart that analyzes the data.

1. Start Excel, open Classic Video.xlsx from the location where you store your Data Files, save it as **Classic Video Report** in the same location, then name the Sheet1 tab Unit Sales and Rentals.
2. Format the worksheet so that the header row is bold and centered and all rows are enclosed by border lines.

3. Create a PivotTable from the data.

4. Click each of the check boxes in the PivotTable Field list.

5. Move Video Title below Genre in the Row Labels area.

6. Name the sheet tab Product Report, then enter **Classic Video** as the title in cell A1 and **Rentals by Genre** as the subtitle in cell A2. Format the titles attractively.

7. Collapse the list so only the genres appear, show only the data for 2010 Unit Rentals, then create a pie chart that shows the breakdown of rentals by genre.

8. Format the chart attractively using the table style of your choice. Include "Breakdown of Rentals" as the chart title.

9. In the Unit Sales and Rentals worksheet, search for "Classic" and replace with "Drama," then update the PivotTable in the Product Report sheet.

10. Add a callout shape containing the text "Comedy and Drama continue to be the most popular genres" that points to the wedges representing Comedy and Drama, then format the shape using the style of your choice.

11. Apply the theme of your choice, set up the document so that it is centered horizontally and includes "Video Report" and your name in the header, print a copy, then save and close the workbook.

INDEPENDENT CHALLENGE 4

You run a sailboat rental business on Maui that caters to adventure-based travelers who rent sailboats for up to two weeks to explore the Hawaiian Islands. During the previous winter, you failed to make a profit on the business. Now you want to project sales for the coming winter months based on your plan to acquire more sailboats, increase advertising, and move into an attractive new boathouse.

1. Create the worksheet shown in Figure D-20, then save the workbook as **Winter Sailboat Rentals**. Fill cell A1 with Purple, Accent 4, Lighter 60%.

FIGURE D-20: Revenue and expenses worksheet

	A	B	C	D	E
1	Tropic Breezes Rentals				
2		Winter Rentals			
3		November	December	January	Totals
4	REVENUE				
5	Rental Income	$ 54,000.00	$ 62,000.00	$ 75,000.00	
6	Less Cancellations: 4%				
7	NET REVENUE				
8	Less Cost of Rentals: 75%				
9	GROSS PROFIT ON RENTALS				
10					
11	EXPENSES				
12	Salaries	$ 8,200.00	$ 8,200.00	$ 8,200.00	
13	Rent	1,500.00	1,500.00	1,500.00	
14	Advertising	2,500.00	2,500.00	2,500.00	
15	Operating Costs	2,000.00	2,000.00	2,000.00	
16	Total Expenses				
17					
18	NET INCOME				
19					
20					

2. Calculate the Cancellations, Net Revenue, Cost of Rentals (75% of Rental Income), Gross Profit on Rentals, Total Expenses, and Net Income.

3. Ensure that your total net income in cell E18 is ($2,490.00). Note that you need to calculate the cost of rentals as 75% of the Rental Income, not the Net Revenue.

4. Create Current scenarios of the data for Rental Income, Rent, and Advertising. Call the scenarios Current Rental Income, Current Rent, and Current Advertising.

5. Create the following Expansion scenarios for the Rental Income, Rent, and Advertising data:

Expansion Rental Income:	**November: $106,000; December: $135,500; January: $177,450**
Expansion Rent:	**$2,200 per month**
Expansion Advertising:	**$3,000 per month**

6. Verify that your net income in cell E18 is $41,779.50 after you have created and then displayed the three Expansion scenarios.

7. With the Expansion scenarios still displayed, create a bar chart that displays the monthly net income. Note the upper limit of the value axis ($25,000). Format the bar chart attractively as shown in Figure D-21.

8. As shown in Figure D-21, apply shading to cells containing changing scenario values and the Net Income total, insert a custom header, then format and print a copy of the worksheet.

9. Display the Current scenarios, modify the header and chart title as shown in Figure D-22, then change the upper limit of the value axis to $25,000 so that it matches the bar chart that shows the Expansion net income.

10. Print a copy of the Current scenarios worksheet, then save and close the workbook.

FIGURE D-21 Projected Winter Rentals worksheet

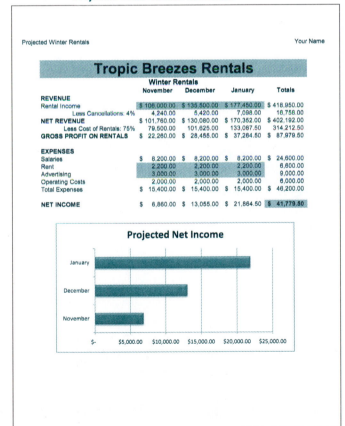

FIGURE D-22 Current Winter Rentals worksheet

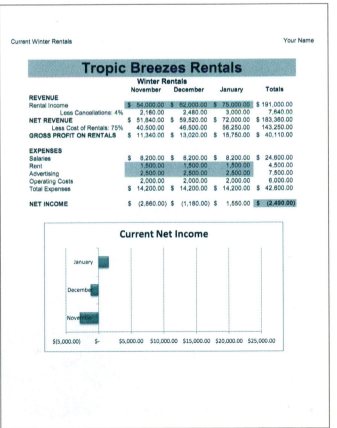

Visual Workshop

You have just completed a survey of the leisure activities most preferred by your classmates in the film program at Gulf Coast College. Now you want to create a chart to display the results of your survey. Create the worksheet shown in Figure D-23, then create a Subtotals list that counts the number of times each activity appears in column B of Sheet1. Once you have created the Subtotals list, create the pie chart shown in Figure D-24. Apply the Urban theme, enter your name in cell A45, save your workbook as **Leisure Activities** in the location where you store your Data Files, print a copy, then save and close the workbook.

FIGURE D-23 Leisure Activities worksheet

	A	B	C
1	Student #	Activity	
2	1	Travel	
3	2	Music	
4	3	Travel	
5	4	Travel	
6	5	Sports	
7	6	Dancing	
8	7	Travel	
9	8	Sports	
10	9	Sports	
11	10	Travel	
12	11	Art	
13	12	Travel	
14	13	Art	
15	14	Sports	
16	15	Art	
17	16	Art	
18	17	Travel	
19	18	Travel	
20	19	Travel	
21	20	Sports	
22			
23			

FIGURE D-24 Leisure Activities pie chart

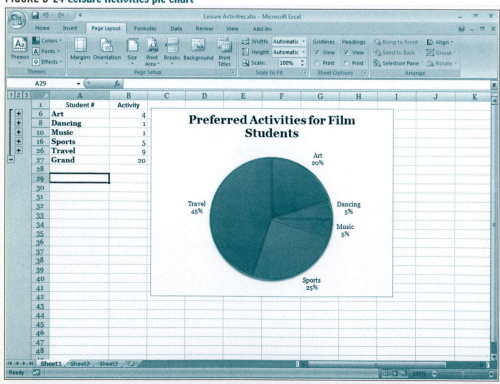

Microsoft
► # Word and Excel
Projects

Unit E

Integration Projects I

In This Unit You Will Create the Following:

 ► ### Job Performance Reviews

 ► ### Sales Report

 ► ### Marketing Report

You can use the integration capabilities of Microsoft Office 2007 to combine text you create in Word with numerical data that you analyze in Excel. For example, suppose you have created a report in Word that references a variety of charts and other data created in Excel. You can copy selected data from Excel and paste it into the Word report as a link. Every time you make a change to the data in Excel, the changes are also made to the data you copied and pasted as a link into the Word report because the two files are linked. In this unit, you will learn how to link documents that combine elements created in both Word and Excel.

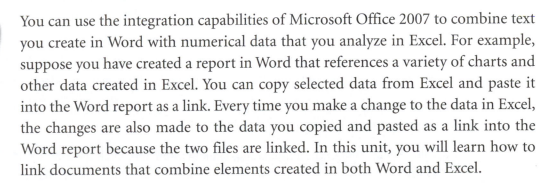

Job Performance Reviews

As a supervisor at Markham Industries, you need to create a form that you can use to compile the results of employee performance reviews. To complete performance reviews for Kelly Lee and Jeff Wheeler, two service agents, you **Create the Form in Word**, **Add Content Controls in Word**, **Compile Results in Excel**, and then **Link the Form and Results** for each employee. The completed performance review for Jeff is shown in Figure E-10 on page 107.

Activity:

Create the Form in Word

You need to set up the performance review form in Word.

Steps:

1. Start a new blank document in Word, click the **Page Layout tab**, click **Margins** in the Page Setup group, click **Custom Margins**, set the top and bottom margin to **.6"**, click **OK**, then save the document as **Performance Review Form** in the location where you store your Data Files

2. Click the **Home tab**, click **Change Styles** in the Styles group, point to **Style Set**, click **Simple**, right-click **Normal** in the Styles gallery, click **Modify**, click the **Font list arrow**, select **Arial Rounded MT Bold**, click the **Decrease Paragraph Spacing button** ⬆≣ two times, then click **OK**

3. Type **Markham Industries**, press **[Enter]**, type **Job Performance Review**, press **[Enter]** twice, apply the **Title** style to **Markham Industries**, apply the **Subtitle** style to Job Performance Review, then center both lines

4. Click the last **blank line** below **Job Performance Review**, click the **Insert tab**, click **Table** in the Tables group, click **Insert Table**, type **4**, press **[Tab]**, type **13**, click **OK**, then type the text for the table as shown in Figure E-1

5. Select all **four cells** in row 1, press and hold **[Ctrl]**, click to the left of the **Rankings cell**, then click to the left of the **Ranking Summary**, **Ranking Chart**, and **Written Evaluation** rows to select them

6. On the **Table Tools Design tab**, click the **Shading list arrow** in the Table Styles group, select **Aqua, Accent 5, Darker 50%**, click the **Home tab**, click the **Font Color list arrow** A⋎ in the Font group, click the **White, Background 1 color**, click the **Grow Font button** A˄ in the Font group once, then click the **Center button** ≣ in the Paragraph group

7. Select all **four cells** in row 1, click the **Table Tools Layout tab**, click the **Merge Cells button** in the Merge group, then use Figure E-2 as your guide to merge cells in selected rows

8. Use **[Ctrl]** to select **rows 1 through 6** (Rankings), and the rows containing **Ranking Summary**, **Ranking Chart**, and **Written Evaluation**

9. Click **Properties** in the Table group, click the **Row tab**, click the **Specify height check box**, press **[Tab]**, type **.3**, click the **Cell tab**, click the **Center option**, click **OK**, deselect the table, then save the document

Hint

You use the [Ctrl] key to quickly select nonadjacent rows and cells in a table so that you can apply formatting all at once.

FIGURE E-1: Table text

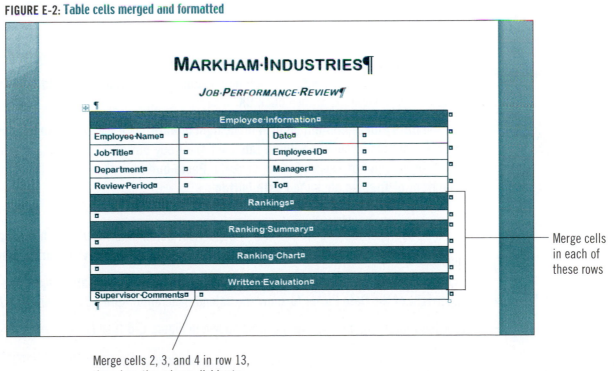

MARKHAM·INDUSTRIES¶

JOB·PERFORMANCE·REVIEW¶

These rows are left blank

Employee·Information¤	¤	¤	¤	¤
Employee·Name¤	¤	Date¤	¤	¤
Job·Title¤	¤	Employee·ID¤	¤	¤
Department¤	¤	Manager¤	¤	¤
Review·Period¤	¤	To¤	¤	¤
Rankings¤	¤	¤	¤	¤
¤	¤	¤	¤	¤
Ranking·Summary¤	¤	¤	¤	¤
¤	¤	¤	¤	¤
Ranking·Chart¤	¤	¤	¤	¤
¤	¤	¤	¤	¤
Written·Evaluation¤	¤	¤	¤	¤
Supervisor·Comments¤	¤	¤	¤	¤

¶

FIGURE E-2: Table cells merged and formatted

MARKHAM·INDUSTRIES¶

JOB·PERFORMANCE·REVIEW¶

Employee·Information¤			
Employee·Name¤	¤	Date¤	¤
Job·Title¤	¤	Employee·ID¤	¤
Department¤	¤	Manager¤	¤
Review·Period¤	¤	To¤	¤
Rankings¤			
¤			
Ranking·Summary¤			
¤			
Ranking·Chart¤			
¤			
Written·Evaluation¤			
Supervisor·Comments¤	¤		

¶

Merge cells in each of these rows

Merge cells 2, 3, and 4 in row 13, then drag the column divider to the right as shown

Activity:

Add Content Controls in Word

You plan to use the same performance review form to record the performance reviews of all the employees you supervise. You make the form an electronic one that includes content controls so you can complete the form on the computer. Your first step is to show the Developer tab so you can access the tools used to create forms.

Steps:

1. Click the **Office Button** ⬛, click **Word Options**, click the **Show Developer tab in the Ribbon check box** to select it, click **OK**, then click the cell to the right of Employee Name

2. Click the **Developer tab**, then click the **Rich Text button** Aa in the Controls group to insert a Rich Text content control as shown in Figure E-3

3. Press **[Tab]** twice to move to the blank cell to the right of Date, click the **Date Picker button** 📅 in the Controls group, click **Properties** in the Controls group, select the date format that corresponds to **May 25, 2010**, then click **OK**

   When you fill in the form, you will only be able to enter a date in the cell to the right of Date.

4. Click the cell to the right of Employee ID, click the **Legacy Tools button** 🔧▾ in the Controls group, click the **Text Form Field button** abl, double-click the **shaded area** to open the Text Form Field Options dialog box, click the **Type list arrow**, click **Number**, select the contents of the **Maximum length text box**, type **4**, compare the Text Form Field Options dialog box to Figure E-4, then click **OK**

   When you fill in the form, you will only be able to enter up to four digits in the cell to the right of Employee ID.

5. Add a **Rich Text content control** in the cells to the right of Job Title and Manager, click the cell to the right of Department, click the **Combo Box button** 🗔 in the Controls group, click **Properties** in the Controls group, click **Add,** type **Administration**, press **[Enter]**, click **Add**, add the four departments shown in Figure E-5, then click **OK**

6. Click the **Date Picker content control** to the right of **Date**, click the **selection handle** (it turns dark blue when selected), click the **Home tab**, click the **Copy button** 📋 in the Clipboard group, click the cell to the right of Review Period, click the **Paste button** in the Clipboard group, click the cell to the right of **To**, then click the **Paste button**

   You can copy and paste fields that contain special formatting to save time.

7. Click the **Developer tab**, click to the right of **Supervisor Comments**, insert a **Rich Text content control**, save the document, then save the document again as **Performance Review Form_Kelly Lee**

8. Click the cell to the right of **Employee Name**, type **Kelly Lee**, press **[Tab]** twice, click the **list arrow** to the right of the Date Picker to show the calendar, scroll to April 2010, then click **April 23**

9. Enter the remaining data for Kelly Lee as shown in Figure E-6 (use [Tab] to move to each control), then save the document

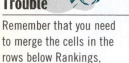

Trouble

Remember that you need to merge the cells in the rows below Rankings, Ranking Summary, and Ranking chart.

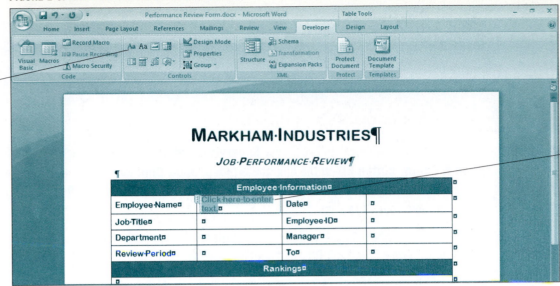

FIGURE E-3: Rich Text content control inserted

Rich Text content control button

Rich text content control inserted in the table cell

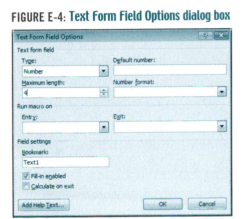

FIGURE E-4: Text Form Field Options dialog box

FIGURE E-5: Drop-Down List Properties

FIGURE E-6: Form text for Kelly Lee

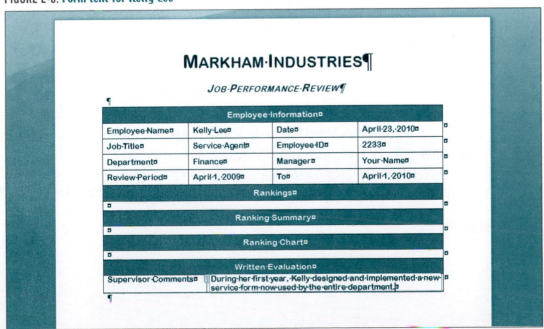

Activity:

Compile Results in Excel

You need to create a worksheet in Excel into which you can enter the numerical results of the performance review. You also need to create a chart in Excel that summarizes the results.

Steps:

1. Start a new blank workbook in Excel, type **Supervisor Rating** in cell A1, select cells **A1:B1**, click the **Merge & Center button** [icon] in the Alignment group, apply **Bold** formatting, enter and enhance the text as shown in Figure E-7, then save the workbook as **Job Performance Reviews** in the location where you save your Data Files

2. Double-click the **Sheet1 tab**, type **Kelly**, press **[Enter]**, click cell **B8**, double-click the **Sum button** [Σ] in the Editing group, click cell **D8**, then double-click [Σ]

3. Click cell **B10**, type **=(B2+D2)/2**, press **[Enter]**, click cell **B10**, then fill cells **B11:B15** with the formula in cell B10

   This formula determines the average score between the supervisor rating and the peer rating.

4. Select cells **A10:B15**, click the **Insert tab**, click the **Column button** in the Charts group, click the upper-left chart type (Clustered Column), click **Layout 1** in the Chart Layouts group, click the **More button** in the Chart Styles group, select **Style 31**, click the **Chart Tools Layout tab**, click the **Chart Title button** in the Labels group, click **None**, click the **Legend button** in the Labels group, then click **None**

5. Size and position the chart so that it extends from cell **C10** through cell **J26**

6. Right-click the **value axis (y-axis)**, click **Format Axis**, click the **Fixed option button** next to Maximum, select **5.0** in the Maximum text box, type **5**, then click **Close**

   Although the value in the Maximum text box is already 5, you need to select and retype 5 because you want this value to be fixed. You set the maximum scale for the value axis at 5 so that the scale remains the same regardless of the data entered in the chart.

7. Double-click the **Sheet2 tab**, type **Jeff**, press **[Enter]**, click the **Kelly sheet tab**, click the **Select All button** [icon] to the left of the **A** at the upper-left corner of the worksheet frame to select the entire worksheet, click the **Copy button** [icon] in the Clipboard group, click the **Jeff sheet tab**, then click the **Paste button** in the Clipboard group

8. Enter values for Jeff in cells **B2:B7** and cells **D2:D7** as shown in Figure E-8, then verify that the totals in row 8 are updated

9. Right-click the **chart**, click **Select Data**, click the **Collapse Dialog Box button** [icon] next to Chart data range, click the **Jeff Sheet tab**, verify that cells **A10:B15** are selected, click the **Expand Dialog Box button** [icon], click **OK**, then save the workbook

   The chart appears as shown in Figure E-9. When you copied the chart from the Kelly worksheet to the Jeff worksheet, the chart still referenced the cells in the Kelly worksheet. You changed the reference so the chart now shows data related to Jeff's rankings.

FIGURE E-7: Worksheet labels and values

	A	B	C	D	E	F
1	Supervisor Rating		Peer Rating			
2	Knowledge	5	Knowledge	4		
3	Work Quality	5	Work Quality	3		
4	Attendance	4	Attendance	4		
5	Initiative	5	Initiative	4		
6	Communication	3	Communication	1		
7	Dependability	4	Dependability	4		
8						
9	Average Rating					
10	Knowledge					
11	Work Quality					
12	Attendance					
13	Initiative					
14	Communication					
15	Dependability					
16						

FIGURE E-8: Values for Jeff

	A	B	C	D	E
1	Supervisor Rating		Peer Rating		
2	Knowledge	2	Knowledge	1	
3	Work Quality	3	Work Quality	1	
4	Attendance	1	Attendance	3	
5	Initiative	1	Initiative	2	
6	Communication	2	Communication	2	
7	Dependability	2	Dependability	1	
8		11		10	

Verify updated values

FIGURE E-9: Jeff's chart

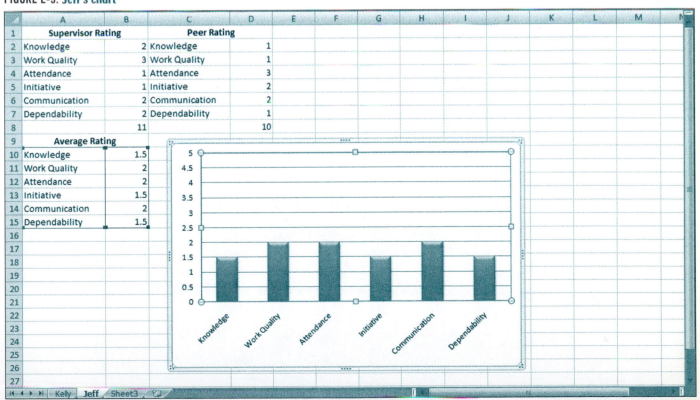

Activity:

Link the Form and Results

You need to copy Kelly's performance results from Excel and paste them into the Word form as linked objects. After completing Kelly's performance review form, you need to save the document as Jeff's, edit the text to reflect Jeff's information, and then change the source for the Excel performance results so the linked objects reflect Jeff's information.

Steps:

1. Click the **Kelly sheet tab**, select cells **A1:D8**, click the **Copy button** in the Clipboard group, switch to Word, click the **cell below Rankings**, click the **Home tab**, click the **Paste list arrow** in the Clipboard group, click **Paste Special**, click the **Paste link option button**, click **Microsoft Office Excel Worksheet Object**, click **OK**, click the **worksheet object**, then click the **Center button** in the Paragraph group

2. Switch to Excel, select cells **A9:B15**, click , switch to Word, click the cell below **Ranking Summary**, click the **Paste list arrow**, click **Paste Special**, click the **Paste link option button**, click **Microsoft Office Excel Worksheet Object**, click **OK**, then center the copied worksheet object

3. Switch to Excel, click a blank area of the **chart**, click , switch to Word, click the **cell below Ranking Chart**, click the **Paste button**, click the **chart**, click the **Chart Tools Format tab**, click the **Size dialog box launcher** , click the **Lock aspect ratio check box** to select it, change the Height to **2.3**, click **Close**, click the **Home tab**, then click

Trouble

If the values have not been updated, right-click each object, then click Update Link.

4. Switch to Excel, change Kelly's ranking for Attendance to **5** from both the Supervisor and the Peers (cell B4 and cell D4), save and close the Excel workbook, switch to Word, verify that the value for attendance is "5" and the top of the Attendance column is even with "5" on the value axis, save the document, then print a copy

   Kelly's rankings for Attendance and the column chart are both updated in the Word document because the data is linked to the Excel workbook.

Trouble

The values in the Excel objects will not yet match Figure E-10.

5. Save the document again as **Performance Review Form_Jeff Wheeler**, click the **Employee Name cell**, press **[Tab]**, then enter text for Jeff in the Employee Information and Written Evaluation sections as shown in the completed form in Figure E-10

6. Click the **Office Button** , point to **Prepare**, click **Edit Links to Files**, if necessary, click **Change Source**, click **Item**, select **Kelly** and type **Jeff** in the Set Item dialog box as shown in Figure E-11, click **OK**, click **Job Performance Reviews.xlsx** in the list of files, click **Open**, repeat the process to change the source for the second link listed in the Links dialog box, then click **OK**

Additional Practice

For additional practice with the skills presented in this project, complete Independent Challenge 1.

7. Click the **chart**, click the **Chart Tools Design tab**, click **Select Data** in the Data group, select **Kelly** in the Chart data range text box, type **Jeff**, click **OK**, then close the Excel workbook

8. Save the document, print a copy, then close the document

   The completed performance review for Jeff appears as shown in Figure E-10. If you later open either linked document to make changes, a message box will appear advising you that the document is linked to an Excel workbook. Click Yes to maintain the link between the document and the workbook.

FIGURE E-10: Jeff Wheeler's Performance Review

MARKHAM INDUSTRIES

JOB PERFORMANCE REVIEW

Employee Information

Employee Name	Jeff Wheeler	Date	April 30, 2010
Job Title	Sales Manager	Employee ID	4455
Department	Marketing	Manager	Your Name
Review Period	April 1, 2009	To	April 1, 2010

Rankings

Supervisor Rating		Peer Rating	
Knowledge	2	Knowledge	1
Work Quality	3	Work Quality	1
Attendance	1	Attendance	3
Initiative	1	Initiative	2
Communication	2	Communication	2
Dependability	2	Dependability	1
	11		10

Ranking Summary

Average Rating	
Knowledge	1.5
Work Quality	2
Attendance	2
Initiative	1.5
Communication	2
Dependability	1.5

Ranking Chart

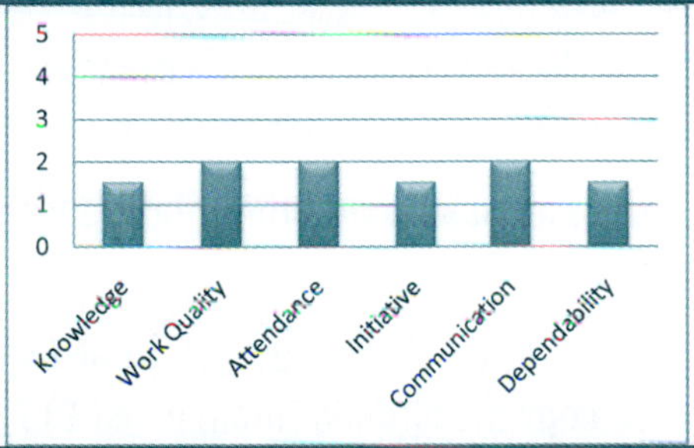

Written Evaluation

Supervisor Comments	Jeff needs to develop a more conventional work ethic.

FIGURE E-11: Set Item dialog box

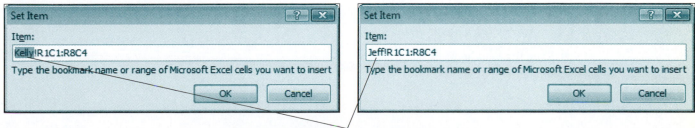

Delete Kelly, replace with Jeff

Sales Report for Gulf Island Resorts

Gulf Island Resorts manages a chain of hotels on four islands near Vancouver, Canada: Saltspring Island, Gabriola Island, Hornby Island, and Bowen Island. As the sales manager for the chain, you want to attract more guests to the hotels in the spring months of April, May, and June. To determine your projected revenue and expenses should you attract more clients in these months, you need to **Summarize Sales**, **Calculate Projected Sales**, and **Create the Sales Report**. The completed sales report appears as shown in Figure E-17 on page 113.

Activity:

Summarize Sales

You need to enter labels and values in an Excel worksheet and then calculate total sales.

Steps:

1. Start a new workbook in Excel, enter and enhance the labels and values so that the worksheet appears as shown in Figure E-12, then save the workbook as **Data for Sales Report** in the location where you store your Data Files

2. Click cell **B8**, enter the formula to multiply the **Average Cost per Room** by the **Total Number of Rooms Rented**, copy the formula through cell **E8**, then increase the column widths, if necessary

   As you complete the required calculations, refer to Figure E-13 to verify your totals.

3. Click cell **B13**, enter the formula to multiply the **Number of Rooms Available** by the **Operating Cost per Room**, then copy the formula through cell **E13**

4. Click cell **B15**, enter the formula to add the **Total Operating Costs** to the **Advertising Costs**, then copy the formula through cell **E15**

5. Calculate the Net Revenue in cell **B17** as the **Total Expenses** subtracted from the **Total Room Rental Revenue**, then copy the formula through cell **E17**

   The hotels on Saltspring Island and Gabriola Island lost money in April, May, and June. Only the Hornby Island and Bowen Island hotels made a profit.

6. Select cells **B7:F8**, click the **Sum button** Σ in the Editing group, then widen **Column F** as needed

7. Select cells **B13:F17**, click Σ, then verify that **$374,800.00** appears in cell F17 as shown in Figure E-13

8. Select cells **B7:E7**, click the **Data tab**, click the **What-If Analysis button** in the Data Tools group, click **Scenario Manager**, click **Add**, type **2010 Rentals**, click **OK**, click **OK**, then click **Close**

   You create a scenario to preserve the existing data because in the next lesson you will change the data in order to calculate projected sales.

9. Save the workbook

FIGURE E-12: Worksheet setup

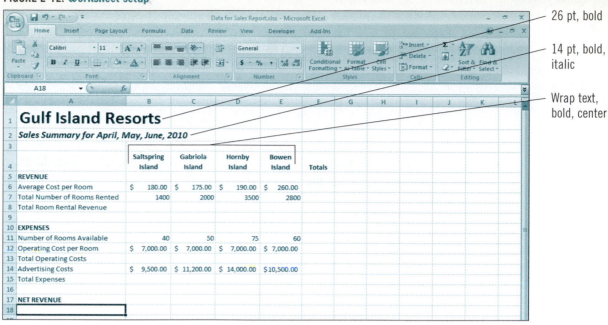

26 pt, bold

14 pt, bold, italic

Wrap text, bold, center

FIGURE E-13: Worksheet complete with calculations

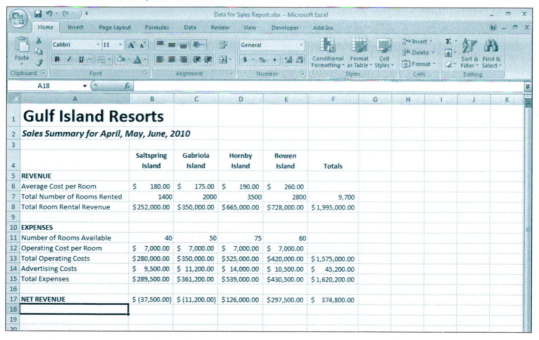

Activity:

Calculate Projected Sales

You use the Goal Seek feature to determine how many rooms to rent at the Saltspring Island and Gabriola Island hotels to increase net revenues, then you create a bar chart.

Steps:

1. Click cell **B17**, click **What-If Analysis** in the Data Tools group, click **Goal Seek**, click the **To value: text box**, type **100000**, press **[Tab]**, type **B7** as shown in Figure E-14, click **OK**, then click **OK**

   You use Goal Seek to determine how many rooms you need to rent at the Saltspring Island hotel to increase the net revenue to $100,000. The value needed, 2163.888889, appears in cell B7.

Trouble

Click the Decrease Decimal button twice to remove the decimal points.

2. Click cell **C17**, click **What-If Analysis**, click **Goal Seek**, enter **120000** as the **To value** and **C7** as the cell to change, click **OK**, click **OK**, select **B7:F7**, then apply the Comma style and remove the decimals

   You need to rent 2,164 rooms at the Saltspring Island hotel to increase net revenue to $100,000 and 2,750 rooms at the Gabriola Island hotel to increase net revenue to $120,000.

3. Click the **Data tab**, click **What-If Analysis**, click **Scenario Manager**, click **Add**, type **Projected Rentals**, enter **B7:C7** as the changing cells, click **OK**, click **OK**, then click **Close**

   You want the sales report to include a bar chart that compares the current and projected revenue at the four hotels. Before you can create the bar chart, you need to have access to both scenarios.

4. Name Sheet1 **2010 Rentals**, click the **Select All button** 🔲, press **[Ctrl][C]**c click the **Sheet2 tab,** press **[Ctrl][V]**, then rename Sheet2 **Projected**

5. Show the **2010 Rentals worksheet**, click **What-If Analysis**, click **Scenario Manager**, click **2010 Rentals**, click **Show**, click **Close**, then click cell **A1**

   The net revenue in cell F17 of the 2010 Rentals sheet is again $374,800.00.

6. Show the **Projected Rentals worksheet**, click cell **A20**, click the **Insert tab**, click the **Bar button** in the Charts group, click the upper-left selection (Clustered Bar), click **Select Data** in the Data group, click the **Collapse Dialog Box button** 🔲 next to Chart data range, click the **2010 Rentals sheet tab**, select cells **B4:E4**, press and hold the **[Ctrl]** key, select cells **B8:E8**, click the **Expand Dialog Box button** 🔲, then click **OK**

7. Move and resize the chart so it extends from cell **A20** to cell **G40**, click **Select Data** in the Data group, click **Series 1** in the Legend Entries section, click **Edit**, type **2010 Rentals** as shown in Figure E-15, click **OK**, click **Add**, type **Projected Rentals**, click 🔲 next to Series values, select cells **B8:E8**, click 🔲, click **OK**, then click **OK**

8. Right-click the **value axis** (x-axis) in the bar chart, click **Format Axis**, click the **Fixed option** next to Maximum, select the contents of the Maximum Fixed text box, type **800000**, click **Number**, select the contents of the **Decimal places text box**, type **0**, then click **Close**

9. As shown in Figure E-16, add a chart title and show the legend at the bottom, then save the workbook.

FIGURE E-14: **Goal Seek dialog box**

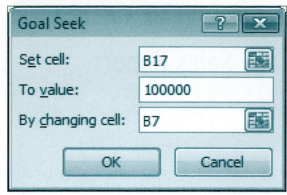

FIGURE E-15: **Edit Series dialog box**

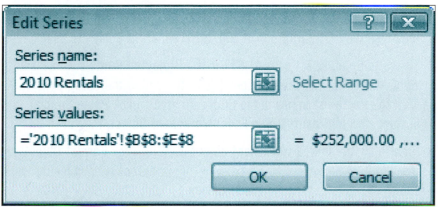

FIGURE E-16: **Bar chart resized and positioned**

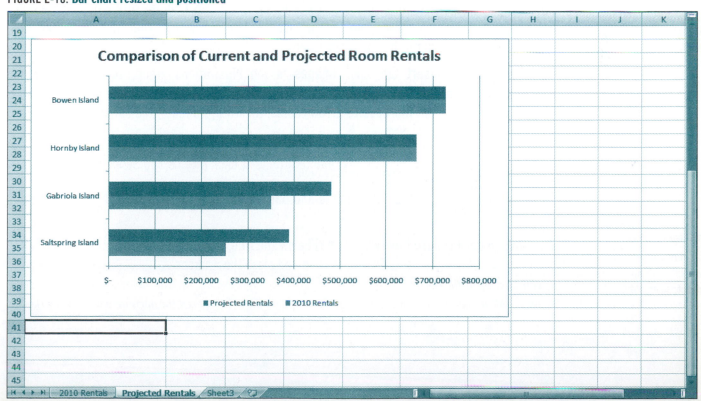

Activity:

Create the Sales Report

You need to compile all the data from the Excel workbook in a report you create in Word. The completed report is shown in Figure E-17.

Trouble

To modify the Title style, right-click it in the Styles gallery, click Modify, then click the Increase Paragraph Spacing button twice.

Steps:

1. Open a new document in Word, change the Top and Bottom margins to **.6"**, type **Sales Report for Gulf Islands Resorts**, apply the **Title style**, press **[Enter]**, select the **Fancy style set**, modify the Title style so the Before and After spacing is **12 pt**, modify the Normal style so the font size is **12 pt**, then save the document as **Sales Report for Gulf Islands Resorts** in the location where you store your Data Files

2. Click the **Change Styles button** in the Styles group, point to **Colors**, select the **Urban color set**, then type the first paragraph of text as shown in the completed sales report in Figure E-17

3. Switch to Excel, select cells **A1:F17** in the **Projected Rentals** worksheet, press **[Ctrl][C]**, switch to Word, verify that the insertion point is at the end of the paragraph you just typed, press **[Enter]**, click the **Paste list arrow** in the Clipboard group, click **Paste Special**, click the **Paste link option button**, click **Microsoft Office Excel Worksheet Object**, then click **OK**

4. Right-click the **linked worksheet object** in Word, click **Format Object**, click the **Size tab**, reduce the Width of the object to **6"**, type the paragraph of text under the copied worksheet object as shown in Figure E-17, then press **[Enter]**

5. Double-click the **copied worksheet object**, click cell **A2**, select **Summary** in the formula bar, type **Projections**, select **2010**, type **2011**, then press **[Enter]**

Trouble

If the link does not update, right-click the worksheet object, then click Update Link.

6. Scroll to the chart, click the chart, press **[Ctrl][C]**, switch to Word, paste the chart into the Word document, set the Height of the chart at **3.1"** and the Width at **6.1"** in the Size group on the Chart Tools Format tab, switch to Excel, change the cost of the Hornby Island rooms (cell D6) to **220**, then return to Word and update the link if necessary

7. In Word, click the **Insert tab**, click **Shapes** in the Illustrations group, select the **Rounded Rectangular Callout shape** in the Callouts section, draw the shape next to the projected rentals for Gabriola Island, type **Increase to 2,750 rooms**, then drag to resize the callout and position it as shown in Figure E-17

   You will need to drag the yellow diamond handle on the callout shape to position the pointer correctly. If necessary, modify the shape fill to match Figure E-17.

8. Draw the callout box for the Saltspring Island bar, then fill it with the required text as shown in Figure E-17

Additional Practice

For additional practice with the skills presented in this project, complete Independent Challenge 2.

9. Type and center **Prepared by [your name]** below the title, save the document, print a copy, close the document, then switch to Excel and save and close the workbook

   If you later open the document to make changes, a message box will appear advising you that the document is linked to an Excel workbook. Click Yes to update the link between the document and the workbook.

Sales Report for Gulf Islands Resorts

Prepared by Your Name

In April, May, and June of 2010, both the Saltspring Island and Gabriola Island hotels lost money. To increase revenue at the Saltspring Island hotel, we need to rent 2,164 rooms instead of the current 1,400 rooms. To increase revenue at the Gabriola Island hotel, we need to rent 2,750 rooms instead of the current 2,000 rooms. By so doing, we will increase revenue to $100,000 from the Saltspring Island hotel and $120,000 from the Gabriola Island hotel.

Gulf Island Resorts

Sales Projections for April, May, June, 2011

	Saltspring Island	Gabriola Island	Hornby Island	Bowen Island	Totals
REVENUE					
Average Cost per Room	$ 180.00	$ 175.00	$ 220.00	$ 260.00	
Total Number of Rooms Rented	2,164	2,750	3,500	2,800	11,214
Total Room Rental Revenue	$389,500.00	$481,200.00	$770,000.00	$728,000.00	$2,368,700.00
EXPENSES					
Number of Rooms Available	40	50	75	60	
Operating Cost per Room	$ 7,000.00	$ 7,000.00	$ 7,000.00	$ 7,000.00	
Total Operating Costs	$280,000.00	$350,000.00	$525,000.00	$420,000.00	$1,575,000.00
Advertising Costs	$ 9,500.00	$ 11,200.00	$ 14,000.00	$ 10,500.00	$ 45,200.00
Total Expenses	$289,500.00	$361,200.00	$539,000.00	$430,500.00	$1,620,200.00
NET REVENUE	$100,000.00	$120,000.00	$231,000.00	$297,500.00	$ 748,500.00

The bar chart shown below compares the current room rentals in April, May, and June of 2010 with the projected room rentals in April, May, and June of 2011.

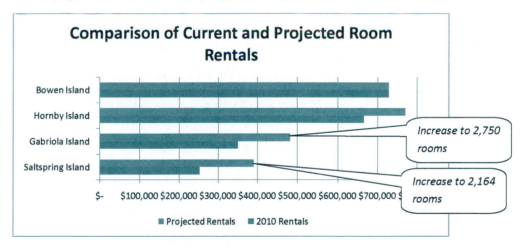

Word and Excel

PROJECT 3

Marketing Report for Midnight Sun Tours

As the office manager of Midnight Sun Tours, you've decided to create the one-page Marketing Report shown in Figure E-21 on page 117 to describe the company's tours to Scandinavia and summarize current sales. You need to **Create the Report in Word** and then **Add Linked Data from Excel**.

Activity:

Create the Report in Word

You need to enter the text for the Marketing Report, use the Research feature to add a picture of a map of Scandinavia, then enter tour sales data in Excel. *This lesson requires an Internet connection.*

Steps:

Trouble

Make sure you select Encarta Encyclopedia from the All Research Sites section, not the Encarta Dictionary section. If you can't find the map shown in the figure, choose another map.

1. Open a blank document in Word, change the Top and Bottom margins to **.6"**, type and format the text as shown in Figure E-18, then save the document as **Midnight Sun Tours Marketing Report** in the location where you store your Data Files

2. Click at the beginning of paragraph 1, click the **Review tab**, click the **Research button** in the Proofing group, type **Scandinavia map** in the Search for text box, click the **All Reference Books list arrow**, click **Encarta Encyclopedia: English (North America)**, then click the link **Dynamic Map from Encarta Encyclopedia**

   Your browser opens and a map of Scandinavia appears.

3. When the browser window opens, scroll if needed to view the picture of the map, right-click the **map**, click **Save Picture As**, navigate to the location where you save your Data Files, type **Scandinavia** in the File name text box, click **Save**, close the browser, return to Word, then close the Research task pane

   The picture is saved as an image file in the .gif format.

4. Click the **Insert tab**, click the **Picture button** in the Illustrations group, navigate to the location where you store your Data Files, click **Scandinavia**, then click **Insert**

5. With the picture selected, click the **Crop button** in the Size group, then use the **Cropping tool** ⊤ to crop the picture as shown in Figure E-19

6. Click **Text Wrapping** in the Arrange group, click **More Layout Options**, click **Square**, click **OK**, drag the map to position it to the right of the text, then save the document

7. Start Excel, apply the **Module theme**, set up the worksheet as shown in Figure E-20, then save the workbook as **Marketing Data** in the location where you store your Data Files

FIGURE E-18: Text for marketing report

Title style

Midnight·Sun·Tours¶

Midnight·Sun·Tours·conducts·five·tours·each·year·to·various·destinations·in·Scandinavia.··These·tours·are· Scandinavian·Odyssey,·Norwegian·Fjords,·Finlandia,··Icelandic·Sagas,·and·Above·the·Arctic·Circle.·All·of· Midnight·Sun's·tours·are·two·weeks·in·duration.¶

Since·its·incorporation·in·1996,·Midnight·Sun·Tours·has·consistently·sold·virtually·all·of·the·Scandinavian· Odyssey·and·Above·the·Arctic·Circle·tours.··In·most·years,·80%·of·the·Finlandia·and·Norwegian·Fjords· tours·are·sold.··The·Icelandic·Sagas·tours·were·first·offered·in·2007·and·are·steadily·gaining·in·popularity.· Shown·below·is·a·breakdown·of·tour·sales·by·category.¶

In·2010,·Midnight·Sun·Tours·offered·a·total·of·xx·tours·and·sold·xx·tours.··The·cylinder·chart·shown·below· displays·the·number·of·tours·sold·in·each·category·relative·to·the·number·of·tours·available.· Scandinavian·Odyssey·tours·rank·the·highest·in·terms·of·the·number·of·tours·sold·relative·to·the·tours· available.··Icelandic·Sagas·tours·rank·the·lowest.¶

You will replace the "xx" references with values in a later lesson

FIGURE E-19: Cropped picture

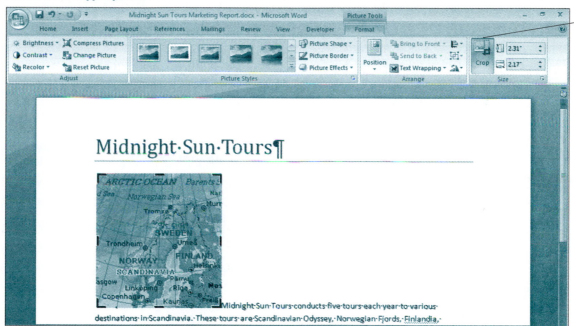

Crop button

FIGURE E-20: Excel worksheet

Use AutoSum to calculate the totals in cells B8 and C8

18-pt, centered across cells A1:C1, filled with Gold, Accent 1, Lighter 60%

Bold

	A	B	C	D
1	2010 Sales by Category			
2	Tour Name	Tours Available	Tours Sold	
3	Scandinavian Odyssey	50	48	
4	Norwegian Fjords	28	28	
5	Finlandia	45	36	
6	Icelandic Sagas	22	14	
7	Above the Arctic Circle	30	29	
8		175	155	
9				

Activity:

Add Linked Data from Excel

You need to create a chart in Excel and then insert the sales data and chart into Word as linked objects. The completed marketing report is shown in Figure E-21.

Steps:

1. Select cells **A2:C7** on the Sales sheet tab, click the **Insert tab**, click the **Column button** in the Charts group, select the **Clustered Cylinder** chart, click the **Move Chart button** in the Location group, click the **Object in list arrow**, click **Chart**, then click **OK**

2. Click the **Chart Tools Layout tab**, add a chart title above the chart containing the text **Tours Sold Compared to Tours Available**, show the legend at the bottom, size and position the chart so that it extends from cell **A1** through cell **J21**, click the **Sales sheet tab**, then save the workbook

3. Select cells **A1:C8**, click the **Copy button** in the Clipboard group, switch to Word, click **after the second paragraph**, press **[Enter]**, click the **Paste list arrow**, click **Paste Special**, click the **Paste link option button**, click **Microsoft Office Excel Worksheet Object**, then click **OK**

   The worksheet is inserted into the Word document as a linked object.

4. Click the worksheet, click the **Center button** in the Paragraph group, then, if necessary, modify the size of the map slightly so the worksheet object appears centered as shown in Figure E-21

5. Switch to Excel, click the **Chart sheet tab**, click the chart, press **[Ctrl][C]**, switch to Word, click **at the end of the last paragraph**, press **[Enter]**, then press **[Ctrl][V]**

6. Drag to resize the cylinder chart, if necessary, so that it fits on page 1 as shown in Figure E-21, then center it

7. Switch to Excel, show the Sales sheet, click cell **B8**, click 📋, switch to Word, select the first **xx** in line 1 of paragraph 3, click the **Paste list arrow**, click **Paste Special**, click the **Paste link option button**, click **Unformatted Text**, click **OK**, then press **[Spacebar]**, if necessary

8. Copy cell **C8** from Excel and paste it as a link (Unformatted Text) over the second **xx** in paragraph 3, switch to Excel, change the number of available tours for Norwegian Fjords in cell B4 to **35** and the number of tours sold to **35**, switch to Word, then verify that the tours available value is 182 and the tours sold value is 162 in the worksheet and the text, and the two cylinders for Norwegian Fjords in the chart are of equal height

   If any link does not update, right-click it, then click Update Link. If you later open the document to make changes, a message box will appear advising you that the document is linked to an Excel workbook. Click Yes to maintain the link between the document and the workbook.

9. Change the Style Set for the document to **Formal**, apply the **Module color scheme**, adjust the position of the map as shown in Figure E-21, type your name right-aligned below the chart, save the document, print a copy, close the document, exit Word, save and close the workbook in Excel, then exit Excel

Trouble

If extra blank columns and rows appear in the worksheet object, double-click the object, then select and delete the extra columns and rows.

Additional Practice

For additional practice with the skills presented in this project, complete Independent Challenge 3.

MIDNIGHT SUN TOURS

Midnight Sun Tours conducts five tours each year to various destinations in Scandinavia. These tours are Scandinavian Odyssey, Norwegian Fjords, Finlandia, Icelandic Sagas, and Above the Arctic Circle. All of Midnight Sun's tours are two weeks in duration.

Since its incorporation in 1996, Midnight Sun Tours has consistently sold virtually all of the Scandinavian Odyssey and Above the Arctic Circle tours. In most years, 80% of the Finlandia and Norwegian Fjords tours are sold. The Icelandic Sagas tours were first offered in 2007 and are steadily gaining in popularity. Shown below is a breakdown of tour sales by category.

2010 Sales by Category		
Tour Name	**Tours Available**	**Tours Sold**
Scandinavian Odyssey	50	48
Norwegian Fjords	35	35
Finlandia	45	36
Icelandic Sagas	22	14
Above the Arctic Circle	30	29
	182	162

In 2010, Midnight Sun Tours offered a total of 182 tours and sold 162 tours. The cylinder chart shown below displays the number of tours sold in each category relative to the number of tours available. Scandinavian Odyssey tours rank the highest in terms of the number of tours sold relative to the tours available. Icelandic Sagas tours rank the lowest.

Your Name

Independent Challenges

INDEPENDENT CHALLENGE 1

Create a form in Word that you can use to record data related to a performance review for a position or situation of your choice. For example, you could create a form to review a course, a workshop, or an employee. Fill in the boxes below with the required information, then set up the form in Word. You need to insert text form fields where required to contain information that will change each time you fill in the form for a different evaluation. You then need to enter data related to the evaluation in an Excel worksheet and finally copy the data and paste it as a link in Word. The completed document in Word should also include a linked chart created from the Excel data.

1. Determine the company name and the position or situation that requires a performance review form. You also need to determine at least five categories to review. For example, if you are creating a form to review a series of workshops, the categories could include Registration Procedure, Instructor, Course Materials, Learning Outcomes, and Facilities. In the box below, write the name of your company and the five categories that you will rank in the performance review:

Company name:

Categories to review:

1. _____

2. _____

3. _____

4. _____

5. _____

2. In the box below, identify information about one individual, course, or workshop that you plan to review. If you're reviewing a person, include the name, department, and position. If you're reviewing a course or workshop, include the title, subject, instructor name, date, and location.

Review subject:

_____

_____

_____

_____

3. In Word, set up a document that includes a title and a subtitle, apply the Style Set of your choice, and modify the Normal style (for example, change the font size or font style).

4. Create an attractively formatted table to contain the performance review form. Use the performance review you created for Project 1 as your guide.

5. Enter content controls where required in the table form. Use at least three types of content controls such as the Rich Text, Combo Box, and Date Picker content controls. Remember that you can use the Legacy Tools form controls when you want to specify exactly how data should be entered in the cell. For example, you can specify that users enter only a 3-digit number. Type your name at the bottom of the page.

6. Save the form as **My Performance Review Form** in the location where you store your Data Files.

7. In Excel, enter labels for the categories you wish to review and determine the ranking scale you will use. For example, you could assign each category a rating from 1 to 10. Format the worksheet attractively.

8. Enter rankings for one individual, course, or workshop you are evaluating.

9. Create a chart that illustrates some aspect of the data. For example, you could create a column chart that shows a ranking for each category or you could create a bar chart that compares the rankings provided by two individuals. Format the chart attractively. Remember to specify the maximum value of the value axis.

10. Save the workbook as **Data for My Performance Review** in the location where you store your Data Files.

11. In Word, enter appropriate information in the form fields related to the individual or course or workshop you wish to evaluate, then save the form as **My Performance Review 1** in the location where you store your Data Files.

12. In Word, copy data from the Excel worksheet and paste it as a link in an appropriate area of the form. Copy the chart and paste it as a link, save the document, print a copy, then close the document.

13. In Excel, copy the data to a new worksheet, then replace the data with data related to another individual, course, or workshop.

14. Modify the chart so that it references data in the second worksheet. Make sure the maximum value on the value axis scale is the same on both charts to ensure a meaningful comparison between the charted results.

15. In Word, save the document as **My Performance Review 2** in the location where you store your Data Files, change the form information excluding the linked data and chart to reflect who or what is being reviewed, open the Edit Links to Files dialog box, then change the links so that they refer to the data in the second Excel worksheet.

16. Click the chart, click the Chart Tools Design tab, click Select Data in the Data group, select the name currently entered in the Chart data range text box, then type the correct reference.

17. Save the document, print a copy, close the document, then save and close the Excel workbook.

INDEPENDENT CHALLENGE 2

In Excel, use the Goal Seek function to analyze a specific goal related to a company of your choice. In Word, create a sales report that includes data from Excel. For example, you could decide to increase your sales in two or three states or countries or increase the number of products of a certain type that you plan to sell.

1. In the box below, write the name of your company and a short description of your business goal. For example, you could name your company "Luxury Landscaping," and describe your goal as increasing your sales of bedding plants.

Company Name: _____

Description of Business Goal: _____

_____

_____

2. Set up a worksheet in Excel similar to the worksheet created for Project 2 for Gulf Island Resorts. Note that you need to include two or three products or locations, the income generated from sales, and your various expenses.

3. Save the workbook as **My Company Goals** in the location where you store your Data Files.

4. Create a current scenario of the data that you will use Goal Seek to change. For example, if you decide to increase the total number of bedding plants you sell in May, you will need to create a current scenario of the sales data related to bedding plants.

5. Use Goal Seek to change the value in one of the cells. Note that the cell you wish to change must not contain a formula. However, the cell must be referenced in a formula contained in another cell, such as a total. You use Goal Seek to specify a set value for the cell containing the formula. For example, you can ask Goal Seek to calculate how many bedding plants you need to sell in May if you want your net income in May to equal $30,000.

6. Create a scenario from the projected data generated by Goal Seek, name the scenario **Projected Rentals**, then show the current scenario.

7. Copy the sales summary from the Current sheet into a new sheet called **Projected Rentals**, then show the Projected scenario sales summary.

8. In the Projected worksheet, create a bar chart that compares the relevant values in the Current scenario (Sheet1) with the new values generated by Goal Seek and shown as the Projected scenario (Sheet2).

9. Format the bar chart attractively.

10. In Word, create a new document that includes the name of the company as a heading. Enter text that describes the company and summarizes the sales data.

11. Save the report as **My Sales Report** in the location where you store your Data Files.

12. Copy the data in the Projected worksheet and paste it as a link into the Word report, then copy the chart from the Projected worksheet and paste it as a link into the Word report. Enter a paragraph above the chart that summarizes the information in the chart.

13. In Word, apply the Style Set of your choice and select a new color scheme.

14. Draw a callout box to highlight any value in the chart that represents projected sales.

15. In Excel, change some of the data, then check that the data is updated correctly in the Word document.

16. Save and close the workbook, include your name in the sales report, print a copy, then save and close the document.

INDEPENDENT CHALLENGE 3

Create a one-page summary in Word that provides information about the sales and marketing efforts for a company of your choice. Use the marketing report you created for Midnight Sun Tours as your model. The summary should include an appropriate picture that you obtain by conducting a search of the Internet from the Research task pane. Make sure you read any copyright restrictions before downloading the picture. Crop the picture if necessary and position it attractively in the document. In Excel, enter data related to your product line and create an appropriate chart in a second worksheet. In Word, insert the data into the document as a linked object, then copy the chart and paste it as a link into the Word document. Make changes to the data in Excel, then update the links in Word. If necessary, crop the worksheet object again so only the data is displayed. Add your name, then save the workbook as My Update Data in the location where you store your Data Files, and store the document as My Update in the same location. Apply the Style Set of your choice, modify styles as needed, and select the color scheme of your choice. (Hint: To update the inserted Excel style to match the color scheme selected for the Word document, double-click the Excel worksheet, then change the color scheme in Excel.) Include your name on the Word document, print a copy, then save and close all open files, and exit all programs you used for this project.

INDEPENDENT CHALLENGE 4

Create an Excel worksheet with the projected income and expenses for Mists of Time, an online bookstore that specializes in historical books, maps, and periodicals. Then use the data in the worksheet to create a chart, which you link to a Projected Sales Summary in Word.

1. Open a blank workbook in Excel, then create the worksheet shown in Figure E-22. Note that the heading in cell A1 is formatted with the Title style. To save time, copy the values entered in column B across through column E, then add border lines as shown.

FIGURE E-22: **Data for Mists of Time Summary**

	A	B	C	D	E	F	G	H	I	J	K	L	M
1			Mists of Time										
2			Projected Income and Expenses										
3		April	May	June	July	Totals							
4	Income												
5	Sales	28,000.00	28,000.00	28,000.00	28,000.00								
6	Total Income												
7													
8	Expenses												
9	Salaries	$ 5,000.00	$ 5,000.00	$ 5,000.00	$ 5,000.00								
10	Rent	1,200.00	1,200.00	1,200.00	1,200.00								
11	Advertising	600.00	600.00	600.00	600.00								
12	Equipment Lease	800.00	800.00	800.00	800.00								
13	Operating Costs	700.00	700.00	700.00	700.00								
14	Cost of Sales												
15	Total Expenses												
16													
17	Total Profit												
18													
19													

2. Save the workbook as **Mists of Time Sales Data** in the location where you store your Data Files.
3. Enter and copy the formulas required to calculate the following amounts:
  a. Total monthly and four-month income (cell F5 and cells B6:F6)
  b. Cost of Sales: sales multiplied by 60% (i.e., B5*.6)
  c. Total monthly (cells B15:F15) and four-month expenses (cells F9:F14)
  d. Total Profit (cells B17:F17): Subtract the total expenses from the total income for each month.
  When you have completed all the calculations, you should see $11,600.00 in cell F17.
4. Create a pie chart that shows the breakdown of expenses by total amount. You will need to use the [Ctrl] key to select cells A9:A14 and cells F9:F14 as the data range. Use the chart title "Breakdown of Expenses" and show the labels as percentages.
5. Move the chart below the worksheet, then increase the chart size so the completed pie chart appears similar to the pie chart shown in the completed sales report in Figure E-24. Your percentages will vary.

6. Start a new, blank document in Word, then enter the text for the Sales Summary, as shown in Figure E-23. Note that you will replace the various "xx" entries with values that you paste as links from the Excel worksheet. Apply the Traditional Style Set, format the title with the Title style and the headings with the Heading 1 style, then select the Concourse color scheme.

FIGURE E-23: Text for Mists of Time Sales Summary

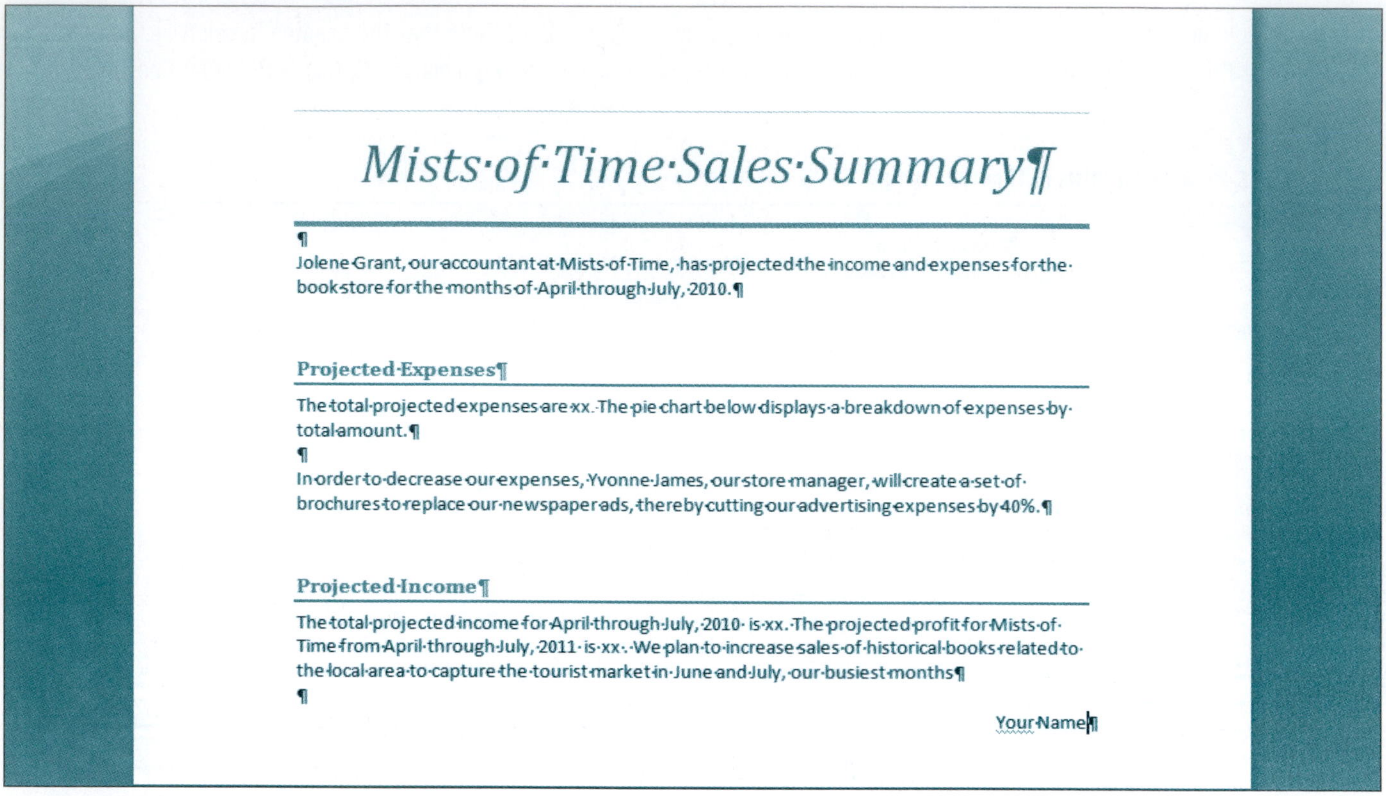

Mists·of·Time·Sales·Summary¶

¶
Jolene·Grant,·our·accountant·at·Mists·of·Time,·has·projected·the·income·and·expenses·for·the·bookstore·for·the·months·of·April·through·July,·2010.¶

Projected·Expenses¶

The·total·projected·expenses·are·xx.·The·pie·chart·below·displays·a·breakdown·of·expenses·by·total·amount.¶
¶
In·order·to·decrease·our·expenses,·Yvonne·James,·our·store·manager,·will·create·a·set·of·brochures·to·replace·our·newspaper·ads,·thereby·cutting·our·advertising·expenses·by·40%.¶

Projected·Income¶

The·total·projected·income·for·April·through·July,·2010·is·xx.·The·projected·profit·for·Mists·of·Time·from·April·through·July,·2011·is·xx.·We·plan·to·increase·sales·of·historical·books·related·to·the·local·area·to·capture·the·tourist·market·in·June·and·July,·our·busiest·months¶
¶

Your·Name¶

7. Save the document as **Mists of Time Sales Summary** in the location where you store your Data Files.
8. Copy the pie chart and any totals required from Excel, and paste them as links into Word, using Figure E-24 as a guide. Make sure you paste the totals as unformatted text.
9. Switch to Excel, increase the salaries expense for June and July to 7,500, then increase the sales income in June and July to 50,000. Note the changes to the pie chart.
10. Switch to Word, update the links if necessary, then remove extra spaces, if necessary.
11. Print a copy of the sales summary, save and close the Word document, add your name to the Excel workbook, then save and close the Excel workbook.

Mists of Time Sales Summary

Jolene Grant, our accountant at Mists of Time, has projected the income and expenses for the book store for the months of April through July, 2010.

Projected Expenses

The total projected expenses are $131,800.00. The pie chart below displays a breakdown of expenses by total amount.

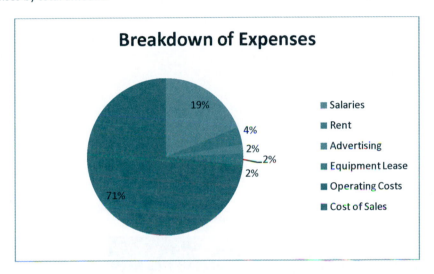

In order to decrease our expenses, Yvonne James, our store manager, will create a set of brochures to replace our newspaper ads, thereby cutting our advertising expenses by 40%.

Projected Income

The total projected income for April through July, 2010 is $156,000.00. The projected profit for Mists of Time Books from April through July, 2011 is $24,200.00. We plan to increase sales of historical books related to the local area to capture the tourist market in June and July, our busiest months

Your Name

Visual Workshop

Create the worksheet shown in Figure E-25 in Excel, then save it as **Classic Mode Sales Data** in the location where you store your Data Files. Calculate the total sales of each item by multiplying the quantity by the price, then calculate the total sales in cell E8. Create the text for the sales report in Word as shown in Figure E-26, entering the values as links to the appropriate figures in the Excel workbook. Save the document as **Classic Mode Sales Report** in the location where you store your Data Files. Apply the Fancy style set and the Verve color scheme, and insert a similar clip-art picture. In Excel, create a cone chart that appears similar to the completed chart shown in Figure E-26. Copy the chart from Excel and paste it into the Word document. In Excel, change the unit price of Haydn's Sonatas to $75, add your name to the worksheet, then save and close the workbook. Update the links in the sales report, add your name under the chart, print a copy, then save and close the document.

FIGURE E-25: Sales data worksheet

	A	B	C	D	E	
1	Title	Composer	Quantity	Price	Total	
2	Complete Preludes and Fugues	Bach	20	$ 78.00		
3	Complete Piano Sonatas	Beethoven	18	$105.00		
4	Complete Piano Sonatas	Mozart	48	$ 48.00		
5	Complete Piano Sonatas	Haydn	45	$ 55.00		
6	Nocturnes	Chopin	19	$ 75.00		
7	Complete Preludes	Debussy	11	$ 48.00		
8						
9						
10						
11						

FIGURE E-26: Sales Report document

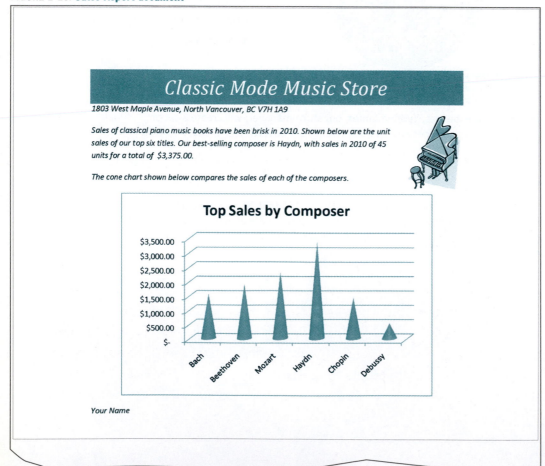

Microsoft
► Access
Projects

Unit **F**

Access Projects

In This Unit You Will Create the Following:

Inventory Database

Author Database

Tour Database

To survive and compete in the contemporary business world, companies and organizations need fast and reliable access to information about their products or services, customers, suppliers, and personnel. Suppose you own an adventure tour company and decide to offer a special incentive to all the clients who signed up for a tour in July of 2010. You could comb through all your files to find the clients, or you could use a relational database program, such as Access, to locate, organize, and print out a list of the clients who joined a tour in July 2010 or during any other time period you choose. A relational database program stores information in related tables that you can use to perform queries and find the information you need. To create a database, you first identify categories—called fields—that describe and organize the contents of your database, such as customers or inventory. Then you formulate queries or questions to retrieve the information you need. In this unit, you will learn how to use Microsoft Access to set up databases and then ask questions to find the information you need to perform specific tasks.

Inventory Database for WorldCraft

Based in Dublin, Ireland, WorldCraft is a distributor of handcrafted items made by artisans from all over the world. As the office manager, you need to create a database that includes the Products table with records for 15 products and the Suppliers table with records for four suppliers. To build the database you **Set Up the Tables**, **Create Forms**, **Create Queries**, and then **Format and Print an Order Report**. The order report is shown in Figure F-11 on page 133.

Activity:

Set Up the Tables

You need to set up the Suppliers table as the "one" table and the Products table as the "many" table, which means that one supplier can supply many products.

Steps:

Hint

If you were setting up a Suppliers table for a real business, you would include full contact information for each supplier.

Trouble

If you press [Enter], click Back to return to the list of values.

1. Start Access, click **Blank Database**, click the **Browse button** 📂, navigate to the location where you store your Data Files, type **WorldCraft Inventory** in the File name text box, click **OK**, then click **Create**

2. Click the **View button** in the Views group, type **WorldCraft Suppliers**, then press **[Enter]**

3. Type **Supplier ID**, press **[↓]** to move the insertion point to the line below Supplier ID, type **Supplier Name**, press **[↓]**, type **Email Address**, press **[Tab]**, click the **Data Type list arrow**, click **Hyperlink**, click the **Close 'WorldCraft Suppliers' button**, then click **Yes** to save the table

4. Click the **Create tab**, click **Table** in the Tables group, click the **View button** in the Views group, type **WorldCraft Products** as the table name, press **[Enter]**, type **Product ID**, press **[↓]**, then enter the remaining field names as shown in Figure F-1

5. Click the **Region Data Type list arrow**, click **Lookup Wizard**, click the **I will type in the values that I want option button**, click **Next**, press **[Tab]**, type **Africa**, press **[↓]**, enter the remaining regions as shown in Figure F-2, click **Next**, then click **Finish**

6. Click the **Category Data Type list arrow**, click **Lookup Wizard**, create the list of lookup values shown in Figure F-3, click **Next**, then click **Finish**

7. Click the **Supplier Name Data Type list arrow**, click **Lookup Wizard**, click **Next** to accept that you want the values to come from an existing table, click **Next**, click **Supplier Name**, click the **Select Single Field button** >, click **Next**, click **Next**, click **Next**, click **Finish**, then click **Yes**

8. Click the **Units in Stock Data Type list arrow**, click **Number**, click the **Unit Price Data Type list arrow**, click **Currency**, click **Currency** in the Field Properties section, click the **list arrow**, then select the **Euro** currency style (€)

9. Close and save the table, click the **Database Tools tab**, click **Relationships**, double-click the **line** between the two tables, click the **Enforce Referential Integrity check box** to select it, click **OK**, compare the Relationships window to Figure F-4, then close the Relationships window

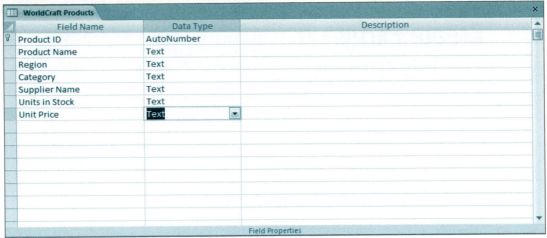

FIGURE F-1: **Fields for the WorldCraft Products table**

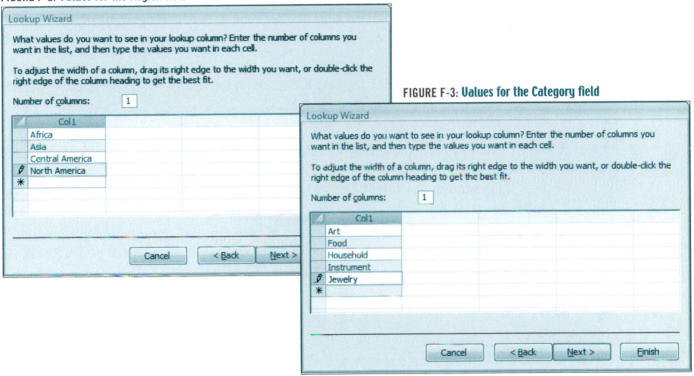

FIGURE F-2: **Values for the Region field**

FIGURE F-3: **Values for the Category field**

FIGURE F-4: **One-to-many relationship**

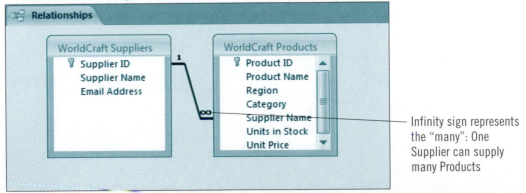

Infinity sign represents the "many": One Supplier can supply many Products

Activity:

Create Forms

You need to create forms into which you can enter the data for the WorldCraft Suppliers table and the WorldCraft Products table.

Steps:

Trouble

The insertion point first tabs through the fields in the related table.

1. Click **WorldCraft Suppliers: Table**, click the **Create tab**, click the **Form button** in the Forms group, click the **More button** in the AutoFormat group, then select the **Trek** format

2. Click the **View button** in the Views group, press **[Tab]**, type **America Arts**, press **[Tab]** until the insertion point appears after Email Address, then type **sales@americaarts.com**

3. Press **[Tab]** twice, type **Kenya Crafts**, enter **sales@kenyacrafts.com** as the Email Address, then create another record for **Rainforest Cooperative** with the address **sales@rainforestcoop.com**

4. Close the form, click **Yes**, click **OK**, click **WorldCraft Products: Table** in the list of tables, click the **Create tab**, click the **Form button**, apply the **Trek** format, click the **Logo button** in the Controls group, navigate to the location where you store your Data Files, then double-click **WorldCraft Logo.jpg**

5. Click the **ProductID label**, click the **Bold button** in the Font group, double-click the **Format Painter button** in the Font group, then click each of the labels to apply bold

6. Click the **View button** in the Views group, press **[Tab]**, type **Carved Polar Bear**, press **[Tab]**, type **N** to show North America, press **[Tab]**, type **A** to show Art, press **[Tab]**, type **A** to show **America Arts**, press **[Tab]**, type **15**, press **[Tab]**, type **250**, press **[Enter]**, click the **Previous record button** at the bottom of the screen to move back to record 1, then compare the form for record 1 to Figure F-5

   Notice how you minimize typing time when you create lookup fields for as many fields as possible.

7. Click the **Next record button** to start a new record, press **[Tab]**, type **Coral Pendant**, press **[Tab]**, type **As** to select Asia, press **[Tab]**, type **J** for Jewelry, then press **[Tab]**

   The supplier you want is not listed. Often when you create a database, you need to go back and add data to related tables.

8. Close and save the form if prompted, double-click **WorldCraft Suppliers** to show the WorldCraft Suppliers form, click the **New button** in the Records group, press **[Tab]**, type **Far East Imports** for the Supplier Name and **sales@fareastimports.com** as the Email Address, then close the form

9. Double-click **WorldCraft Products** to show the WorldCraft Products form, go to record 2, enter **Far East Imports**, **9**, and **220** in the appropriate fields, press **[Enter]**, enter data for records 3 to 15 as shown in Figure F-6, then close the final form

   Figure F-6 shows all the records in Datasheet view so that you can see them. You are entering the records into the form.

FIGURE F-5: Completed record for product 1

WorldCraft Products	✕

WorldCraft Products

Product ID:	1
Product Name:	Carved Polar Bear
Region:	North America ▼
Category:	Art ▼
Supplier Name:	America Arts ▼
Units in Stock:	15
Unit Price:	€250.00

FIGURE F-6: Datasheet for WorldCraft Products table

Product ID ▾	Product Name ▾	Region ▾	Category ▾	Supplier Name ▾	Units in Stoc ▾	Unit Price ▾	Add
1	Carved Polar Bear	North America	Art	America Arts	15	€250.00	
2	Coral Pendant	Asia	Jewelry	Far East Imports	9	€220.00	
3	Turquoise Pendant	North America	Jewelry	America Arts	8	€50.00	
4	Mahogany Bowl	Central America	Household	Rainforest Cooperative	5	€40.00	
5	Smoked Salmon	North America	Food	America Arts	9	€25.00	
6	Hippo Carving	Africa	Art	Kenya Crafts	11	€150.00	
7	Jade Ring	Asia	Jewelry	Far East Imports	7	€200.00	
8	Soapstone Seal	North America	Art	America Arts	8	€400.00	
9	Aztec Mask	Central America	Art	Rainforest Cooperative	14	€150.00	
10	Maple Sugar Treats	North America	Food	America Arts	6	€15.00	
11	Ebony Carving	Africa	Art	Kenya Crafts	8	€160.00	
12	Talking Drum	Africa	Instrument	Kenya Crafts	13	€75.00	
13	Lacquer Dinner Set	Asia	Household	Far East Imports	13	€120.00	
14	Opal Earrings	Asia	Jewelry	Far East Imports	5	€180.00	
15	Hand Pipes	Central America	Instrument	Rainforest Cooperative	9	€60.00	
* (New)							

Activity:

Create Queries

First, you view the records that relate to each of the four suppliers, and then you use the two tables that you've created to ask two questions, called *queries*. You create a query to find out how many products you have from Asia in the Art category, and then you create a query to determine the number of products with fewer than 10 items in the inventory.

Steps:

1. Double-click **WorldCraft Suppliers** to open the form, then click the **Next record button** ▶ to view the records associated with each of the four suppliers

   As a result of the one-to-many relationship you created between the Suppliers table and the Products table, you can create queries that list all the products purchased from a specific supplier.

2. Close the WorldCraft Suppliers form, click the **Create tab**, click the **Query Wizard button** in the Other group, then click **OK** to accept Simple Query Wizard

Trouble

If the WorldCraft Suppliers table is selected, click the list arrow, then click Table: WorldCraft Products.

3. Verify that **Table: WorldCraft Products** is selected in the Tables/Queries text box, click the **Select All Fields button** >> to select all the fields in the Products table, click **Next**, click **Next** to accept a Detail query, select the **contents** of the Title text box, type **Asia Jewelry** as the query name, click the **Modify the query design option button**, then click **Finish**

4. Click the **Region Criteria cell**, type **Asia**, click the **Category Criteria cell**, type **Jewelry** as shown in Figure F-7, then click the **Run button** in the Results group

   Three of the products from Asia are from the Jewelry category—the Coral Pendant, the Jade Ring, and the Opal Earrings.

5. Click the **Close 'Asia Jewelry' button**, then click **Yes** to save the query

6. Click the **Create tab**, click the **Query Wizard button** in the Other group, click **OK**, select the **WorldCraft Products table**, add all the fields, click **Next**, click **Next**, change the name to **Items to Order**, click the **Modify the query design option button**, then click **Finish**

7. Click the **Units In Stock Criteria cell**, type **<10**, then click the **Run button** in the Results group

   A datasheet listing all the products with fewer than 10 units in stock appears. These are the items that you need to order.

8. Click the **View button**, click in the **blank cell** to the right of Unit Price, click **Builder** in the Query Setup group, type the formula: **Units to Order: (10-[Units in Stock])** as shown in Figure F-8, then click **OK**

   This formula calculates how many units you need to order if fewer than 10 items are in stock. For example, if 8 units are in stock, you need to order 2 units so that you always have at least 10 units.

9. Click in the blank cell to the right of Units to Order, type **Total: [Units to Order]*[Unit Price]**, click the **Run button**, scroll right to view the Units to Order and Total columns, adjust column widths where needed, compare the query to Figure F-9, then close and save the query

FIGURE F-7: **Selecting criteria**

Run button

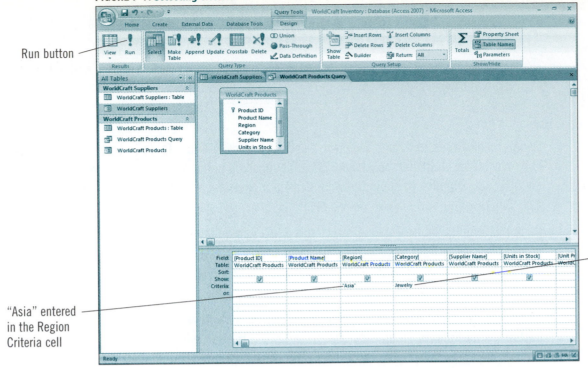

"Asia" entered
in the Region
Criteria cell

Jewelry entered
in the Category
Criteria cell;
quotation marks
appear when you
exit the cell

FIGURE F-8: **Formula in the Expression Builder**

FIGURE F-9: **Datasheet view of query results**

Category	Supplier Name	Units in Stock	Unit Price	Units to Order	Total
Jewelry	Far East Imports	9	€220.00	1	$220.00
Jewelry	America Arts	8	€50.00	2	$100.00
Household	Rainforest Cooperative	5	€40.00	5	$200.00
Food	America Arts	9	€25.00	1	$25.00
Jewelry	Far East Imports	7	€200.00	3	$600.00
Art	America Arts	8	€400.00	2	$800.00
Food	America Arts	6	€15.00	4	$60.00
Art	Kenya Crafts	8	€160.00	2	$320.00
Jewelry	Far East Imports	5	€180.00	5	$900.00
Instrument	Rainforest Cooperative	9	€60.00	1	$60.00

Activity:

Format and Print an Order Report

You modify the Items to Order query so it includes two fields from the Suppliers table; then format and print the Order report shown in Figure F-11.

Steps:

1. Double-click **Items to Order**, switch to Design view, click **Show Table** in the Query Setup group, click **WorldCraft Suppliers**, click **Add**, click **Close**, scroll to the right to view the next blank column, double-click **Supplier Name** in the WorldCraft Suppliers table, then double-click **Email Address**
   The Supplier Name and Email Address fields are added to the query design grid.

2. Click the **SupplierName Sort cell list arrow**, click **Ascending**, click the **Run button** in the Results group, then scroll right to view the Suppliers
   The list of 10 products to order includes the names and e-mail addresses of the suppliers to contact sorted by supplier name.

Trouble

Make sure you add Units to Order before Unit Price.

3. Close and save the Items to Order query table, click the **Create tab**, click the **Report Wizard button** in the Reports group, then select and move the following fields from the Query: Items to Order table to the Selected Fields list box in the order specified: **Product Name**, **Region**, **Category**, **Units in Stock**, **Units to Order**, **Unit Price**, **Total**, **WorldCraft Suppliers:Supplier Name**, and **Email Address**

4. Click **Next**, click **Next**, click **WorldCraft Suppliers: Supplier Name** in the list of groupings, click the **Select Single Field button** $>$, click **Next**, click **Next** again, click the **Landscape option button**, click **Next**, select the **Trek** report style, click **Next**, then click **Finish**
   The report is shown in Print Preview. Too much space appears between some of the fields.

5. Click the **Close Print Preview button** in the Close Preview group, click the **View list arrow** in the Views group, click **Layout View**, click **Region**, then press **[Delete]**
   You can change your mind in the report formatting process and remove or add fields.

6. Right-click any cell in the Total column, click **Properties**, click the **Format list arrow** in the list of Properties, click **Euro**, then close the Property Sheet

7. Click **[WorldCraft Suppliers].[Supplier Name]**, double-click, delete all the text, type **Supplier**, click **America Arts**, increase the font size to **14 pt**, click **Total**, click the **Center button** in the Font group, then adjust the height and width of selected fields and labels so all the data is visible and columns are attractively spaced as shown in Figure F-10

8. Click the title **WorldCraft Products**, click the **Home tab**, increase the font size to **24 pt**, increase the height of the label so that it appears as shown in Figure F-11, click the **Report Layout Tools Format tab**, click the **Logo button** in the Controls group, navigate to the location where you store your Data Files, double-click **WorldCraft Logo.jpg**, then enlarge and position the logo as shown in Figure F-11

Additional Practice

For additional practice with the skills presented in this project, complete Independent Challenge 1.

9. Click in the blank space between the title and the logo to select both items, click the **Fill/back Color list arrow**, click **Brown 2** (appears as a light orange color), add your name to the title and widen the text box to fit, click the **View list arrow**, click **Print Preview**, click the **Zoom list arrow**, click **75%**, compare the completed report to Figure F-11, click the **Print button** in the Print group, click **OK**, close the report, click **Yes**, then close the database

FIGURE F-10: Formatting the report

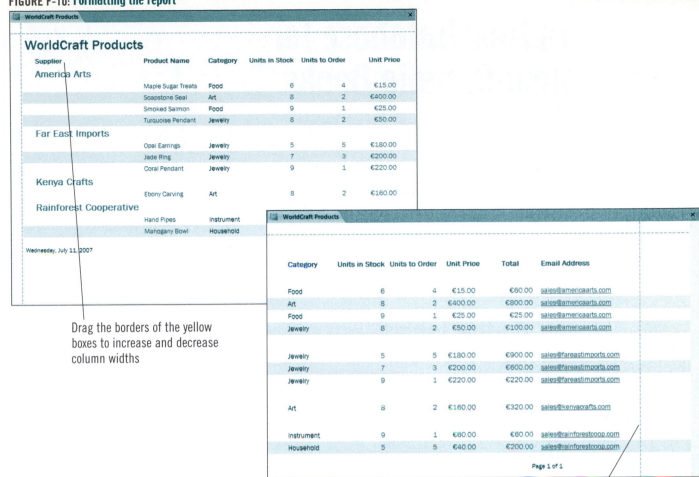

Drag the borders of the yellow boxes to increase and decrease column widths

Dotted vertical line represents the edge of the page; don't extend the column beyond the line

FIGURE F-11: Completed report in Print Preview

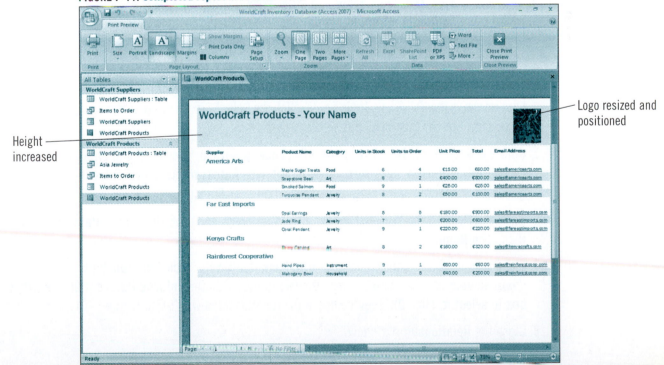

Height increased

Logo resized and positioned

Author Database for New Arcadia Books

Based in Denver, Colorado, New Arcadia Books publishes nonfiction books that inspire people to action in the service of their communities, and by extension, the planet. Categories include Activism, Diversity, Environment, Family, Cooking, Gardening, Globalization, and Sustainability. As the managing editor, you decide to set up a database that you can use to identify the authors who have sold the most books, the titles that have realized revenues in excess of $50,000 during the last year, and the most popular categories purchased. To create the database, you **Set Up the Tables**, **Enter Records and Create Queries**, and then **Create and Format a Report**. The completed report is shown in Figure F-20 on page 139.

Activity:

Set Up the Tables

Your first task is to set up the two tables in the New Arcadia Books database: the Authors table and the Books table. Because one author can write many books, you set up the Authors table as the "one" table and the Books table as the "many" table.

Steps:

1. Start Access, click **Blank Database**, click the **Browse button** 📂, navigate to the location where you store your Data Files, type **New Arcadia Books** in the File name text box, click **OK**, then click **Create**

2. Click the **View button** in the Views group, type **New Arcadia Authors** as the table name, press **[Enter]**, enter the fields shown in Figure F-12, then close and save the table

3. Click the **Create tab**, click **Table**, click the **View button**, type **New Arcadia Books** as the table name, press **[Enter]**, then enter the following fields: **Book ID**, **Book Title**, **Author**, **Topic**, **Price**, and **Units Sold**

4. Click the **Author Data Type list arrow**, click **Lookup Wizard**, click **Next** to accept that you want the values to come from an existing table, click **Next** to accept the New Arcadia Authors table, click **Last Name** in the list of available fields, click the **Select Single Field button** [>], click **Next**, click **Next**, click **Finish**, then click **Yes**

5. Click the **Topic Data Type list arrow**, click **Lookup Wizard**, click the **I will type in the values that I want option button**, click **Next**, press **[Tab]**, type **Activism**, press **[↓]**, enter the remaining categories as shown in Figure F-13, click **Next**, then click **Finish**

6. Click the **Price Data Type list arrow**, click **Currency**, click the **Units Sold Data Type list arrow**, then click **Number**

7. Close and save the table, click the **Database Tools tab**, click **Relationships** in the Show/Hide group, double-click the **line** between the two tables, click the **Enforce Referential Integrity check box** to select it, click **OK**, then compare the Relationships window to Figure F-14

8. Close the Relationships window

FIGURE F-12: Fields for the New Arcadia Authors table

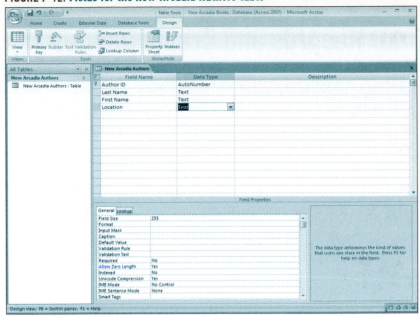

FIGURE F-13: Values for the Topic field

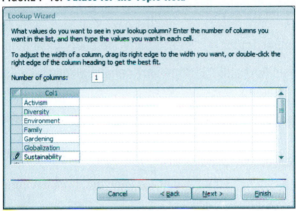

FIGURE F-14: One-to-many relationship

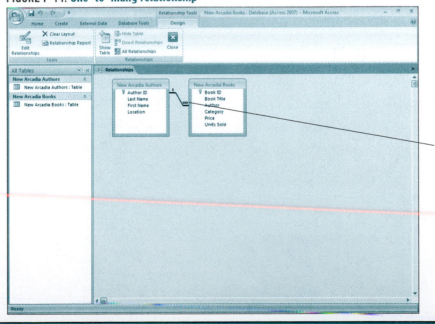

The line indicates a one-to-many relationship: One Author can write many Books

Activity:

Enter Records and Create Queries

Your market researchers have found that readers want more titles on the Globalization and Sustainability topics, so you decide to create a query that shows how many titles on these topics you have in stock. You then modify this query to list only those authors who sold more than $50,000 worth of books. Before you can create the query, you need to enter records for the Authors and Books tables.

Hint

Remember that you can save time by typing only the first letter or two to show the required record for the Author and Topic fields.

Steps:

1. Open the **New Arcadia Authors table**, enter the records shown in Figure F-15, then close and save the table

2. Open the **New Arcadia Books table**, enter the records shown in Figure F-16, then close the table, saving if prompted

3. Click the **Create tab**, click the **Query Wizard button** in the Other group, click **OK**, select **Table: New Arcadia Authors** in the Tables/Queries text box, then add only the **Last Name**, **First Name**, and **Location** fields to the Selected Fields list box

4. Click the **Tables/Queries list arrow**, click **Table: New Arcadia Books**, add all the fields except the Book ID field to the Selected Fields list box, click **Next**, click **Next** again, change the name of the query to **Popular Topics**, click the **Modify the query design option button**, then click **Finish**

5. Click the **Topic Sort cell**, click the **Sort cell list arrow**, click **Ascending**, then click the **Run button** in the Results group

Hint

The required formula is Total Sales: [Units Sold]*[Price].

6. Switch to Design view, scroll to view the blank column to the right of Units Sold, click in the **blank cell**, then enter a formula that will designate "Total Sales" as the field name and multiply the Units Sold by the Price

7. Click the **Topic Criteria cell**, type **Globalization**, click the **Total Sales Criteria cell**, type **>30000**, complete the criteria as shown in Figure F-17, then click the **Run button**
   Seven books match the criteria.

8. Scroll right, adjust the column widths, compare your screen to Figure F-18, close the Query Results window, then click **Yes** to save the modified query

FIGURE F-15: Records for the New Arcadia Authors table

	Author ID	Last Name	First Name	Location	Add New Field
⊞	1	Knutson	Gabriel	Montreal, Quebec	
⊞	2	Lamont	Michele	New York, New York	
⊞	3	Deville	Pierre	Miami, Florida	
⊞	4	Sanchez	Teresa	San Diego, California	
⊞	5	Quire	Elsie	Sydney, Australia	
⊞	6	Watts	Harriet	London, England	
⊞	7	O'Brian	Hamish	Dublin, Ireland	
⊞	8	Owen	Marcus	Chicago, Illinois	
*	(New)				

FIGURE F-16: Records for the New Arcadia Books table

Book ID	Book Title	Author	Topic	Price	Units Sold	Add New Field
1	Zero Emission Cars	Deville	Environment	$22.00	3000	
2	Going Green	Sanchez	Sustainability	$25.00	4000	
3	Bringing up Citizens	Quire	Family	$28.00	11000	
4	Conserving Water	Owen	Sustainability	$32.00	2200	
5	All Together	O'Brian	Globalization	$18.00	1800	
6	Make Do with Less	Sanchez	Sustainability	$26.00	700	
7	Village Economies	Deville	Globalization	$18.00	700	
8	Organic Medley	Knutson	Gardening	$42.00	1200	
9	Community Ties	Lamont	Sustainability	$27.00	500	
10	Lobbying for Results	Owen	Activism	$18.00	2000	
11	Our Planet	Sanchez	Sustainability	$28.00	3000	
12	Celebration	Quire	Diversity	$12.00	1000	
13	Sustain to Survive	O'Brian	Sustainability	$25.00	2000	
14	Peace Proposals	Lamont	Globalization	$22.00	2200	
15	Greening of the Land	O'Brian	Sustainability	$27.00	3000	
*	(New)					

FIGURE F-17: Selecting criteria

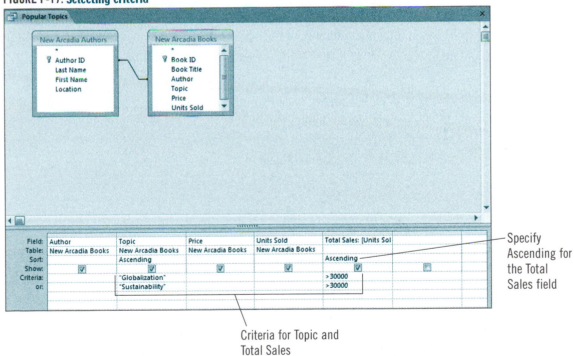

Specify Ascending for the Total Sales field

Criteria for Topic and Total Sales

FIGURE F-18: Popular Topics query

Book Title	Author	Topic	Price	Units Sold	Total Sales
All Together	O'Brian	Globalization	$18.00	1800	$32,400.00
Peace Proposals	Lamont	Globalization	$22.00	2200	$48,400.00
Sustain to Survive	O'Brian	Sustainability	$25.00	2000	$50,000.00
Conserving Water	Owen	Sustainability	$32.00	2200	$70,400.00
Greening of the Land	O'Brian	Sustainability	$27.00	3000	$81,000.00
Our Planet	Sanchez	Sustainability	$28.00	3000	$84,000.00
Going Green	Sanchez	Sustainability	$25.00	4000	$100,000.00
*					

PROJECT 2

Activity:

Create and Format a Report

You need to create a report and then format it to present to your colleagues at a meeting. Your finished report will look similar to the one shown in Figure F-20.

Steps:

1. Verify that **Popular Topics** is selected, click the **Create tab**, then click the **Report button** in the Reports group

2. Click the **AutoFormat button** in the AutoFormat group, select the **Concourse** style, click the **Group & Sort button** in the Grouping & Totals group, click **Add a Group** at the bottom of the screen, then click **Author**

3. Click the **First Name field**, press **[Delete]**, then delete the **Last Name field**

4. Scroll to and click the **Total Sales label**, click the **Totals button** in the Grouping & Totals group, then click **Sum**

   The total sales for each of the four authors is calculated.

5. Right-click the first author's subtotal (**48400**), click **Properties**, click the **All tab**, click the blank cell to the right of Format, click the **list arrow**, click **Currency** as shown in Figure F-19, then close the Property sheet

6. Scroll to the bottom of the report, then change the format of the grand total (466200) to Currency

7. Scroll to the top of the report, double-click **Popular Topics** in the title box, change the name of the report to **New Arcadia Books Popular Topics**, modify the column widths so the completed report appears as shown in Figure F-20, click the **Save button**, then save the report as **New Arcadia Books Popular Topics**

Additional Practice

For additional practice with the skills presented in this project, complete Independent Challenge 2.

8. Click the **View list arrow**, click **Print Preview**, click the **Zoom list arrow** in the Zoom group, click **75%**, compare the completed report to Figure F-20, add your name to the title and reduce the font size to fit, if necessary, click the **Print button** in the Print group, click **OK**, close and save the report, click **Yes**, then close the database

FIGURE F-19: Selecting the Currency format

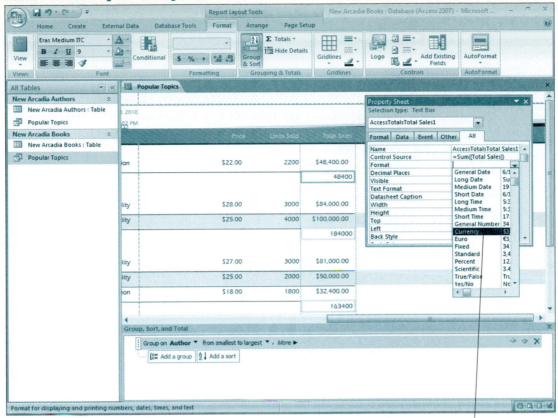

Click the list arrow to
show the list of formats

FIGURE F-20: Completed report in Print Preview

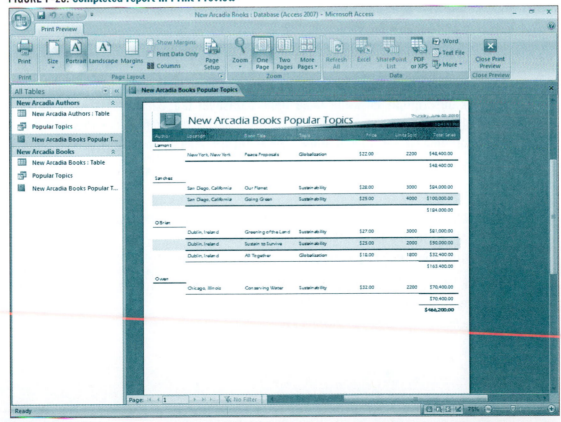

Database for Off the Path Tours

Off the Path Tours conducts tours for groups of 10 to 15 people to locations around North America. You have decided to use the Events Table Template in Access to create a database containing information about each tour. You then relate this table to a list of tour participants that you import from another database. First, you need to **Create the Tours Table**, and then you need to **Import the Participants Table**.

Activity:

Create the Tours Table

You need to create the Off the Path database and then create the Off the Path Tours table based on the Events Table Template. The Off the Path Tours table will include attachments in the form of Word documents and pictures. In Access 2007, you use the Attachments data type to attach files to a record.

Steps:

1. Start Access, then create a database called **Off the Path Tours** saved in the location where you store your Data Files

2. Click the **Create tab**, click the **Table Templates button** in the Tables group, then click **Events**
   A table already containing field names is created.

3. Click the **Home tab**, click the **View button**, type **Off the Path Tour List**, press **[Enter]**, change Title to **Tour**, change Start Time and End Time to **Start Date** and **End Date**, click **Location**, click the **Delete Rows button** in the Tools group, then compare the field list to Figure F-21
   You will add the Category field in a later step.

4. Switch to Datasheet view and save the table when prompted, press **[Tab]**, type **Coastal Islands**, press **[Tab]**, click the **Date button** ▦, select **June 10, 2010**, press **[Tab]**, select **June 15, 2010**, then press **[Tab]**

5. Click **Description**, click the **Table Tools Datasheet tab**, click the **Lookup Column button** in the Fields & Columns group, follow the steps in the Lookup Wizard to create a lookup column consisting of three entries: **City**, **Cultural**, and **Outdoors**, then name the column **Category**

6. For Coastal Islands, select the **Outdoors** category, press **[Tab]**, type **Relaxing island jaunt**, then press **[Tab]**

7. Double-click the cell to show the Attachments dialog box, click **Add**, navigate to the location where you store your Data Files, then double-click **Island.jpg**
   The Attachments dialog box appears as shown in Figure F-22.

8. Click **OK**, press **[Tab]**, enter data for the remaining four records as shown in Figure F-23, close the table, then answer **Yes** to save the table if prompted
   Note that you need to add the attachments indicated in Figure F-23.

FIGURE F-21: Revised field list for the Off the Path Tour List table

	Field Name	Data Type
🔑	ID	AutoNumber
	Tour	Text
	Start Date	Date/Time
	End Date	Date/Time
	Description	Memo
	Attachments	Attachment

Off the Path Tour List

FIGURE F-22: Attachments dialog box

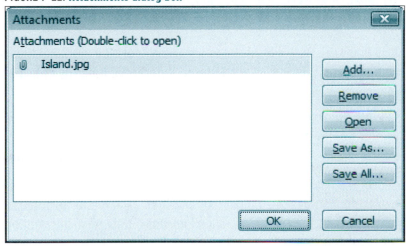

FIGURE F-23: Records for the Off the Path Tour List table

	ID	Tour	Start Date	End Date	Category	Description	📎	Add N
	1	Coastal Islands	6/10/2010	6/15/2010	Outdoors	Relaxing island jaunt	📎(1)	
	2	Second City Culture	6/17/2010	6/22/2010	Cultural	Chicago art, music, architecture	📎(1)	
	3	Texas Roundup	7/5/2010	7/10/2010	City	Highlights of Texas	📎(1)	
	4	Gardens Galore	7/14/2010	7/19/2010	Outdoors	Gardens of Washington	📎(1)	
	5	Mountain Madness	7/25/2010	7/31/2010	Outdoors	Hiking in Montana	📎(1)	
*	(New)						📎(0)	

Off the Path Tour List

San Antonio.jpg   Hollyhock.jpg   Hiking.jpg   Chicago.jpg

Activity:

Import the Participants Table

You import the Participants table from another database, then create a relationship between the Off the Path Tour List table and the imported table. The relationship will be a one-to-many relationship because one tour can host many participants. The Off the Path Tour List table is the "one" table, and the Participants table is the "Many" table. Finally, you create two reports. One report shows all the tours and includes the picture of each tour, and the other report shows all the participants according to the tour they are taking.

Steps:

1. Click the **External Data tab**, click **Access** in the Import group, click the **Browse button**, navigate to the location of your Data Files, double-click **Tour Participants.accdb**, click **OK**, click **Tour Participants** in the list of tables, click **OK**, then click **Close**

2. Double-click **Tour Participants: Table** to open it, scroll right to the first blank cell, click **Add New Field**, click the **Table Tools Datasheet tab**, click the **Add Existing Fields button** in the Fields and Columns group, click the **plus sign** ⊞ next to Off the Path Tour List, double-click **Tour**, click **Next**, click **Next**, click **Next**, then click **Finish**

3. Close the Field List, then as shown in Figure F-24, select a tour for each of the participants

4. Close and save the table, click the **Database Tools tab**, click **Relationships**, double-click the line joining the two tables, click the **Enforce Referential Integrity check box**, click **OK**, then close the Relationships window

5. Click **Off the Path Tour List: Table**, click the **Create tab**, click the **Report button** in the Reports group, apply the **Opulent AutoFormat**, modify the column widths as shown in Figure F-25, add your name to the report title, print a copy, then close and save it as **Off the Path Tour List**

6. With Off the Path Tour List: Table still selected, click the **Create tab**, click the **Report button** in the Reports group, apply the **Opulent AutoFormat**, click the **ID field**, press **[Delete]**, click **Start Date**, press and hold the **[Shift]** key, click **End Date**, **Category**, **Description**, and **Attachments** (scroll right) to select them, then press **[Delete]**
   You've deleted all the fields in the report except the Tour field.

7. Click the **Add Existing Fields button** in the Controls group, click **Show all tables**, click the **plus sign** ⊞ next to Tour Participants, double-click **First Name**, double-click **Last Name**, then close the field list

8. Click the **Group & Sort button** in the Grouping & Totals group if necessary, click **Add a group**, click **Tour**, click **Add a sort**, click **Tour**, click **Add a Sort**, then click **Last Name**

9. Click the **Save button** 🖫 on the Quick Access toolbar, type **Tour Participants**, click **OK**, compare the report in Print Preview to Figure F-26, add your name to the title, print a copy, close the report, save your changes, then close the database

Additional Practice

For additional practice with the skills presented in this project, complete Independent Challenge 3.

FIGURE F-24: Matching tours with participants

ID	First Name	Last Name	Address	City	Sta	ZIP/Posta	Country/I	Tour	Add Ne
1	Mary	Anton	1208 Elm Stree	Vancouver	BC	V7H 1A7	Canada	Coastal Islands	
2	Arthur	Harrison	18 Grand Road	Littleton	CO	80122	United State	Second City Culture	
3	Wanda	Renfrew	3809 Maple Str	Boston	MA	02111	United State	Second City Culture	
4	Jay	Ng	1200 Green Str	Cincinnati	OH	45206	United State	Texas Roundup	
5	Tom	Watson	398 Seabreeze	Halifax	NS	B9A 1P3	Canada	Gardens Galore	
6	Paula	Saunders	344 Cowan Roa	Green Bay	WI	54311	United State	Gardens Galore	
7	David	Steinberg	122 West 40th	New York	NY	10010	United State	Second City Culture	
8	Gary	Gutzmann	890 Glenayre D	Toronto	ON	M5W 1E6	Canada	Coastal Islands	
9	Lisa	Morales	67 Pacific Way	Santa Monic	CA	90405	United State	Gardens Galore	
10	Ranjit	Singh	80 The Mews	London		SW1X 8PZ	United King	Gardens Galore	
11	Darius	Morelli	Via Principe Ar	Roma		00187	Italy	Coastal Islands	
12	Kevin	Washington	678 Hood Road	Seattle	WA	98110	United State	Coastal Islands	
13	Lance	Lee	34 Atlantic Stre	Savannah	GA	31405	United State	Coastal Islands	
14	Julie	Roan	230 Olive Road	Sacramento	CA	94822	United State	Gardens Galore	
15	Beryl	Wade	450 Park Street	Toronto	ON	M5E 3R5	Canada	Second City Culture	
*	(New)								

Press the first letter of each entry, then press the down arrow to quickly select all the tour titles

FIGURE F-25: Off the Path Tour List report

FIGURE F-26: Tour Participants report

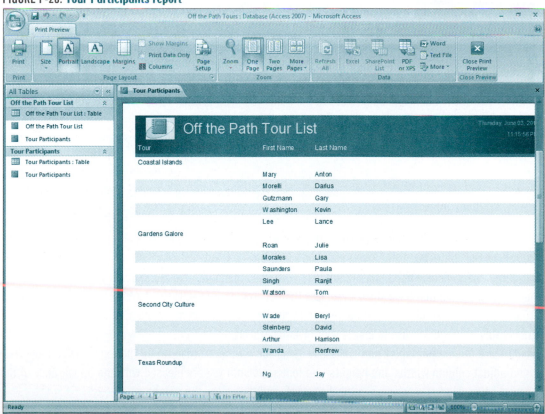

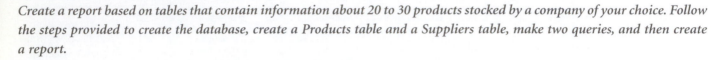

Independent Challenges

INDEPENDENT CHALLENGE 1

Create a report based on tables that contain information about 20 to 30 products stocked by a company of your choice. Follow the steps provided to create the database, create a Products table and a Suppliers table, make two queries, and then create a report.

1. Choose a name for your company and determine the type of products it sells. For example, you could call your company Tee to Green and describe it as a retail operation that sells golf equipment and accessories, such as golf clubs, bags, shoes, umbrellas, and clothing. Write the name of your company and a brief description of the products it sells in the box below:

> Company name: _____
>
> Description: _____
>
> _____
>
> _____

2. Start Access, then create a database called **My Inventory**, and save it in the location where you store your Data Files for this book.
3. Create a Suppliers table similar to the table you created for Project 1 that includes the Supplier ID, Supplier Name, and one or two additional fields such as Email Address or Phone Number.
4. Create a Products table similar to the table you created for Project 1. Include at least six fields, including the Supplier Name field and a Units in Stock field.
5. Identify fields that require a limited selection of responses. For example, a Category field for the Golf database could include the values "Shoes," "Accessories," "Clubs," "Clothing," and "Bags."
6. In the Products table, use the Lookup Wizard to create lookup values for the fields you identified in the previous step.
7. Use the Lookup Wizard to create a relationship between the "Supplier Name" field in the Products table and the "Supplier Name" field in the Suppliers table.
8. Open the Relationships window and enforce referential integrity. One Supplier can supply many Products.
9. Create a form for each table, and apply the AutoFormat of your choice.
10. Enter records for each table. You should enter a minimum of 15 records for the Products table and four records for the Suppliers table.
11. In the box below, describe two queries you plan to make based on the Products and Suppliers tables. For example, you could ask which products are handled by a certain supplier, which products conform to a specific category, and which suppliers are located in a specific area. One of the queries should relate to the items you need to order to keep stock levels at 10 for all items. Call the query **Items to Order**.

> Query 1: _____
>
> _____
>
> Query 2: _____
>
> _____

12. Use the Query Wizard to create the queries. Make sure you specify the criteria for each query in Design view and then rename each query to reflect the contents.
13. In the Items to Order query, include appropriate formulas to calculate the total value of the items you need to order. For example, if you decide you need to order items that have stock levels less than 10, you need to enter two formulas. One formula subtracts Units in Stock from 10 and the other formula multiplies the result by the Unit Price to determine the total worth of the units you need to order.
14. Select the query table that you will use to create your inventory report.
15. Use the Report Wizard to create a report that will show items you need to reorder. Group the report by Supplier Name. Apply an AutoFormat and adjust column widths and heights and font sizes until you are pleased with the appearance of the report.
16. Be sure the report title includes your name, print the report, and then close the database.

INDEPENDENT CHALLENGE 2

Create a database that contains information related to a company such as a publisher, art gallery, or talent agency that deals with people and the products they create. For example, you could create a database for a recording company that includes two tables—one table lists the recordings and the other table lists the recording artists. Plan and then create the database as follows.

1. Start Access, then create a database called **My People List** and save it in the location where you store your Data Files.
2. Plan your database on paper by first listing all the fields you require. Here are some sample fields for an art gallery, in no particular order: Artist Name, Painting Title, Artist Phone Number, Painting Medium, Painting Size, Painting Genre, and Painting Price.
3. Sort the fields into two tables and determine the relationship between the tables. For example, the fields for the art gallery database could be sorted into an Artists table and a Paintings table as follows:
   Artists table: Artist ID, Artist First Name, Artist Last Name, Phone Number
   Paintings table: Painting ID, Painting Title, Medium, Size, Genre, Price, and Artist Name
4. Determine the relationship between the two tables. For example, the Artists and Paintings tables are related through the Artist field. The two tables are related through the Artist Name field because one artist can create many paintings.
5. Determine which fields require a limited selection of responses. For example, the Genre field in the Art Gallery database could include the values "Abstract," "Landscape," and "Photography."
6. Create the two tables in Access. Make sure you assign appropriate data types and that you use the Lookup Wizard to create lookup values for the fields you identified.
7. Use the Lookup Wizard to create a relationship between the two tables. For example, in the Art Gallery database, a relationship would be created between "Artist Name" in the Artist table (the "one" table) and "Artist Name" in the Painting table (the "many" table).
8. Modify the relationship so referential integrity is enforced.
9. Enter records for the two tables. You should enter a minimum of 15 records for the "many" table and 4 records for the "one" table.
10. View the relationship between the two tables. Figure F-27 shows the relationship between the two tables in the Art Gallery database. Notice how you can view the related records (the many), by clicking the plus sign next to a record in the "one" table. Figure F-27 clearly shows that one artist can create many paintings.

FIGURE F-27: Sample relationship

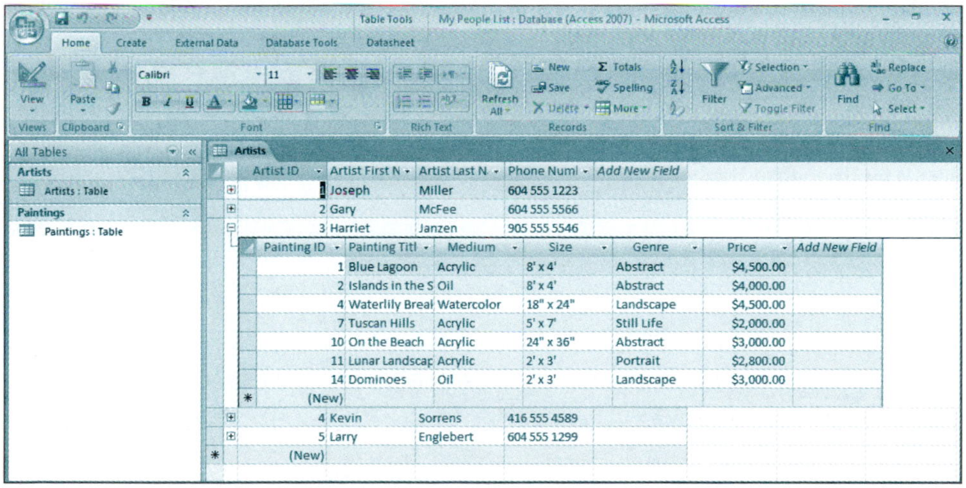

11. Determine two queries you could make based on the data in the two tables. If appropriate, include a formula in one of the queries. For example, you could include a formula that multiplied the Units Sold by the Unit Price to determine total revenue.
12. Select one query to use as the basis for a report. For example, you could create a report that lists only painters who have sold more than $10,000 worth of paintings.
13. Format the report attractively, include your name in the report title, print a copy, then close the database.

INDEPENDENT CHALLENGE 3

Create a database called My Pet Walking Service that contains information about all the dogs and their human walkers at a small pet walking service in your hometown. Follow the steps provided to create the database, create a Walker table and a Dogs table, and then create a report. Note that the relationship is created on the basis that one walker can walk many dogs. You enter records for the Walker table, and then you import the Dogs table from another database.

1. Start Access, then create a database called **My Pet Walking Service** and save it in the location where you store your Data Files.
2. Create a table named **Walkers**, then add fields and specify data types as shown in Figure F-28.
3. Switch to Datasheet view, then add a lookup column called Region after the Email Address field that contains four values: Burnaby, Downtown, North Shore, and Woodlands. Note that several walkers could work in the same region.
4. Enter data for four records as shown in Figure F-29 below. Note that you need to add the **Janice Bio.docx** attachment to the record for Janice Grant and the **Tom Bio.docx** to the record for Tom O'Grady. These documents are located where you are storing Data files for this book.
5. Double-click one of the attachments to view the Attachments dialog box, then double-click the attachment to open and view it. Close the Word document, then save and close the table.
6. Import the Dogs.accdb database from the location where you are storing Data Files for this book, then select the Dogs table.
7. Open the Dogs table, then add the First Name field from the Walker table.
8. Close the Field List dialog box, name the column Walker, then select a walker for each of the dogs. You can determine which walker goes with which dog.
9. Close and save the table, then modify the relationship so referential integrity is enforced.
10. From the Dogs table, use the Report button to create a report that lists only the Walkers, Region, Pet Name, and Breeds (remove the ID and Owner Family fields).
11. Add the Region field after the Walker field, then group the report by Walker sorted in alphabetical order and then by Region.
12. Apply the AutoFormat of your choice, modify the column widths and row heights so that the report presents the information attractively, change the title to "Dogs and Walkers - Your Name," then save the report as **Dogs and Walkers**.
13. Print a copy, close the report, then close the database and exit Access.

FIGURE F-28: Fields for the Walkers table

Walkers	
Field Name	**Data Type**
Walker ID	AutoNumber
First Name	Text
Last Name	Text
Email Address	Hyperlink
Cell Phone	Text
Attachments	Attachment

FIGURE F-29: Records for the Walkers table

Walker ID	First Name	Last Name	Email Address	Region	Cell Phone	📎	A
1	Tom	O'Grady	ogrady@vancouveronline.com	Burnaby	604 555 7788	(1)	
2	Zheni	Vladzova	zheni@vancouverinternet.com	Downtown	604 555 7766	(0)	
3	Janice	Grant	jgrant@northshoreinternet.com	North Shore	604 555 1277	(1)	
4	Yani	Deville	yani@yanishome.com	Woodlands	604 555 6112	(0)	
(New)						(0)	

INDEPENDENT CHALLENGE 4

You've decided that you would like to investigate the possibility of studying in a foreign country for a summer, an academic term, or even a full year. From the hundreds of programs offered, you need to select one that suits your academic interests and is located in a country you want to visit. To help you choose the best program, you will search the World Wide Web for information about programs for studying abroad, and then you will create an Access database that contains data related to at least three programs.

1. Start Access, then create a database called **Study Abroad**, and save it in the location where you store your Data Files.
2. In Design view, enter field names and select data types as shown in Figure F-30. Note that the data type for the Description field is Memo. You select this data type so that you can enter several lines of text into the table. You do not select the Currency data type for Cost because you want to be able to enter "N/A" when you are not able to find cost information. The data type for the Web Address field is Hyperlink. When you copy the address of a Web page into this field it will be formatted as a hyperlink that you can click and follow to open the related Web page.

FIGURE F-30: Field names and data types for Study Abroad Programs table

⊞ Study Programs		
Field Name	**Data Type**	
⚷ Program ID	AutoNumber	
Field of Study	Text	
Country	Text	
Location	Text	
Description	Memo ———	——— Memo data type
Cost	Text	
Web Address	Hyperlink ———	——— Hyperlink data type

3. Save the table with the name **Study Programs**.
4. Open Internet Explorer, connect to the Internet, and then conduct a search for studying abroad programs. Use keywords such as "study abroad," "international study," and "overseas study." To narrow your search further, include the field of study and location that interests you. For example, you could search for "art history programs in Italy." You could also explore study abroad Web sites such as www.studyabroad.com.
5. Identify a field of study and two or three countries that interest you. For example, you could decide to investigate archeological study programs in Italy, France, and Israel, or anthropology programs in Belize, Mexico, and Ecuador.
6. Explore some of the Web sites you've found to gather information about three programs that you think look interesting. As you explore the sites, copy and paste relevant information to the Study Abroad Programs table in the Study Abroad database. Note that you can copy and then edit a paragraph of text into the Description field because you chose the Memo data type, which allows you to enter unlimited text. You will need to follow several links to find the information required for each program. In some cases, you will not find all the information; for example, you may not be able to find cost information. You can enter N/A where applicable in the table.
7. For the Web Address field, enter the Web page address (URL) of the page that contains most of the information you've gathered about a particular program. To copy a URL, click the Address box in your browser, press [Ctrl][C], return to Access, click the appropriate cell in the Web Address field, and then press [Ctrl][V]. The Web site address appears as a hyperlink because you selected the Hyperlink data type for the field.
8. When you have gathered information about at least three programs, create a report. Apply the AutoFormat of your choice, select the Landscape layout, modify column widths, then include your name in the report title.
9. Print a copy of the report, and then close the Study Abroad database.

Visual Workshop

Start Access, and then create a database called **Staff Travel** using the table shown in Figure F-31. Create a lookup field for Region that includes the values shown. Create a query that includes a field called Total that multiplies the Daily Rate by the Days. The required formula is Total: [Daily Rate]*[Days]. Create the report shown in Figure F-32. Note that the Urban AutoFormat is used.

FIGURE F-31: Travel Expenses table

	ID	Last Name	First Name	Destination	Region	Daily Rate	Days	Add New Field
	1	Ralston	Terri	Rome	Europe	$250.00	10	
	2	Sanchez	Maria	Paris	Europe	$250.00	11	
	3	Yaretz	Gordon	New York	North America	$150.00	14	
	4	Harmon	Walter	Tokyo	Asia	$200.00	12	
	5	Tisdale	Andrew	Singapore	Asia	$200.00	13	
	6	Evans	Michelle	New Orleans	North America	$150.00	16	
	7	Vernon	Ron	Barcelona	Europe	$250.00	7	
	8	Ralston	Terri	Stockholm	Europe	$250.00	8	
	9	Yaretz	Gordon	Prague	Europe	$250.00	12	
	10	Evans	Michelle	Hong Kong	Asia	$200.00	13	
*	(New)						0	

FIGURE F-32: Staff Travel Expenses report

Staff Travel Expenses - Your Name

Region	Last Name	First Name	Destination	Daily Rate	Days	Total
Asia						
	Evans	Michelle	Hong Kong	$200.00	13	$2,600.00
	Tisdale	Andrew	Singapore	$200.00	13	$2,600.00
	Harmon	Walter	Tokyo	$200.00	12	$2,400.00
						$7,600.00
Europe						
	Yaretz	Gordon	Prague	$250.00	12	$3,000.00
	Ralston	Terri	Stockholm	$250.00	8	$2,000.00
	Vernon	Ron	Barcelona	$250.00	7	$1,750.00
	Sanchez	Maria	Paris	$250.00	11	$2,750.00
	Ralston	Terri	Rome	$250.00	10	$2,500.00
						$12,000.00
North America						
	Evans	Michelle	New Orleans	$150.00	16	$2,400.00
	Yaretz	Gordon	New York	$150.00	14	$2,100.00
						$4,500.00
						$24,100.00

Microsoft
►Word, Excel, and Access Projects

Unit **G**

Integration Projects II

In This Unit You Will Create the Following:

 **Job Search Database**

 **Multipage Proposal**

 **Art Collection Catalogue**

You can use Word, Access, and Excel in a variety of ways to perform business tasks quickly and easily. The key is to use each program in the Office suite efficiently. You often start by building an Access database that contains the names and addresses of customers and suppliers, information about inventory, and sales records. You can then combine the database information in Word to produce form letters, labels, and other documents such as reports and proposals. You can also analyze database information in Excel so that you can then create charts and spreadsheets. In this unit you will use Access, Word, and Excel to create a variety of common business documents.

Job Search Database for Kevin Lowe

Kevin Lowe needs to find a job in the Miami area as an office manager or management trainee. To help coordinate his job search efforts, you need to **Create the Contacts Table**, **Create the Results Form**, **Create the Job Application Letter**, and then **Analyze the Job Search Results**. The form letter is shown in Figure G-9 on page 155.

Activity:

Create the Contacts Table

First, you need to create the Job Search database, and then you need to create a table to contain information about Kevin's job contacts. You design the Contacts table to include a lookup field.

Steps:

1. Start Access, click **Blank Database**, click the **Browse button** , navigate to the location where you store your Data Files, type **Job Search Database** in the File name text box, click **OK**, then click **Create**

2. Click the **View button** in the Views group, type **Contacts** as the table name, then press **[Enter]**

3. Type **Job ID**, press **[↓]** to move the insertion point to the line below Job ID, then enter the remaining fields as shown in Figure G-1

4. Click the **City/State field**, click the **Default Value text box** in the General tab of the Field Properties area, type **"Miami, FL"** including the quotation marks, then press **[Enter]**

   Kevin makes Miami, FL, the default value because every company he has contacted is located in Miami.

5. Click the **Position Data Type list arrow**, click **Lookup Wizard**, click the **I will type in the values that I want option button**, then click **Next**

6. Press **[Tab]**, type **Junior Manager**, press **[↓]**, type **Manager Trainee**, enter the remaining positions as shown in Figure G-2, then click **Finish**

7. Click the **View button**, then click **Yes** to save the table

8. Press **[Tab]** to move to the First Name field, type **Lucinda**, press **[Tab]**, type **Johnson**, press **[Tab]**, type **100 Palm Drive**, press **[Tab]** two times (Miami, FL will be entered automatically), type **33172**, press **[Tab]**, type **First Fashions**, press **[Tab]**, click the **list arrow**, then select **Manager Trainee**

9. Enter the data for the remaining records in the Contacts table as shown in Figure G-3, adjust column widths as needed, then close and save the table

Trouble

If you press [Enter] instead of [↓] you go to the next screen; click Back to return to the list of values to finish entering them.

FIGURE G-1: Field names for Contacts table

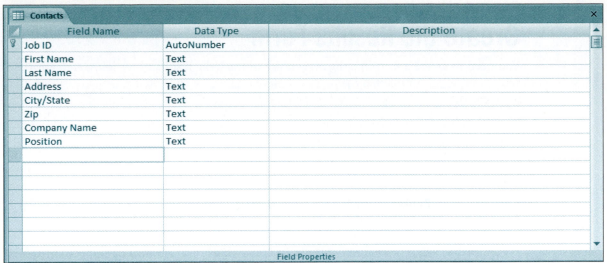

Field Name	Data Type	Description
Job ID	AutoNumber	
First Name	Text	
Last Name	Text	
Address	Text	
City/State	Text	
Zip	Text	
Company Name	Text	
Position	Text	

Field Properties

FIGURE G-2: Lookup Wizard

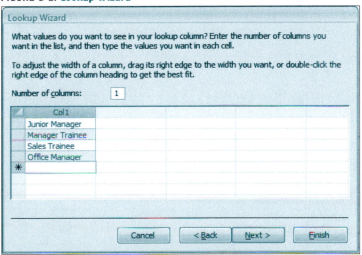

Lookup Wizard

What values do you want to see in your lookup column? Enter the number of columns you want in the list, and then type the values you want in each cell.

To adjust the width of a column, drag its right edge to the width you want, or double-click the right edge of the column heading to get the best fit.

Number of columns: 1

Col1
Junior Manager
Manager Trainee
Sales Trainee
Office Manager

Cancel   < Back   Next >   Finish

FIGURE G-3: Records for the Contacts table

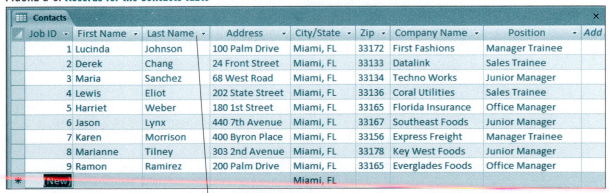

Job ID	First Name	Last Name	Address	City/State	Zip	Company Name	Position	Add
1	Lucinda	Johnson	100 Palm Drive	Miami, FL	33172	First Fashions	Manager Trainee	
2	Derek	Chang	24 Front Street	Miami, FL	33133	Datalink	Sales Trainee	
3	Maria	Sanchez	68 West Road	Miami, FL	33134	Techno Works	Junior Manager	
4	Lewis	Eliot	202 State Street	Miami, FL	33136	Coral Utilities	Sales Trainee	
5	Harriet	Weber	180 1st Street	Miami, FL	33165	Florida Insurance	Office Manager	
6	Jason	Lynx	440 7th Avenue	Miami, FL	33167	Southeast Foods	Junior Manager	
7	Karen	Morrison	400 Byron Place	Miami, FL	33156	Express Freight	Manager Trainee	
8	Marianne	Tilney	303 2nd Avenue	Miami, FL	33178	Key West Foods	Junior Manager	
9	Ramon	Ramirez	200 Palm Drive	Miami, FL	33165	Everglades Foods	Office Manager	
* (New)				Miami, FL				

Double-click column dividers to autofit the columns to the text

Activity:

Create the Results Form

You need to create a form that Kevin can use to track the results of his job search efforts. The form needs to include all the fields from the Contacts table as well as two new fields. One field is a check box that Kevin can click if he receives a positive response to his job application; the other field is a Date/Time field that Kevin can use to enter each interview date. You create the form in Design view so that you can customize its appearance.

Steps:

1. Double-click **Contacts: Table**, click the **View button**, click the blank cell below Position, type **Response**, press **[Tab]**, click the **Data Type list arrow**, then click **Yes/No**

2. Press **[Tab]** twice, type **Interview Date**, press **[Tab]**, select the **Date/Time** data type, click the **Format text box** in the General tab, click the **list arrow** and select **Medium Date**, then close and save the Contacts table

3. With the Contacts table still selected, click the **Create tab**, click the **Form Design button** in the Forms group, click the **Add Existing Fields button** in the Tools group, then click the **plus sign** ⊞ next to Contacts to show all the fields if necessary

   A blank grid appears. You use the grid and rulers to position the labels and text boxes representing the fields from the Contacts table.

4. Double-click **Job ID** in the Field List to place it in the grid, double-click **First Name**, double-click each of the remaining fields in turn to place them in the grid, then close the Field List

5. Place the mouse pointer above and to the left of the Job ID label, then click and drag to select all the labels and text boxes as shown in Figure G-4

6. With all the labels and text boxes selected, drag to position them so the left edge of the labels lines up with **2** on the horizontal ruler bar and the top edge lines up with **1** on the vertical ruler bar as shown in Figure G-5

7. Click the **Label button** in the Controls group, point just below **1** on the horizontal ruler bar, click and drag to create a box between 1 and 5 that is approximately **.5"** in height, type **Job Search Results**, click a blank area of the grid, click the **label**, click the **Font Size list arrow** in the Font group, click **24**, click the **Bold button** 𝐁 in the Font group, then click the **Center button** ▤

8. Click the **View button**, click the **Response check box** in Form1 for First Fashions to select it, enter **June 1, 2010** as the interview date, click the **Next record button** ▶ on the Navigation bar twice to move to record 3, then enter the responses and the dates for selected records as shown below:

Company Name	Response	Interview Date
Techno Works	**Yes**	**June 2, 2010**
Coral Utilities	**Yes**	**June 3, 2010**
Florida Insurance	**Yes**	**June 6, 2010**
Everglades Foods	**Yes**	**June 8, 2010**

9. Click the **View button**, click the **Company Name text box**, then drag to widen it so Everglades Foods fits, widen the Position text box, click the **View button**, click the **Save button** 💾 on the Quick Access toolbar, type **Job Search Results**, click **OK**, compare the form for Everglades Foods to Figure G-6, then close the form

FIGURE G-4: Selecting the fields in the Form grid

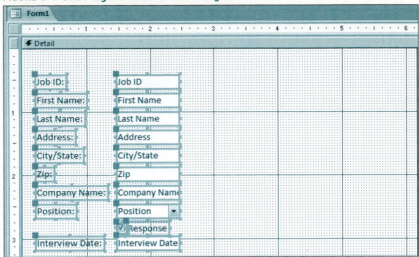

FIGURE G-5: Positioning fields on the design grid

2" on the horizontal ruler bar

1" on the vertical ruler bar

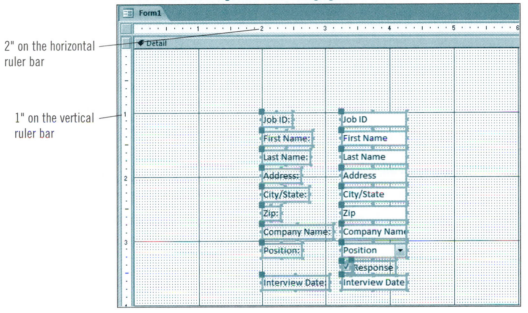

FIGURE G-6: Completed form for Everglades Foods

Center, bold, 24 pt

Resized text boxes

PROJECT 1

Activity:

Create the Job Application Letter

You need to switch to Word and create the letter that Kevin plans to send to each job prospect. You then need to merge the letter with the Job Search database to produce individually addressed letters.

Hint

Text in square brackets is placeholder text for the merge fields.

Steps:

1. Start Word, click the **Office button**, click **Open**, navigate to the location where you store your Data Files, open **Application Letter.docx**, then save the document as **Job Search Form Letter.docx**

2. Close the document and exit Word, return to Access, click **Contacts: Table**, if necessary, click the **External Data tab**, click the **More button** in the Export group, click **Merge it with Microsoft Office Word**, then click **OK** to accept the warning

   By default the database is in exclusive mode. You need to close it and then reopen it before you can complete the merge.

3. Click **Open**, click the **Office button**, click **Close Database**, click the **Office button** again, click **Job Search Database** in the list of database files, click **Options**, click the **Enable this content option button**, then click **OK**

4. Click the **External Data tab**, click the **More button** in the Export group, click **Merge it with Microsoft Office Word**, click **OK** to use an existing Microsoft Word document, navigate to the location where you store your Data Files, click **Job Search Form Letter.docx**, click **Open**, then click **OK**

5. Click **Job Search Form Letter** on the taskbar, maximize the Word window, click **Next: Write your letter** in the Mail Merge task pane, replace **Current Date** in the letter with the current date, press **[Enter]** twice, click **Address block** in the Mail Merge task pane, then click **OK**

   When you run the mail merge, the address will be inserted in place of the field code.

6. Click after **Dear** in the letter, click **Greeting line** in the Mail Merge task pane, click **OK**, select **[Position]** in the first paragraph, click **More items** in the Mail Merge task pane, click **Position**, click **Insert**, click **Close**, press **[Spacebar]** if necessary, select **[Company Name]**, then replace it with the **Company Name** field

7. Replace **[Company Name]** and **[Position]** in the fourth paragraph with the **Company Name** and **Position fields**, press **[Ctrl][Home]** to move to the top of the document, then click **Next: Preview your letters**

   As you can see, the address and salutation appear incorrectly. Manager Trainee Lucinda Johnson is the name, the city and state are missing, and the salutation includes "Dear" two times.

8. Click **Previous: Write your letter** in the Mail Merge task pane, select **<<AddressBlock>>** in the letter, press **[Delete]**, click **Address block** in the Mail Merge task pane, click **Match Fields**, make changes in the Match Fields dialog box as shown in Figure G-7, click **OK**, click **OK**, then press **[Enter]** following <<Address Block>>

9. Select and delete **<<GreetingLine>>**, click **Greeting line** in the Mail Merge task pane, make the change to the Greeting line dialog box as shown in Figure G-8, then click **OK**

10. Click **Next: Preview your letters**, select the four lines of the address for Lucinda Johnson, click the **Page Layout tab**, change the After spacing in the Paragraph group to **0**, deselect the text, compare the address and salutation text to Figure G-9, click **Next: Complete the merge**, click **Print** in the task pane, type **1** in the From box, type **2** in the To box, click **OK**, click **OK**, save and close the document, then close Word

FIGURE G-7: Match Fields dialog box

FIGURE G-8: Insert Greeting Line dialog box

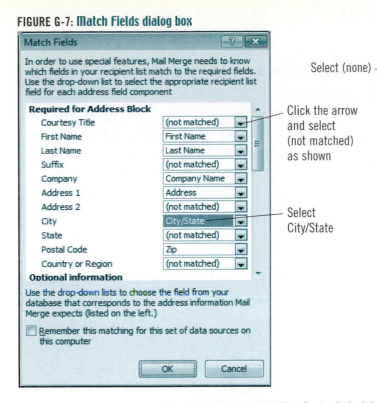

Click the arrow and select (not matched) as shown

Select City/State

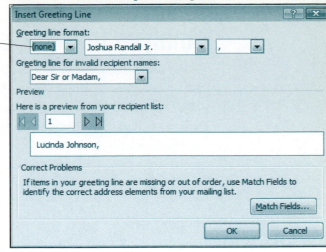

Select (none)

FIGURE G-9: Completed letter for Lucinda Johnson

PROJECT 1

Activity:

Analyze the Job Search Results

All of the companies that interviewed Kevin have offered him employment. Now he needs to decide which company to accept. To help him make a wise decision, you create a query table in Access that lists only those companies that interviewed him. Then you need to add several new fields that can be used to rank each company in terms of its location, pay, benefits, and opportunities for advancement. Kevin decides on a rating scale as follows: 3 = Poor, 6 = Good, 9 = Excellent. Once you have completed the table, you need to analyze it in Excel and then create a chart to illustrate the overall ranking for each company.

Steps:

1. Return to Access, click **Contacts: Table** if necessary, click the **Create tab**, click the **Query Wizard button** in the Other group, then click **OK** to accept Simple Query Wizard

2. Click **Company Name** in the list of available fields, click the **Select Single Field button** `>`, then add the **Position** and **Response** fields to the Selected Fields list, click **Next**, click **Next**, type **Positive Results** as the query title, click the **Modify the query design option button**, then click **Finish**

3. Click the **Response Criteria cell**, type **Yes**, then click the **Run button** in the Results group
   All five of the companies that responded positively to Kevin's form letter appear.

4. Click the gray box in the upper-left corner of the datasheet to select the entire query as shown in Figure G-10, click the **Copy button** in the Clipboard group, close the query datasheet, save changes if prompted, click the **Create tab**, click **Table** in the Tables group, click the **Home tab**, click the **Paste button**, then click **Yes**

5. Click the **View button**, type **Ratings**, enter the **Location**, **Pay**, and **Benefits** and **Advancement** labels, change the data type to **Number** for all four fields, click the **View button**, click **Yes**, then enter the values as shown in Figure G-11

6. Close the table, click **Ratings: Table**, click the **External Data tab**, click **Excel** in the Export group, click **Browse**, navigate to the location where you store your Data Files, click **Save**, click **OK**, then click **Close**

7. Open Excel, open **Ratings.xlsx** from the location where you store your Data Files, select cells **E2:I6**, click the **Sum button** Σ in the Editing group, then click away from the selected cells

8. Select cells **B2:B6**, press and hold the **[Ctrl]** key, select cells **I2:I6**, click the **Insert tab**, click the **Column button** in the Charts group, then select the Clustered Column chart type (top left type)

9. Click the **Chart Styles More button** `≡`, select **Style 30**, click the **Chart Tools Layout tab**, click **Chart Title** in the Labels group, click **Above Chart**, type **Employer Ratings**, press **[Enter]**, click **Legend** in the Labels group, then click **None**

10. Adjust column widths, size and position the chart as shown in Figure G-12, type your name below the chart, print a copy of the worksheet, save and close the workbook, close the database, then exit all programs
    Kevin can see at a glance that the job offered by Coral Utilities most closely matches his employment criteria.

FIGURE G-10: Selecting the Positive Results query datasheet

Click here to select the entire datasheet

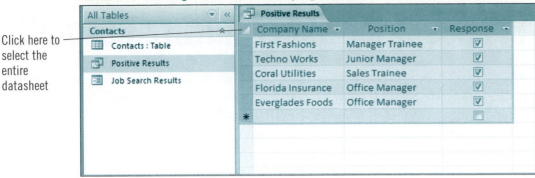

FIGURE G-11: Records for the Ratings table

ID	Company Na	Position	Response	Location	Pay	Benefits	Advanceme	Ad
1	First Fashions	Manager Traine	☑	3	3	6	3	
2	Techno Works	Junior Manage	☑	3	3	3	3	
3	Coral Utilities	Sales Trainee	☑	3	6	9	9	
4	Florida Insuran	Office Manage	☑	6	3	3	3	
5	Everglades Foc	Office Manage	☑	9	6	3	3	
*	(New)		☐					

FIGURE G-12: Completed column chart in Excel

Proposal for Sheer Nature Cosmetics

You are the owner of Sheer Nature Cosmetics, a small business that sells organically made beauty products. To increase sales, you've decided to propose a partnership with Cloud Nine Spa, a local health resort. To create the proposal, you need to **Import an Excel Workbook**, **Create the Proposal in Word**, and then **Add Excel and Access Objects to Word**. The three pages of the completed proposal are shown in Figure G-20 on page 163.

Activity:

Import an Excel Workbook

The owner of Cloud Nine Spa has asked Sheer Nature Cosmetics to supply a product database. Information about the aromatherapy products that most interest Cloud Nine Spa is currently stored in an Excel workbook. You need to import the Excel data into a table in an Access database that contains information about the other products distributed by Sheer Nature Cosmetics.

Steps:

Hint

Make sure you change the data type for Price to Currency.

1. Start Access, then create a new database called **Partnership Products.accdb** saved to the location where you store your Data Files

2. Click the **View button**, save the table as **Sheer Nature Products**, type **Product #**, change the Data Type to **Number**, then enter the remaining fields as shown in Figure G-13

3. Click the **Category Data Type list arrow**, click **Lookup Wizard**, click the **I will type in the values that I want option button**, click **Next**, enter **Bath** and **Cleansing** as the two lookup values, then click **Finish**

4. Click the **View button**, click **Yes**, enter the data as shown in Figure G-14, then close and save the table

5. Start Excel, open the file **Sheer Nature Products.xlsx** from the location where you store your Data Files, then save the file as **Partnership Data.xlsx**

   The worksheet contains three columns. Before you can import this worksheet into the Access table, you need to ensure that both the Excel worksheet and the Access table contain the exact same column headings and data types.

6. Select **column C**, click the **right mouse button**, click **Insert**, type **Category** in cell **C1**, click cell **C2**, type **Essential Oil**, then drag the fill handle to cell **C32** to fill all the cells with the Essential Oil label

7. Save and close the workbook, return to the Partnership Products database in Access, click **Sheer Nature Products: Table**, click the **External Data tab**, click **Excel** in the Import group, click the **Browse button**, navigate to the location where you store your Data Files, then double-click **Partnership Data.xlsx**

8. Click the **Append a copy of the records to the table: option button**, click **OK**, click **Next**, click **Next**, click **Finish**, then click **Close**

9. Double-click **Sheer Nature Products: Table** to open it, scroll down so you can see the records you entered and some of the new records, widen the Description column as shown in Figure G-15, then close the table

FIGURE G-13: Fields for the Sheer Nature Products table

Sheer Nature Products		
Field Name	Data Type	
⚲ Product #	Number	
Description	Text	
Category	Text	
Price	Currency ——————	

— Select the Currency data type

FIGURE G-14: Records for the Sheer Nature Products table

Sheer Nature Products				
Product # ▾	Description ▾	Category ▾	Price ▾	Add New Field
7888	Lavender Spray	Bath	$4.50	
7889	Peppermint Bath Oil	Bath	$5.50	
7890	Citrus Wash	Cleansing	$6.50	
7891	Lemon Mist	Cleansing	$4.50	
7892	Raspberry Wash	Cleansing	$5.50	
7893	Mango-Papaya Spray	Bath	$6.50	
7894	Sage Bath Oil	Bath	$5.50	
7895	Green Apple Soap	Cleansing	$4.50	
7896	Orange Body Scrub	Cleansing	$5.50	
*				

FIGURE G-15: Excel data imported into the Sheer Nature Products table

Sheer Nature Products				
Product # ▾	Description ▾	Category ▾	Price ▾	Add New Field
3564	Jasmine	Essential Oil	$6.00	
3565	Juniper	Essential Oil	$6.50	
3566	Lavender	Essential Oil	$6.00	
3567	Lemon	Essential Oil	$5.50	
3568	Lemon Grass	Essential Oil	$5.00	
3569	Lime	Essential Oil	$5.00	
3570	Myrrh	Essential Oil	$7.00	
3571	Patchouli	Essential Oil	$6.50	
3572	Peppermint	Essential Oil	$6.00	
3573	Pine Needle	Essential Oil	$4.50	
3574	Rosemary	Essential Oil	$5.00	
3575	Rosewood	Essential Oil	$4.50	
3576	Sandalwood	Essential Oil	$7.00	
3577	Spearmint	Essential Oil	$5.00	
3578	Tea Tree	Essential Oil	$5.50	
3579	Vanilla	Essential Oil	$5.50	
3580	Ylang Ylang	Essential Oil	$6.50	
7888	Lavender Spray	Bath	$4.50	
7889	Peppermint Bath Oil	Bath	$5.50	
7890	Citrus Wash	Cleansing	$6.50	
7891	Lemon Mist	Cleansing	$4.50	
7892	Raspberry Wash	Cleansing	$5.50	
7893	Mango-Papaya Spray	Bath	$6.50	
7894	Sage Bath Oil	Bath	$5.50	
7895	Green Apple Soap	Cleansing	$4.50	
7896	Orange Body Scrub	Cleansing	$5.50	

PROPOSAL FOR SHEER NATURE COSMETICS

Activity:

Create the Proposal in Word

The proposal consists of three pages that include objects copied from Excel and Access. First, you need to set up the document in Word and then you need to insert the text. You will insert the objects in the next lesson.

Steps:

1. Start Word, click the **Page Layout tab**, click the **Margins button** in the Page Setup group, click **Custom Margins**, change the Left margin to **2.5**, click **OK**, then save the document as **Partnership Proposal.docx** in the location where you store your Data Files

2. Click the **Insert tab**, click the **Header button** in the Header & Footer group, click **Blank**, click the **Insert tab**, click the **WordArt button** in the Text group, click the **upper-left selection**, type **Proposal**, select the **Calibri** font, click the **Bold button** **B**, click the **Italic button** _I_, compare the Edit WordArt Text dialog box to Figure G-16, then click **OK**

3. With the **WordArt object** still selected, click the **Shape Fill list arrow** in the WordArt Styles group, select **Aqua, Accent 5, Lighter 80%**, click the **Shape Outline list arrow** , then click **No Outline**

Trouble

Drag the sizing handles to adjust the width and height of the WordArt object.

4. Click the **WordArt Vertical Text button** in the Text group, click the **Text Wrapping button** in the Arrange group, click **Square**, click the **View tab**, click the **One Page button** in the Zoom group, then size and position the WordArt object as shown in Figure G-17

5. Switch back to 100% view, click the **Header & Footer Tools Design tab**, click the **Go to Footer button** in the Navigation group, type your name at the left margin, press **[Tab]** twice, then click at **4.9** on the ruler bar to place a left tab marker as shown in Figure G-18

6. Click the **Page Number button** in the Header & Footer group, point to **Current Position**, click **Plain Number**, then click the **Close Header and Footer button**

7. Click the **Insert tab**, click the **Object list arrow** in the Text group, click **Text from File**, navigate to the location where you store your Data Files, then double-click **Partnership Proposal Text.docx**
   The text required for the proposal is inserted into the document.

8. Scroll to the top of the document, select **INTRODUCTION**, click the **Home tab**, then click **Heading 1** in the Styles gallery

9. Format all the headings that appear in all capitals with the Heading 1 style, format all the headings in title case with the Heading 2 style, then save the document
   Figure G-19 shows some of the formatted headings.

FIGURE G-16: Formatting options for the WordArt object

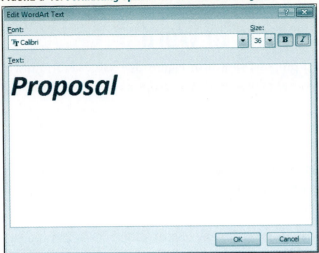

FIGURE G-17: Completed WordArt object in One Page view

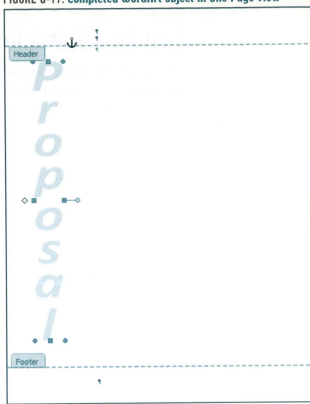

FIGURE G-18: Setting a new left tab

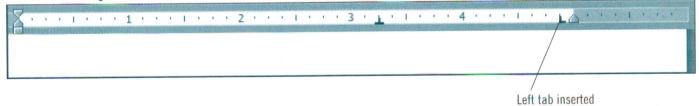

Left tab inserted

FIGURE G-19: Heading styles applied to selected text

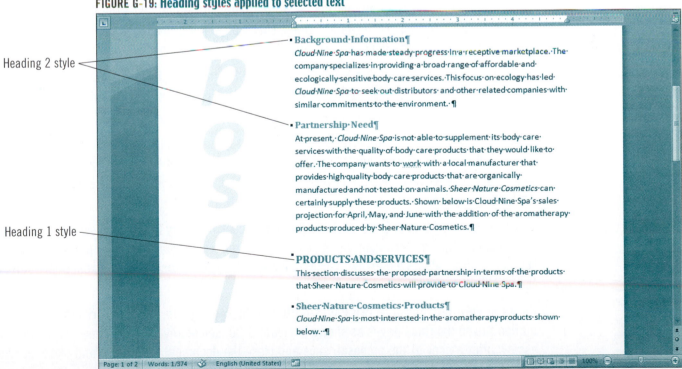

Heading 2 style

Heading 1 style

Activity:

Add Excel and Access Objects to Word

To produce the three pages of the completed proposal shown in Figure G-20, you need to insert spreadsheet data, create a query table in Access and publish it in Word, copy a chart from Excel, and finally, generate a table of contents.

Steps:

1. Switch to Excel, open the file **Cloud Nine Spa Products.xlsx** from the location where you store your Data Files, save the file as **Cloud Nine Spa Partnership Data.xlsx**, select cells **A1:E14**, click the **Copy button**  in the Clipboard group, then switch to Word

2. Click at the end of the **Partnership Need paragraph** (following "Sheer Nature Cosmetics"), press **[Enter]**, click the **Paste list arrow** in the Clipboard group, click **Paste Special**, click **Microsoft Office Excel Worksheet Object**, click **OK**, click the pasted object, point to the lower-left corner, then click and drag up to reduce the width of the object so that it fits at the bottom of page 1 as shown in Figure G-20

3. Switch to Access, click the **Create tab**, click the **Query Wizard button** in the Other group, click **OK**, move all the records in the Sheer Nature Products table to the Selected Fields list box, click **Next**, click **Next**, then click **Finish**

4. Switch to Design view, type **Essential Oil** in the Criteria cell for Category, click the **Run button** in the Results group, then close and save the query

5. Click the **External Data tab**, click the **Word button** in the Export group, click the **Browse** button, navigate to the location where you store Data Files, click **Save**, click the **Open the destination file after the export operation is complete check box**, then click **OK**

   The table is pasted into a new document named Sheer Nature Products Query.rtf. The .rtf extension stands for Rich Text Format.

6. Select the **table**, click the **Copy button** in the Clipboard group, click the **View tab**, click the **Switch Windows button** in the Window group, click **Partnership Proposal**, click at the end of the **Sheer Nature Cosmetics Products paragraph**, press **[Enter]**, then click the **Paste button**

7. Select the table, click the **Table Tools Design tab**, click the **More button** in the Table Styles group to show the Table Styles Gallery, select the **Light Grid-Accent 5 style**, click the **Home tab**, then click the **Center button** in the Paragraph group

8. Switch to Excel, click the **Projected Revenue sheet tab**, select cells **A1:E3**, click the **Insert tab**, click the **Column button** in the Charts group, click the **Clustered Pyramid** chart style, click the **Chart Tools Layout tab**, click the **Legend button** in the Labels group, then click **Show Legend at Bottom**

9. With the chart selected in Excel, click the **Home tab**, click the **Copy button**, switch to the Word Partnership Proposal document, click at the end of the **Projected Revenues paragraph**, press **[Enter]**, click the **Paste list arrow**, click **Paste Special**, click **Microsoft Office Excel Chart Object**, then click **OK**

10. Click the **View tab**, click the **Two Pages button** in the Zoom group, scroll to verify that the information fits on the three pages as shown in Figure G-20, delete any extra hard returns where necessary, print a copy of the proposal, save and close the document, then save and close all files and all programs

Additional Practice

For additional practice with the skills presented in this project, complete Independent Challenge 2.

FIGURE G-20: Completed Partnership Proposal

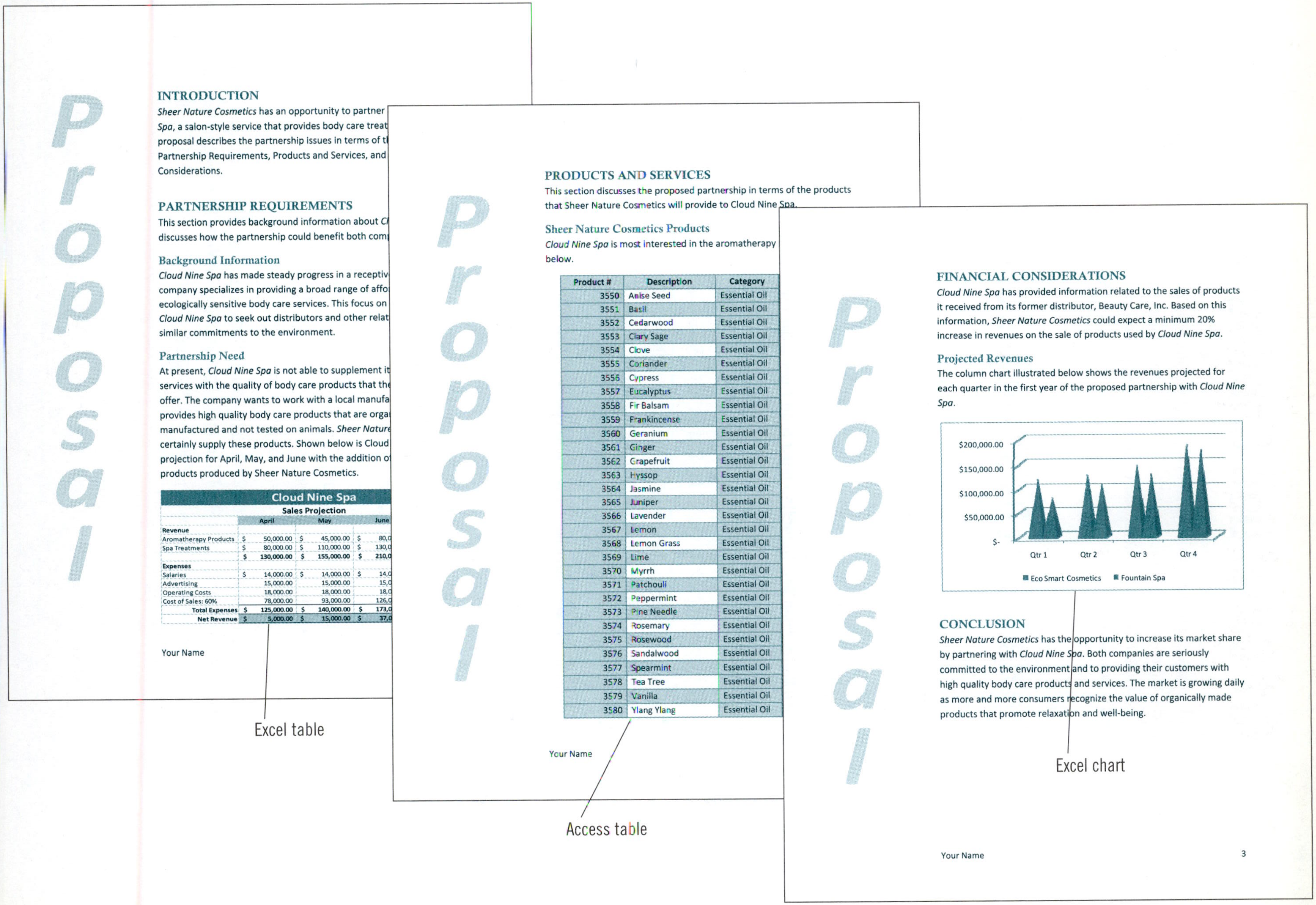

INTRODUCTION

Sheer Nature Cosmetics has an opportunity to partner *Cloud Nine Spa*, a salon-style service that provides body care treat proposal describes the partnership issues in terms of t Partnership Requirements, Products and Services, and Considerations.

PARTNERSHIP REQUIREMENTS

This section provides background information about *C* discusses how the partnership could benefit both com

Background Information

Cloud Nine Spa has made steady progress in a receptive company specializes in providing a broad range of affo ecologically sensitive body care services. This focus on *Cloud Nine Spa* to seek out distributors and other relat similar commitments to the environment.

Partnership Need

At present, *Cloud Nine Spa* is not able to supplement it services with the quality of body care products that the offer. The company wants to work with a local manufa provides high quality body care products that are orga manufactured and not tested on animals. *Sheer Nature* certainly supply these products. Shown below is Cloud projection for April, May, and June with the addition o products produced by Sheer Nature Cosmetics.

Cloud Nine Spa
Sales Projection

	April	May	June
Revenue			
Aromatherapy Products	$ 50,000.00	$ 45,000.00	$ 80,0
Spa Treatments	$ 80,000.00	$ 110,000.00	$ 130,0
	$ 130,000.00	$ 155,000.00	$ 210,0
Expenses			
Salaries	$ 14,000.00	$ 14,000.00	$ 14,0
Advertising	15,000.00	15,000.00	15,0
Operating Costs	18,000.00	18,000.00	18,0
Cost of Sales: 60%	78,000.00	93,000.00	126,0
Total Expenses	$ 125,000.00	$ 140,000.00	$ 173,0
Net Revenue	$ 5,000.00	$ 15,000.00	$ 37,0

Your Name

Excel table

PRODUCTS AND SERVICES

This section discusses the proposed partnership in terms of the products that *Sheer Nature Cosmetics* will provide to Cloud Nine Spa.

Sheer Nature Cosmetics Products

Cloud Nine Spa is most interested in the aromatherapy below.

Product #	Description	Category
3550	Anise Seed	Essential Oil
3551	Basil	Essential Oil
3552	Cedarwood	Essential Oil
3553	Clary Sage	Essential Oil
3554	Clove	Essential Oil
3555	Coriander	Essential Oil
3556	Cypress	Essential Oil
3557	Eucalyptus	Essential Oil
3558	Fir Balsam	Essential Oil
3559	Frankincense	Essential Oil
3560	Geranium	Essential Oil
3561	Ginger	Essential Oil
3562	Grapefruit	Essential Oil
3563	Hyssop	Essential Oil
3564	Jasmine	Essential Oil
3565	Juniper	Essential Oil
3566	Lavender	Essential Oil
3567	Lemon	Essential Oil
3568	Lemon Grass	Essential Oil
3569	Lime	Essential Oil
3570	Myrrh	Essential Oil
3571	Patchouli	Essential Oil
3572	Peppermint	Essential Oil
3573	Pine Needle	Essential Oil
3574	Rosemary	Essential Oil
3575	Rosewood	Essential Oil
3576	Sandalwood	Essential Oil
3577	Spearmint	Essential Oil
3578	Tea Tree	Essential Oil
3579	Vanilla	Essential Oil
3580	Ylang Ylang	Essential Oil

Your Name

Access table

FINANCIAL CONSIDERATIONS

Cloud Nine Spa has provided information related to the sales of products it received from its former distributor, Beauty Care, Inc. Based on this information, *Sheer Nature Cosmetics* could expect a minimum 20% increase in revenues on the sale of products used by *Cloud Nine Spa.*

Projected Revenues

The column chart illustrated below shows the revenues projected for each quarter in the first year of the proposed partnership with *Cloud Nine Spa.*

Excel chart

CONCLUSION

Sheer Nature Cosmetics has the opportunity to increase its market share by partnering with *Cloud Nine Spa.* Both companies are seriously committed to the environment and to providing their customers with high quality body care products and services. The market is growing daily as more and more consumers recognize the value of organically made products that promote relaxation and well-being.

Your Name

3

Art Collection Catalogue

As the office manager of the Raven Wing Art Gallery, you decide to create a database that lists the art pieces currently being shown at the gallery, produce identification labels to affix to each piece, and create a chart showing the breakdown of paintings by price category. First, you need to **Create the Art Database and Set Up the Merge** and then you need to **Merge the Labels and Create a Chart**.

Activity:

Create the Art Database and Set Up the Merge

You need to create the database by copying a table from Word. Then you need to create a query and merge the data in the query with identification labels you create in Word.

Steps:

1. Create a new database called **Art Collection.accdb** saved in the location where you store your Data Files

2. Open Word, open **Art Collection.docx** from the location where you store your Data Files, select the table, click the **Copy button** 📑 in the Clipboard group, close the document, switch to Access, click the **Home tab**, click the **Paste button**, then click **Yes**

3. Close the table, click **Yes**, type **Art List** as the table name, then press **[Enter]**

4. Click **Art List: Table**, click the **Create tab**, click **Query Wizard** in the Other group, click **OK**, select all the fields *except* the ID and Price Category fields, click **Next**, click **Next**, name the query **Identification Labels**, then click **Finish**

5. Switch to **Design view**, click the **Date Sort cell**, click the **list arrow**, select **Ascending**, click the **Run button** in the Results group, close and save the query, then close the database

   Before you use the Merge function, you need to close and then reopen the database.

6. Open **Art Collection.accdb**, enable content if necessary, click **Identification Labels**, click the **External Data tab**, click the **More button** in the Export group, click **Merge it with Microsoft Office Word**, click the **Create a new document and then link the data to it option button**, then click **OK**

7. Click the **Microsoft Word button** on the taskbar, maximize the Word window, click the **Labels option button** in the Mail Merge task pane, click **Next: Starting document**, click **Label options**, click the **Label vendors list arrow**, click **Avery US Letter** if necessary, scroll to and select **5163** in the Product number list as shown in Figure G-21, then click **OK**

   A sheet of labels formatted as a table appears in a new Word document.

8. Save the document as **Art Identification Labels.docx** in the location where you store your Data Files, select the table, click the **Table Tools Layout tab**, click **View Gridlines** in the Table group to turn on the gridlines if necessary, click a blank area, change the zoom to 100%, then compare the Word window to Figure G-22

FIGURE G-21: Selecting the label type

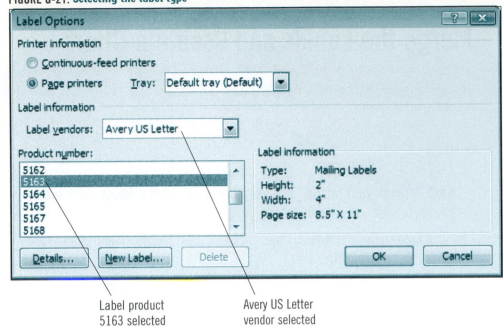

Label product
5163 selected

Avery US Letter
vendor selected

FIGURE G-22: Label sheet in Word

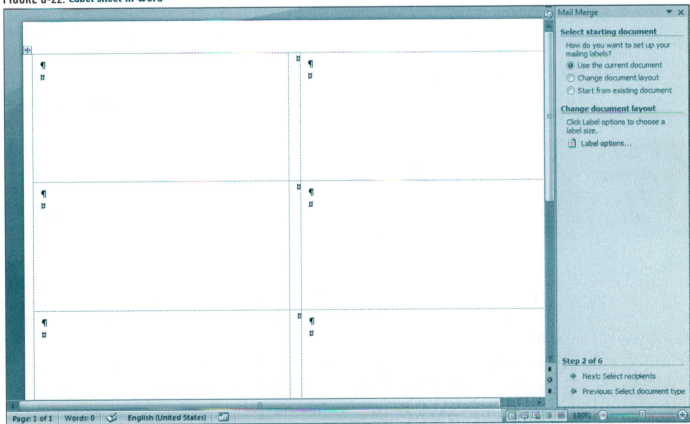

Word, Excel, and Access

Activity:

Merge the Labels and Create a Chart

You need to add fields to the identification labels, and then print the sheet of completed labels. Then you need to analyze the Art List table in Excel so that you can create a separate chart that shows the breakdown of paintings by price category.

Steps:

1. Click in the top left table cell, click **Next: Select recipients** in the Mail Merge task pane, click **Next: Arrange your labels**, click **More items**, click **Artist Name**, click **Insert**, then click **Close**
   The Artist field is inserted.

2. Press **Enter**, click the **Mailings tab**, click the **Insert Merge Field button** in the Write & Insert Fields group, double-click **Title**, then insert the remaining fields, arranging them as shown in Figure G-23

3. Format the field labels as shown in Figure G-24, click the **Artist** field, click the **Page Layout tab**, change the Before spacing to **24 pt**, click **Update all labels** in the Mail Merge task pane, click **Next: Preview your labels**, click **Next: Complete the merge**, close the Mail Merge task pane, compare the completed label sheet to Figure G-25, print a copy of the document, then save and close it

4. Switch to Access, click **Art List: Table**, click the **External Data tab**, click the **Excel button** in the Export group, click **Browse**, navigate to the location where you store Data Files, click **Save**, click **OK**, then click **Close**

5. Start Excel, open **Art List.xlsx**, widen columns as necessary, select cells **A1:H16**, click the **Sort & Filter button** in the Editing group, click **Custom Sort**, click the **Sort by list arrow**, click **Price Category**, then click **OK**

6. Click the **Data tab**, click **Subtotal** in the Outline group, click the **At each change in list arrow**, click **Price Category**, click **OK**, then click a blank cell to deselect the table

7. Widen the Price column, click the **Home tab**, click the **Find & Select button** in the Editing group, click **Replace**, type **Count**, in the Find what text box, press **[Tab]**, click **Replace All**, click **OK**, then click **Close**

8. Select cells **G6:H6**, press and hold the **[Ctrl]** key, select cells **G15:H15** and cells **G19:H19**, click the **Insert tab**, click the **Other Charts button** in the Charts group, click the **Doughnut chart**, then drag the chart below the data

9. Select **Layout 6** in the Chart Layouts group, click the **chart title**, type **Breakdown by Price Category**, press **[Enter]**, click the **Chart Tools Layout tab**, click **Data Labels** in the Labels group, click **More Data Label Options**, click the **Value check box** to select it, click the **Percentage check box** to deselect it, then click **Close**

10. Size and position the doughnut chart as shown in Figure G-26, type your name below the chart, save and print the workbook, then close all files and exit all programs

Additional Practice

For additional practice with the skills presented in this project, complete Independent Challenge 3.

FIGURE G-23: Fields for the art identification labels

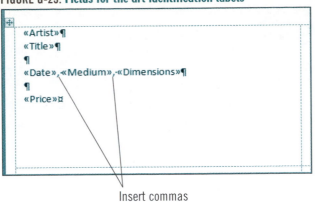

Insert commas

FIGURE G-24: Formatted fields

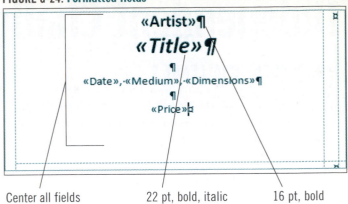

Center all fields

22 pt, bold, italic

16 pt, bold

FIGURE G-25: Completed label sheet

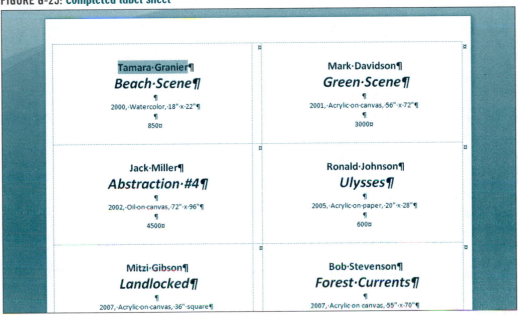

FIGURE G-26: Completed Doughnut chart

Independent Challenges

INDEPENDENT CHALLENGE 1

Create a Job Search database similar to the database you created for Project 1 to track your own job search efforts. Even if you are not currently seeking employment, create a practice database and accompanying form letter for your dream job. You can then modify these files when you are ready to seek employment. Follow the steps provided to create the database, merge it with a form letter you create in Word, and then create a chart in Excel that graphically displays your ratings of the companies that responded positively to your form letter.

1. Your first task is to determine the type of job position you are seeking and the type of company or organization you would like to work for. For example, you could seek a job as an office manager at a real estate or architectural company. In the box below, write the job positions you are seeking and the types of companies you would like to work for:

   Job Positions: _____

   Companies: _____

2. You need at least 10 employers for your job search database. Look through the employment advertisements in your local paper to find potential employers, or, if you can't find advertisements for the specific jobs you require, look through the Yellow Pages to find the names and addresses of at least 10 companies that you think you would like to work for and that may be interested in an applicant with your qualifications. Try to include as many realistic records in your job search database as possible.

3. Create a database called **My Job Search.accdb** in the location where you save your Data Files.

4. Create a **Contacts** table similar to the Contacts table you created for Project 1. Include at least six fields and make one field a lookup field. Make sure you include a primary key in the table.

5. Switch to Word and set up an application form letter. Use the form letter you created in Project 1 to help you determine the information to include. Make sure you fully describe your qualifications and experience. Select the records in the Contacts table as the data source for the form letter, and include the appropriate fields.

6. Merge the data source with the form letter, match fields where needed for the address, change the After spacing for the address lines, print two or three of the letters, then save the form letter as **My Job Application Letter.docx** to the location where you store your Data Files.

7. Switch back to Access and create a custom form called **Job Search** that includes the fields from the Contacts table and two additional fields: a Yes/No field called Response, and a text field for a date. Remember that you need to add the new fields to the Contacts table first and then you can create the form in Design view.

8. Use the form to enter positive responses for at least five of the employers.

9. Create a query that lists only the companies that responded positively to your form letter.

10. Copy the Company Name and Position records from the query to a new table called **My Job Ratings**, then enter your ratings for each company in terms of four criteria of your choice. For example, you could rank the employers on Location, Pay, Benefits, and Advancement.

11. Export the My Ratings table to Excel, then create a column chart that shows the breakdown of companies according to your ratings. Remember that you will need to total the ratings for each company and then use the Chart Wizard to create a column chart that includes only the company names and the total ratings. Include a title on the column chart and remove the legend.

12. Type your name below the chart, print the workbook containing the Excel chart, then close all the files and applications. Be sure the Excel workbook is saved as **My Job Ratings.xlsx** in the location where you store your Data Files.

13. Save all files, and close all applications.

INDEPENDENT CHALLENGE 2

Write a three-page proposal that discusses partnership opportunities between two companies of your choice. For example, you could write about the benefits of a partnership between a small computer store and a bookkeeping business. For ideas, refer to the proposal you created for Project 2. Follow the steps provided to create data in Excel, import it into an Access database, create an attractively formatted proposal in Word, and then add objects from Excel and Access.

1. Start Excel, then in Sheet1 create a product list that contains information about some of the products you plan to mention in the proposal. Save the Excel file as **My Partnership Data.xlsx** in the location where you store your Data Files.
2. Start Access, create a new database called **My Partnership.accdb**, save it in the location where you store your Data Files, then import the Excel worksheet.
3. Name the new table **My Products**.
4. Start Word, then save the new document as **My Partnership Proposal.docx** in the location where you store your Data Files.
5. Show the Header and Footer ribbon, then use WordArt to create an interesting background for your proposal similar to the background you created in Project 2. You can choose to create "Proposal" or the name of your company as shaded text behind or to the left of the proposal text.
6. Switch to the footer, enter your name at the left margin, then insert the page number at the right margin.
7. Write approximately one page of text for the proposal. Make sure that you include text that introduces a table that you'll publish from Access, a worksheet that you'll copy from Excel, and a chart that you'll copy from Excel.
8. Include several headings and subheadings that you format with the Heading 1 or Heading 2 style.
9. Switch to the My Partnership Data.xlsx workbook, enter appropriate financial data regarding revenue and expenses in Sheet2, then enter projected quarterly data and create a chart on Sheet3.
10. Copy the cells containing the financial data to an appropriate place in the proposal. Use Paste Special to paste them as a Microsoft Office Excel Worksheet Object.
11. Copy the chart to an appropriate place in the proposal. Use Paste Special to paste it as a Microsoft Office Excel Chart Object, *not* as a linked object.
12. From Access, publish the My Products table in Word. Be sure the table is saved as **My Products.rtf** in the location where you store your Data Files.
13. Copy the table that appears in Word to an appropriate place in the proposal, then format it attractively by applying one of the available Table styles.
14. Add a title at the top of the first page, scroll through the document, add page breaks where appropriate, print a copy of the completed proposal, save and close the document, then save and close all files and all programs.

INDEPENDENT CHALLENGE 3

Create a database that contains information about your personal collection of CDs, records, tapes, videos, photographs, or a collection of your choice. Use the database to create labels for items in your collection. Plan and create the database as follows.

1. In Word, create a table containing headings that will differentiate the various records in your collection in terms of genre, category, or type, as appropriate. If your table lists all your videos, for example, you could include fields for Title, Genre, Date, and Price.
2. Save the Word document as **My Collection.docx** in the location where you store your Data Files.
3. Create a database called **My Collection.accdb** and save it in the location where you store your Data Files, create a table for entering data, then copy the table from the Word document into the Access table.
4. Replace the field labels with the labels in the first record, then remove the first record.
5. Save the table as **Collection List**.
6. Merge the table to a new document in Word, and then follow the steps in the Mail Merge task pane to select a label, insert fields, and then format the label. Look through the list of labels available in the Label Options dialog box to find a label appropriate for the items in your collection.

7. Complete the merge and print one sheet of labels. Save the label sheet as **My Collection Labels.docx** in the location where you store your Data Files.

8. Switch back to Access and export the table to Excel as a workbook called **My Collection List.xlsx**.

9. In Excel, sort one of the fields (for example, the category field) in ascending order, apply a Subtotals list that calculates the total number of items in each category, replace "Count" with nothing, then create a chart that shows the breakdown of items by category. Add a title to the chart, type your name below the chart, then print the Excel worksheet.

10. Save and close all open files, and exit all programs.

INDEPENDENT CHALLENGE 4

You work for a company called Diversion, Inc., that creates imaginative computer games for teens and adults. The games sell worldwide on the Internet. You've decided to analyze the types of customers who have purchased your games in the past month in terms of occupation and country. Follow the instructions provided to create the report shown in Figure G-28. This document includes a table published from Access and a cone chart created in Excel.

1. Start Access, create a database called **Diversion Computers.accdb**, and save it in the location where you store your Data Files.

2. Create a table called **Customer List** as shown in Figure G-27. Note that the Occupation field is a lookup field (**Artist, Consultant, Lawyer, Manager, Teacher**), and the Country field is a lookup field (**Canada, India, Ireland, United Kingdom, United States**).

3. Export the Customer List table to an Excel workbook that you name **Diversion Analysis.xlsx**. Create a pyramid chart that shows the breakdown of customers by country. You will need to sort the worksheet by country and create a Subtotal list to count the number of records in each occu-

FIGURE G-27: Customers table

ID	Last Name	First Name	Occupation	Country	Product	Add New Field
1	Janzen	David	Teacher	United Kingdom	Trail Blazer	
2	Yaretz	Wanda	Lawyer	Canada	Venus Voyager	
3	Pryce	Wyndam	Consultant	United Kingdom	Grand Prix Racer	
4	Singh	Manjit	Manager	India	Medieval Odyssey	
5	O'Brian	Sean	Teacher	Ireland	Art Quest	
6	St. Pierre	Brigitte	Manager	Canada	Trail Blazer	
7	Wallace	Diane	Artist	United States	Star Gazer	
8	Knutson	Olga	Lawyer	United Kingdom	Venus Voyager	
9	Morrison	Dawn	Lawyer	United States	Medieval Odyssey	
10	Li	Doris	Teacher	United States	Deep Sea Diver	
11	Stephensen	Hugh	Manager	Canada	Art Quest	
12	McDonald	Ewan	Teacher	United States	Animalia	
13	Reilly	Patrick	Teacher	Ireland	Roman World	
14	Kanaka	Hiromi	Teacher	Canada	Art Quest	
15	Fuentes	Diego	Consultant	United States	Deep Sea Diver	
*	(New)					

pation before you create the pyramid chart. In the Subtotal dialog box, you'll need to select "Country" as the At each change in selection. You will also need to remove "Count" from the worksheet so that it does not appear in the chart labels. (*Hint:* Search for Count so that Excel does not also remove the "count" in "Country.")

4. Format the chart so that it appears as shown in the completed report in Figure G-28.

5. Start Word, enter just the text shown in Figure G-28, apply the Metro theme, then change the top margin to .5". Note that the Title style is applied to the title.

6. Save the document as **Diversion Report.docx** in the location where you store your Data Files.

7. Switch to Access, then publish the table in Word (it becomes a file called Customer List.rtf).

8. Copy the table and then paste it below the first paragraph of text in the Word document.

9. Apply the Light Grid - Accent 1 table style, deselect the Banded Columns check box in the Table Style Options group, then adjust column widths, as shown in Figure G-28.

10. Switch to Excel, and then use the Paste Special command to copy the pyramid chart and paste it as a Microsoft Office Excel Chart Object below the last paragraph in the Word document. Double-click the chart, click the Page Layout tab in Excel, then select the Metro theme. Click outside the chart, then resize the chart so that it fits on page 1 of the document.

11. Center the chart, format the page attractively in Word, type your name below the chart, print a copy, then save and close all files and exit all programs.

DIVERSION, INC.

Diversion, Inc., sells the majority of its computer games to teens and adults directly from its Web site. We have analyzed the types of customers who have bought our computer games during the month of December 2006 in terms of occupation and country. The following table shows the breakdown of customers by Occupation and Country for December 2006:

ID	Last Name	First Name	Occupation	Country	Product
1	Janzen	David	Teacher	United Kingdom	Trail Blazer
2	Yaretz	Wanda	Lawyer	Canada	Venus Voyager
3	Pryce	Wyndam	Consultant	United Kingdom	Grand Prix Racer
4	Singh	Manjit	Manager	India	Medieval Odyssey
5	O'Brian	Sean	Teacher	Ireland	Art Quest
6	St. Pierre	Brigitte	Manager	Canada	Trail Blazer
7	Wallace	Diane	Artist	United States	Star Gazer
8	Knutson	Olga	Lawyer	United Kingdom	Venus Voyager
9	Morrison	Dawn	Lawyer	United States	Medieval Odyssey
10	Li	Doris	Teacher	United States	Deep Sea Diver
11	Stephensen	Hugh	Manager	Canada	Art Quest
12	McDonald	Ewan	Teacher	United States	Animalia
13	Reilly	Patrick	Teacher	Ireland	Roman World
14	Kanaka	Hiromi	Teacher	Canada	Art Quest
15	Fuentes	Diego	Consultant	United States	Deep Sea Diver

As shown in the pyramid chart illustrated below, the majority of our customers live in Canada or the United States. A significant number of customers live in the United Kingdom and Ireland. To continue serving the British and Irish markets, Diversion plans to develop a marketing strategy in consultation with contacts in London and Dublin.

Visual Workshop

Start Word, create the table shown in Figure G-29, then save the file as **Serenity Landscaping.docx** in the location where you store your Data Files. Start Access, create a database called **Serenity Landscaping.accdb**, copy the table from the Word document to a new table in the Access database, then save the table as **Neighborhood Sales**. Add the fields and values as shown in Figure G-30. Export the table to an Excel file called **Serenity Landscaping Analysis.xlsx**, and then create a column chart in Excel as shown in Figure G-31. Enter your name in cell A33, save and print the Excel worksheet, then save and close all files and exit all programs.

FIGURE G-29: Table in Word

Neighborhood¤	Landscape·Services¤	Garden·Products¤	¤
Richmond¤	45000¤	75000¤	¤
North·Delta¤	55000¤	72000¤	¤
Rockridge¤	60000¤	80000¤	¤
West·River¤	36000¤	28000¤	¤

¶

FIGURE G-30: Neighborhood Sales table

ID	Neighborhood	Landscape Services	Garden Products	Design Services	Add New Field
1	Richmond	45000	75000	50000	
2	North Delta	55000	72000	30000	
3	Rockridge	60000	80000	10000	
4	West River	36000	28000	20000	
* (New)					

FIGURE G-31: Sales by Neighborhood

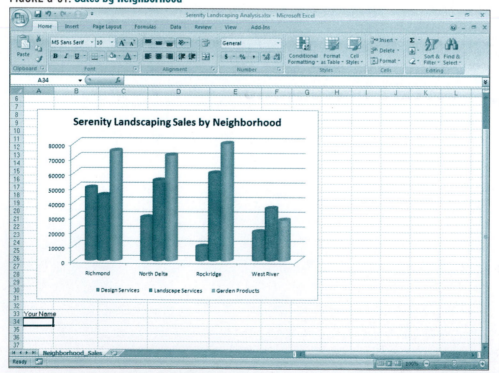

Microsoft
▶ PowerPoint
Projects

Unit H

PowerPoint Projects

In This Unit You Will Create the Following:

▶ **Training Presentation**

▶ **Poster**

▶ **Lecture Presentation**

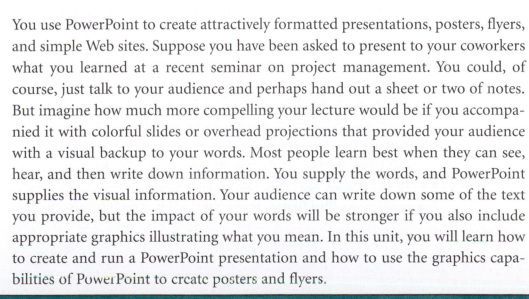

You use PowerPoint to create attractively formatted presentations, posters, flyers, and simple Web sites. Suppose you have been asked to present to your coworkers what you learned at a recent seminar on project management. You could, of course, just talk to your audience and perhaps hand out a sheet or two of notes. But imagine how much more compelling your lecture would be if you accompanied it with colorful slides or overhead projections that provided your audience with a visual backup to your words. Most people learn best when they can see, hear, and then write down information. You supply the words, and PowerPoint supplies the visual information. Your audience can write down some of the text you provide, but the impact of your words will be stronger if you also include appropriate graphics illustrating what you mean. In this unit, you will learn how to create and run a PowerPoint presentation and how to use the graphics capabilities of PowerPoint to create posters and flyers.

Training Presentation on Oral Presentation Skills

You have been asked to teach your coworkers how to give an oral presentation. To help emphasize the points you make, you plan to accompany your lecture with an on-screen presentation that you create in PowerPoint. To complete the training presentation, you need to **Create the Presentation Outline**, **Customize a Theme**, **Modify Individual Slides**, and **Edit and Show the Presentation**.

Activity:

Create the Presentation Outline

You need to enter the information you plan to display on the slides in the Oral Presentation Skills presentation.

Steps:

1. Start PowerPoint, click the **Outline tab**, then click to the right of the **slide icon** on the Outline tab

2. Type **Oral Presentation Skills**, then press **[Enter]**

3. Press **[Tab]** to indicate you want to type subtext on Slide 1, type your name, then save the presentation as **Oral Presentation Skills** in the location where you store your Data Files

   Slide 1 of the presentation appears as shown in Figure H-1. Notice how the text appears in the Outline tab and in the Slide pane.

4. Press **[Enter]**, press **[Shift][Tab]** to start a new slide, type **Overview**, press **[Enter]**, press **[Tab]**, then type **Choose Topic**

   The text you just typed appears as the first bulleted item on the slide titled "Overview."

5. Press **[Enter]**, type **Create Outline**, press **[Enter]**, type **Prepare Slides**, press **[Enter]**, type **Deliver Presentation**, then press **[Enter]**

   A bullet appears each time you press [Enter].

6. Press **[Shift][Tab]** to create a new slide, type **Step 1: Choose Topic**, press **[Enter]**, press **[Tab]**, type **Persuade your audience to take a specific action or approve a specific request**, press **[Enter]**, type **Sample Topics**, then press **[Enter]**

7. Press **[Tab]**, enter the three items under Sample Topics as shown in Figure H-2, press **[Enter]**, then press **[Shift][Tab]** to return to the left margin

8. Enter the information for Slides 4 through 7 as shown in Figure H-2

   Remember to press [Tab] to move the insertion point to the right and [Shift][Tab] to move the insertion point to the left. You can also click the Increase Indent button or the Decrease Indent button to change the outline level for the selected line.

9. Click the **Review tab**, click the **Spelling button** in the Proofing group, make any corrections required, press **[Ctrl][Home]** to move to the title slide, then save the presentation

Hint

You can modify the width of the Outline pane by using the pointer to drag the splitter bar to the left or right.

PowerPoint

FIGURE H-1: Title slide

Outline tab

Slides tab

Text appears
on the slide
and in the
Outline tab

Drag the splitter bar to
change the width of
the Outline tab

Slide pane

Oral Presentation Skills

Your Name

Notes pane

FIGURE H-2: Outline for Oral Presentation Skills

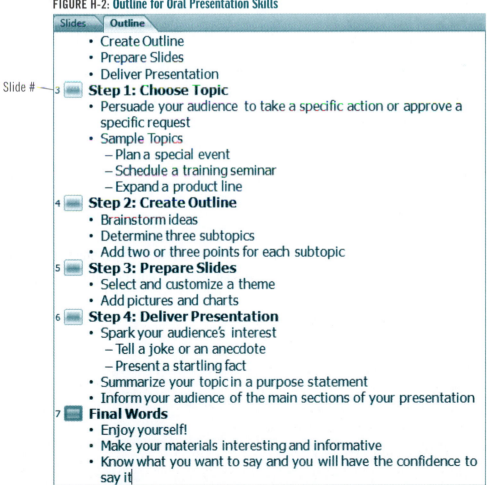

Slide #

| Slides | Outline |

- Create Outline
- Prepare Slides
- Deliver Presentation

3 **Step 1: Choose Topic**
- Persuade your audience to take a specific action or approve a specific request
- Sample Topics
  - Plan a special event
  - Schedule a training seminar
  - Expand a product line

4 **Step 2: Create Outline**
- Brainstorm ideas
- Determine three subtopics
- Add two or three points for each subtopic

5 **Step 3: Prepare Slides**
- Select and customize a theme
- Add pictures and charts

6 **Step 4: Deliver Presentation**
- Spark your audience's interest
  - Tell a joke or an anecdote
  - Present a startling fact
- Summarize your topic in a purpose statement
- Inform your audience of the main sections of your presentation

7 **Final Words**
- Enjoy yourself!
- Make your materials interesting and informative
- Know what you want to say and you will have the confidence to say it

Activity:

Customize a Theme

PowerPoint includes 20 built-in themes that you can use to format a presentation. You can give your presentation a unique look by changing the color and font schemes, applying a new background style, and then working in the slide master to apply new formats to specific parts of each slide. You apply the Urban theme to the presentation and then customize it.

Steps:

1. Click the **Slides tab**, click the **Design tab**, click the **More button** ⬇ in the Themes group to show the full selection of themes, move your mouse over each theme to see the live preview, then select the **Urban** theme as shown in Figure H-3

2. Click the **Colors button** in the Themes group, click the **Apex** color scheme, click the **Fonts button** in the Themes group, then click the **Module** font scheme

3. Click the **Background Styles button** in the Background group, click **Format Background**, then click the **Picture or texture fill option button**

4. Click the **Texture button**, select the **Canvas** texture as shown in Figure H-4, click **Apply to All**, then click **Close**

   You can create hundreds of interesting presentation designs just by mixing and matching the various themes with new color schemes, font schemes, and background effects. You can also work in the slide master to make changes to specific portions of the presentation design.

5. Click the **View tab**, click the **Slide Master button** in the Presentation Views group, click the top slide in the Slides pane, then click **Second level** on the slide master (very light green text)

6. Click the **Home tab**, click the **Font Color list arrow** 🅰⁻ in the Font group, then click **Aqua, Accent 3, Darker 50%**

   The text of all second level text is changed for the entire presentation.

7. Click the **dark grey rectangle** at the top of the slide master, click the **Shape Fill button** in the Drawing group, then click **Aqua, Accent 3, Darker 50%** as shown in Figure H-5

8. Click the **Title Slide Layout** (second slide in the task pane), click the **dark grey rectangle**, then fill it with **Aqua, Accent 3, Darker 50%**

9. Click below the rectangle, click the **View tab**, click the **Normal button** in the Presentation Views group, then save the presentation

FIGURE H-3: Selecting the Urban theme

Urban theme
selected

FIGURE H-4: Selecting the Canvas texture

Texture button

Canvas texture
selected

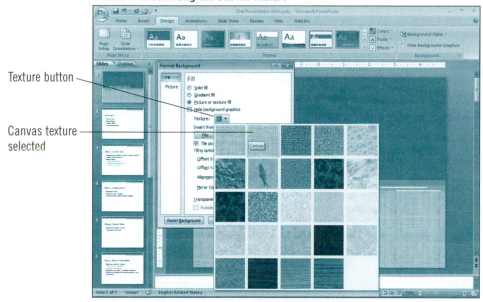

FIGURE H-5: Filling an object on the slide master

Rectangle object
selected and filled
with a new color

Activity:

Modify Individual Slides

You need to add a clip-art picture on Slide 2, and then insert a new slide and create a SmartArt graphic on it.

Steps:

Trouble

You need to be connected to the Internet to find the clip art of the checkmark. Also verify that All Collections is selected in the Clip Art task pane. If it is not, click the Search in list arrow and select the Everywhere check box.

Trouble

Use [↓] to move to each level; if you press [Enter] and insert a new circle, click the Undo button.

1. Click the **Next Slide button** ⊻ on the vertical scroll bar to display Slide 2, click the **Insert tab**, click the **Clip Art button** in the Illustrations group, select the contents of the **Search for** text box, type **checkmarks**, click **Go**, click the **picture of the check box** (see Figure H-6), then close the Clip Art task pane

2. Use the mouse to drag the corner handles to resize the clip-art picture, then position it as shown in Figure H-6

3. Click the **Next Slide button** ⊻ until Slide 6 appears (containing "Step 4: Deliver Presentation"), click the **Home tab**, click the **New Slide button** in the Slides group, click in the title placeholder, then type **Four-Step Process**

4. Click the **Insert SmartArt Graphic button** 🖼 in the body placeholder, click **Cycle**, select the **Basic Radial** diagram type (third row, second from left), then click **OK**

5. If necessary, click the **Text Pane button** in the Create Graphic group to show the text pane, type **Great Presenting**, press the **[↓]**, type **Topic**, then enter the labels for the remaining three circles as shown in Figure H-7

6. Click the **More button** in the SmartArt Styles group, then select the **Polished design** (the upper-left design) in the 3-D section

7. Click the **Change Colors button** in the SmartArt Styles group, then click **Colorful – Accent Colors** (the far-left choice in the Colorful group)

8. Click the **border** surrounding the SmartArt graphic, click the **Home tab**, click the **Font Color list arrow** 🅰 ▾ in the Font group, then click a **Black box**

9. Click the **circle** containing the Great Presenting text, press and hold **[Shift]**, drag the **upper-right sizing handle** up and to the right to increase the size of the circle as shown in Figure H-8, then save the presentation

The completed SmartArt graphic appears as shown in Figure H-8.

FIGURE H-6: Clip-art picture

FIGURE H-7: Text for the SmartArt graphic

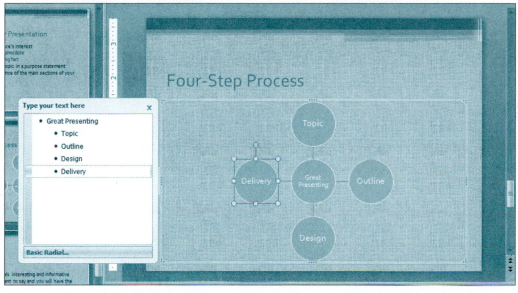

FIGURE H-8: Completed SmartArt graphic

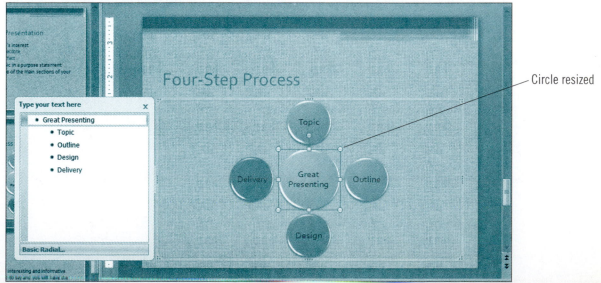

Circle resized

Activity:

Edit and Show the Presentation

You need to select an animation scheme in Slide Sorter view, and then apply a custom animation scheme to the SmartArt graphic. Finally, you run the presentation in Slide Show view, and then print a copy of the presentation as a sheet of handouts with all nine slides on one page.

Steps:

1. Click the **View tab**, click the **Slide Sorter button** in the Presentation Views group, verify that **Slide 7** is selected, then drag Slide 7 to the left of Slide 3 as shown in Figure H-9

2. Click the **Animations tab**, click the **More button** in the Transition to This Slide group, then select the **Shape Diamond Wipe** as shown in Figure H-10

   A preview of the animation effect is shown on the selected slide.

3. Click the **Apply to All button** in the Transition to This Slide group

4. Verify that **Slide 3** is still selected (it contains the SmartArt graphic), then click the **Normal button** on the status bar at the bottom of the screen

5. Click the **SmartArt graphic** to select it (be careful not to select any one circle), click the **Custom Animation button** in the Animations group, click **Add Effect** in the Custom Animation task pane, point to **Entrance**, click **More Effects**, then click **Diamond** in the list of Basic effects in the Add Entrance Effect dialog box

6. Click **OK**, click the **list arrow** next to Content Placeholder in the Custom Animation task pane, click **Effect Options**, click the **SmartArt Animation tab**, click the **Group graphic list arrow**, click **One by one**, then click **OK**

   A preview of the custom animation effect is shown on the slide. As you can see, each circle appears in turn, starting from the Great Presenting circle.

7. Close the Custom Animation task pane, press **[Ctrl][Home]**, click the **View tab**, click the **Slide Show button** in the Presentation Views group, then press **[Spacebar]** or click the **left mouse button** to move through the presentation

   The animation scheme works nicely, and the custom animation effect on the SmartArt graphic adds interest.

Additional Practice

For additional practice with the skills presented in this project, complete Independent Challenge 1.

8. Click the **Office Button**, click **Print**, click the **Print what list arrow**, click **Handouts**, click the **Slides per page list arrow**, click **9** as shown in Figure H-11, click **OK**, then save and close the presentation

   Your presentation is printed on one page.

FIGURE H-9: Slide 7 moved in Slide Sorter view

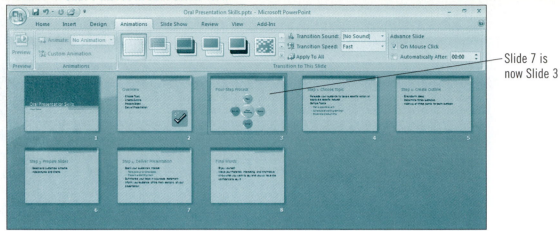

Slide 7 is now Slide 3

FIGURE H-10: Shape Diamond animation scheme selected

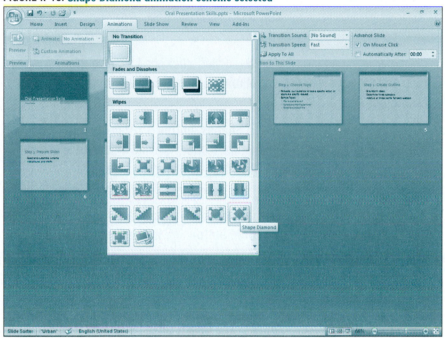

FIGURE H-11: Print dialog box

Handouts selected

Slides per page is 9

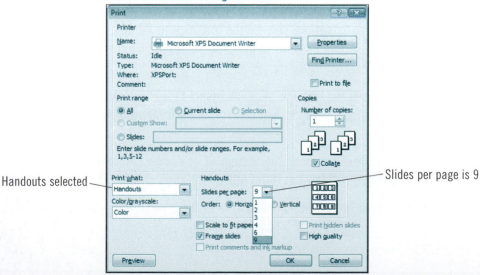

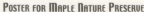
Poster for Maple Nature Preserve

You are in charge of advertising the monthly information meetings held from May through August at Maple Nature Preserve Area in North Vancouver, British Columbia. You have decided to create a poster to advertise the dates and times of these information meetings. The poster can be displayed on bulletin boards in libraries, community centers, and other areas throughout the neighborhood. To create the poster, you need to **Insert Text Objects**, **Create a Table**, and then **Add Graphics**. The completed poster is shown in Figure H-20 on page 187.

Activity:

Insert Text Objects

You need to start a new presentation, draw a shape, and then enter and format text.

Steps:

1. Create a new presentation in PowerPoint, click the **Layout button** in the Slides group, click **Blank**, then save the presentation as **Maple Nature Preserve Poster** in the location where you store your Data Files

2. Click the **Insert tab**, click the **Shapes button** in the Illustrations group, select the **Rounded Rectangle** shape in the Rectangles section (second from the left), draw a box approximately 8" wide anywhere on the screen, then type **Information Meeting**
   You do not need to worry about sizing the rectangle shape exactly at this point.

3. Click a blank area of the text box, click the **Home tab**, click the **Font Size list arrow** in the Font group, click **32**, then click the **Bold button** 🅱 in the Font group

4. Click the **Drawing Tools Format tab**, select the contents of the **Height text box** in the Size group, type **1**, press **[Enter]**, select the contents of the Width text box, type **7.75**, press **[Enter]**, then drag the rounded rectangle object to position it as shown in Figure H-12

5. Click away from the text box, click the **Insert tab**, click the **Text Box button** in the Text group, click below the rounded rectangle, type **Location**, press **[Enter]**, then type the address text, as shown in Figure H-13
   You do not need to worry about positioning the text box exactly at this point.

Hint

You select the border so that any changes you make will be applied to all the text in the box.

6. Select the word **Location**, change the font size to **20 pt** and apply **Bold**, select the **two address lines**, change the font size to **16 pt**, click the **text box border**, then click the **Center button** 🗏 in the Paragraph group to center all the text

7. Click away from the text box, click the **Insert tab**, click **Text Box** in the Text group, click in a blank area of the slide below the address, type **2010 Meeting Times**, then format the text with **Bold** and **24 pt**

8. Add another text box near the bottom of the slide containing the text, **For more information, please call [Your Name] at (604) 555-1188**, then format the text with **14 pt**

Hint

You will align the boxes precisely when you complete the project in the next lesson.

9. Drag the three text boxes to the positions shown in Figure H-14, then save the presentation

FIGURE H-12: Rounded rectangle object sized and positioned

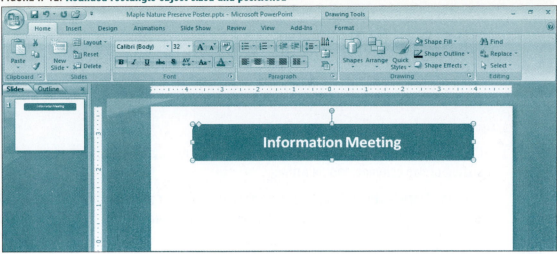

FIGURE H-13: Address text

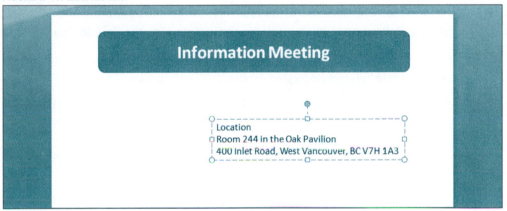

FIGURE H-14: Completed text objects

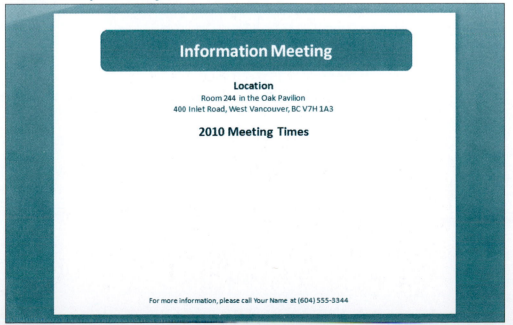

PowerPoint

Activity:

Create a Table

The poster includes a table that lists the meeting times for the months of May, June, and July. You need to create and then modify the table.

Steps:

1. Click the **Insert tab**, click the **Table button** in the Tables group, then drag to create a table consisting of two columns and four rows

2. Click the **More button** ⊽ in the Table Styles group, select the **Light Style 2 – Accent 3** table style (in the green column), then click the **Banded Columns check box** in the Table Style Options group to select it

3. Move the pointer over the top border to show the ⬚, then drag to position the table as shown in Figure H-15

4. Click in the first cell, then type the text for the table as shown in Figure H-16

5. Select the top row, click the **Home tab**, click the **Center button** ▤ in the Paragraph group, select the three cells containing dates in column 1, then click the **Bold button** **B** in the Font group

6. Move the pointer over the **column divider** between columns 1 and 2 to show the ↔, then double-click to autofit the text in column 1

7. Move the pointer over the right border of column 2 to show ↔, then double-click to autofit the text in column 2

8. Click the table border, click the **Table Tools Layout tab**, click the **Center Vertically button** ▤ in the Alignment group, then as shown in Figure H-17, drag the bottom border down slightly to increase the height of the table, and then position the table below 2010 Meeting Times

9. Click the **rounded rectangle**, click the **Drawing Tools Format tab**, click the **More button** ⊽ in the Shape Styles group, select **Intense Effect – Accent 3** (the center style in the bottom row), click away from the shape to deselect it, then save the presentation

FIGURE H-15: **Table positioned**

FIGURE H-16: **Table text**

FIGURE H-17: **Table sized and positioned**

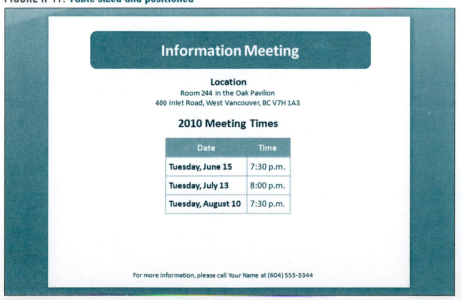

Activity:

Add Graphics

You need to insert two photographs and create a WordArt object using the text "Maple Nature Preserve" so the completed poster appears as shown in Figure H-20.

Steps:

1. Click the **Insert tab**, click the **WordArt button** in the Text group, click **Fill – Accent 3, Powder Bevel** (fifth row, green selection), type **Maple Nature Preserve**, then drag the WordArt object below the table (don't worry about precise positioning at this point)

2. Select the text, click the **Text Effects button** Ⓐ˅ in the WordArt Styles group, point to **Bevel**, click **3-D Options**, then modify settings in the 3-D Format dialog box as shown in Figure H-18

3. Click **Close**, click the **Home tab**, reduce the font size to **44 pt**, then position the WordArt object just above the information line

4. Click the **Select button** in the Editing group, click **Select All**, click the **Drawing Tools Format tab**, click the **Align button** in the Arrange group, click **Align Center**, then if necessary, use the right or left arrow keys to nudge the selected objects right or left so that they appear centered between the left and right edges of the slide

   You use the Align function to precisely align objects with relation to each other.

5. Click a blank area of the slide to deselect the objects, click the **Insert tab**, click the **Picture button** in the Illustrations group, navigate to the location where you store your Data Files, then double-click **Holly.jpg**

6. Click the **Crop button** in the Size group, then drag the middle right crop mark to the left to crop the picture as shown in Figure H-19

7. Click away from the picture, click the picture again, then size and position the picture so that it appears as shown in the completed poster in Figure H-20

8. Click the **Insert tab**, click the **Picture button** in the Illustrations group, navigate to the location where you store your Data Files, then double-click **Swan.jpg**

9. Move the swan to the upper-right corner of the slide so that it overlaps the rounded rectangle, click the **Send to Back button** in the Arrange group, then crop and position the picture as shown in Figure H-20

10. Print a copy of the presentation, then save and close it

Additional Practice

For additional practice with the skills presented in this project, complete Independent Challenge 2.

FIGURE H-18: 3-D Format options

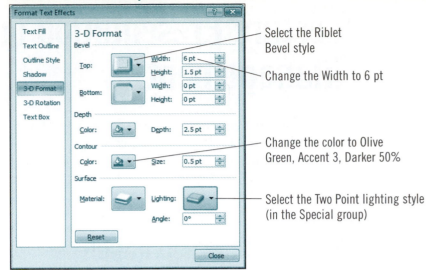

Select the Riblet Bevel style

Change the Width to 6 pt

Change the color to Olive Green, Accent 3, Darker 50%

Select the Two Point lighting style (in the Special group)

FIGURE H-19: Holly picture cropped

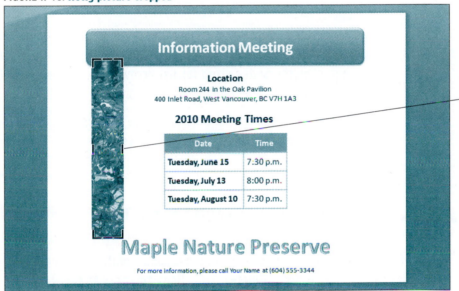

Drag the right middle crop handle to crop the picture

FIGURE H-20: Completed poster

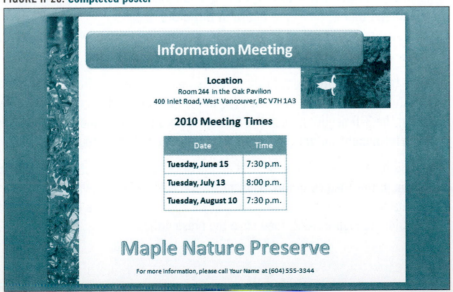

Lecture Presentation on Project Management

You need to give a presentation to your classmates on the basic concepts of project management. You decide to use PowerPoint to create overhead transparencies. You need to **Set Up the Presentation** and **Modify Graphics**. The completed presentation is shown in Slide Sorter view in Figure H-25 on page 191.

Activity:

Set Up the Presentation

You need to enter and then edit text for the presentation in Outline view. Then you need to insert an organizational chart on Slide 6.

Steps:

1. Create a new presentation in PowerPoint, click the **Design tab**, click the **Page Setup button** in the Page Setup group, click the **Slides sized for list arrow**, click **Letter Paper (8.5×11 in)**, click the **Portrait option button** in the Orientation Slides section, then click **OK**

2. Click the **Outline tab**, enter the text for the seven slides shown in Figure H-21, check the spelling, then save the presentation as **Project Management Lecture** in the location where you store your Data Files

3. Click the **Design tab**, then select the **Origin** theme

4. Move to **Slide 5**, click the **Insert SmartArt graphic button** in the object placeholder, click **Hierarchy**, select **Organization Chart** (far-left selection in the top row), then click **OK**

5. Type **Project Manager**, click the edge of the box immediately below and slightly left of the top box (the assistant box), press **[Delete]**, type **Department Managers**, click the **middle box**, type **Vendors**, click the **right box**, then type **Customers**

6. Click the **Project Manager box**, click the **Add Shape list arrow** in the Create Graphic group, click **Add Shape Below**, then type **Board of Directors**

   The organization chart now contains a total of five boxes—one for the Project Manager and one each for the four stakeholders.

7. Click the **More button** in the Layouts group, select the **Horizontal Hierarchy layout** (middle selection in the middle row), click in the SmartArt Styles group, select **Cartoon** (third from the left in the 3-D section), click the **Change Colors button** in the SmartArt Styles group, then select **Colorful-Accent Colors** (the far-left option in the Colorful group)

8. Click a blank area of the slide outside the SmartArt graphic, click the **Design tab**, click the **Colors button** in the Themes group, point to several color schemes, view how the organization chart colors change, depending on the color scheme applied, select the **Concourse color scheme**, compare your slide to Figure H-22, then save the presentation

FIGURE H-21: Outline for the Project Management lecture

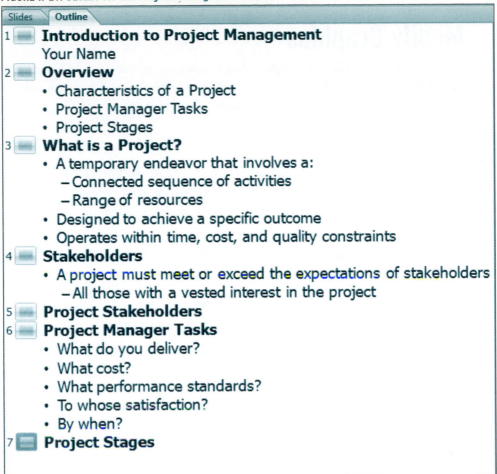

FIGURE H-22: Completed organization chart

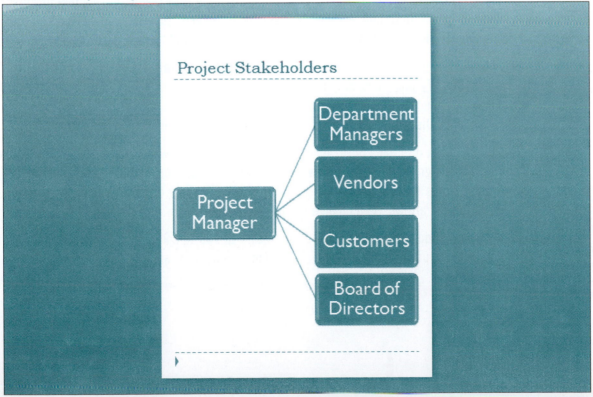

Activity:

Modify Graphics

You need to insert a clip-art picture and then modify it by removing an object in the picture that you do not want. You then need to create five aligned text boxes and draw arrows to connect them. The completed presentation in Slide Sorter view is shown in Figure H-25.

Steps:

Trouble

You need to be connected to the Internet to find the clip art of the checkmark. Also verify that All Collections is selected in the Clip Art task pane.

Hint

Sometimes you need to ungroup a picture two or more times before you can select and delete specific objects.

1. Move to **Slide 4**, click the **Insert tab**, click the **Clip Art button**, type **project** in the Search for text box, find and insert the picture shown in Figure H-23, then close the Clip Art task pane
   The picture you insert will include a light yellow background, which you will remove in a later step.

2. Move the picture so it fills the lower-right area of the slide, click the **Group button** in the Arrange group, click **Ungroup**, click **Yes** to convert it to a drawing object, then increase the zoom to 100%

3. Click away from the picture, right-click the picture, point to **Group**, click **Ungroup**, click away from the selected objects, click the **yellow background,** then press **[Delete]**
   Most of the picture is deleted—which isn't quite what you had in mind.

4. Click the **Undo button** 🔄 on the Quick Access toolbar, right-click the **yellow background**, point to **Group**, click **Ungroup**, click away from the picture again, click just the **yellow background** again, then press **[Delete]**
   The yellow background object is removed from the picture.

5. Position the mouse pointer above and to the left of the clip-art picture, click and drag to select all the remaining objects that make up the picture, click the **Drawing Tools Format tab**, click **Group** in the Arrange group, then click **Group**
   The modified clip-art object appears as shown in Figure H-23.

6. Move to **Slide 7**, click the **View tab**, click the **Fit to Window button** in the Zoom group, click the **Home tab**, click **Layout** in the Slides group, click the **Title Only slide layout**, draw a **text box** just below the slide title, type **Initiating**, fill the text box with **Turquoise, Accent 1, Darker 25%**, select the text, change the font color to **white**, change the font size to **28 pt**, center the text, then apply **bold**

7. With the text box selected, click the **Drawing Tools Format tab**, set the width at **4"**, press **[Ctrl][C]**, press **[Ctrl][V]** four times, drag the currently selected text box to the bottom of the slide (just above the dotted line), use your mouse to select all five text boxes, click the **Align button** in the Arrange group, click **Distribute Vertically**, click the **Align button** again, then click **Align Center**

8. Change the text in each of the four copied text boxes as shown in Figure H-24, click **Shapes** in the Illustrations group, click the **Arrow shape** in the Lines section, draw a **vertical arrow** between the top two boxes (see Figure H-25), copy it and paste it three times, position the arrows as shown, select all the arrows, then change the Weight to **6 pt**

Additional Practice

For additional practice with the skills presented in this project, complete Independent Challenge 3.

9. Switch to **Slide Sorter** view, change the Zoom to 100%, compare the completed presentation to Figure H-25, print a copy of the presentation as handouts, six to a page, then save and close the presentation

FIGURE H-23: Modified clip-art object

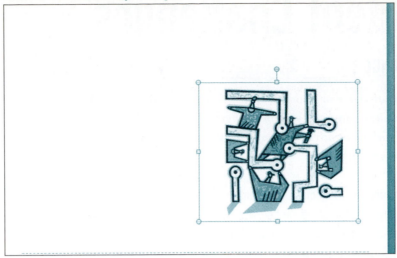

FIGURE H-24: Text boxes and arrows on Slide 8

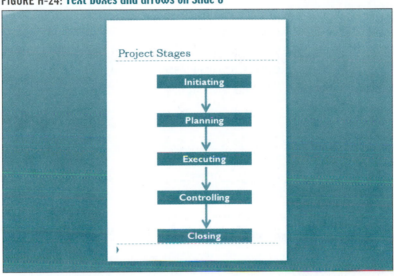

FIGURE H-25: Completed presentation in Slide Sorter view

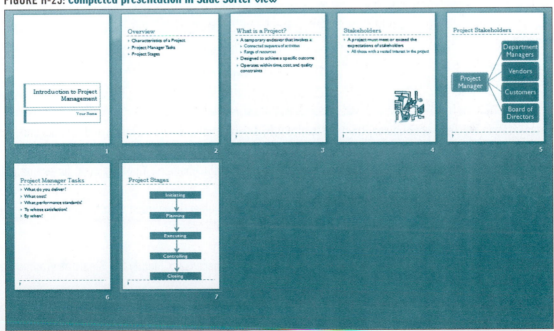

Independent Challenges

INDEPENDENT CHALLENGE 1

Create a six-slide presentation that you could use to help teach a specific concept or task. For example, your presentation could offer guidelines for purchasing a computer system or buying a used car, tips for taking effective vacation photographs or planning an event such as a wedding, or advice for enjoying the major sites in your hometown. Follow the steps provided to create the presentation in PowerPoint.

1. Your first task is to determine the topic of your presentation. Think about an activity or task that you know well and that you can present in short, easy-to-understand steps. To help get started, write the words "How to", followed by a verb and then the activity. For example, your presentation topic could be "How to Create a Balcony Garden" or "How to Plan a Backpacking Trip." In the box below, write the topic of your presentation:

> **Presentation Topic:** _____

2. You need to determine three main sections for your presentation. Each of these sections should cover a specific activity related to your topic. For example, the three sections for a presentation titled "How to Find a Job" could be: 1. Personal Profile, 2. Employment Sources, and 3. Interview Techniques. You should present each of these sections on separate slides along with three or four bulleted points that describe it. Write the sections of your presentation in the box below:

> **Section 1:** _____
>
> **Section 2:** _____
>
> **Section 3:** _____

3. Start PowerPoint and create an outline of your presentation. Save the presentation as **My Training Presentation** in the location where you store your Data Files. Here's a suggested format:

Slide #	Slide Title	Text
1	Presentation Topic	Your Name
2	Overview	List the three sections in your presentation
3	Section 1 Title	List three or four bulleted points related to Section 1
4	Section 2 Title	List three or four bulleted points related to Section 2
5	Section 3 Title	List three or four bulleted points related to Section 3
6	Conclusion	Create a "motivational" slide to summarize your presentation

4. Apply the presentation theme of your choice, then customize it by selecting a new color scheme and font scheme.
5. Change the background style. For example, you could apply a texture fill or a gradient fill.
6. Switch to Slide Master view and modify the appearance of the text in the placeholders. You may wish, for example, to change the font size and style of the text in the Master Title Style placeholder.
7. In Slide Master view, modify the appearance of one or more of the graphic objects included with the design. For example, you can fill an object with a different color.
8. Exit the slide master, then add clip-art pictures to selected slides.
9. Insert an appropriate SmartArt graphic on one slide. Insert a new slide if necessary. Modify the SmartArt graphic attractively by applying a new style and color scheme.

10. When you are satisfied with the appearance of your slides, switch to Slide Sorter view, add an animation scheme, add a custom animation effect to the SmartArt graphic, and then switch to Slide Show view and run the presentation.

11. Save the presentation, print a copy of it as handouts with four to a page, and then close the presentation.

INDEPENDENT CHALLENGE 2

Create a poster that announces some kind of event, such as a concert series, sports tournament, or club meeting.

1. Determine the type of event you will announce. Think of your own interests. In what type of event are you most likely to participate? If you are involved in sports, you could create a poster to advertise an upcoming game or tournament. If you belong to a club, you could create a poster and Web page to advertise a special event such as a fund-raising bake sale or craft fair.

2. Think of an interesting title for your event. For example, a poster that announces a celebrity golf tournament could be called "Stars on Par," or a Web page that advertises running events for cash prizes could be called "Dash for Cash."

3. Determine the details that readers of your poster will need to know in order to participate in the event that you plan to advertise. You need to specify where the event will be held, when it will be held (date and time), what activities will occur at the event, and your name as the person readers should contact for more information.

4. On a blank piece of paper, create a rough draft of your poster. Determine where you will place the various blocks of text and one or two photographs or clip-art images.

5. Create the poster on a blank PowerPoint slide. Add at least one clip-art image or photograph and a WordArt object. Experiment with the many options available to customize the WordArt object.

6. Include a table on your poster. Format the table attractively with one of the table styles.

7. Save the presentation as **My Poster** in the location where you store your Data Files, then print a copy.

INDEPENDENT CHALLENGE 3

1. Create a short presentation that presents information about an academic topic of your choice. Then format and print the presentation in portrait orientation, which is appropriate for delivery on an overhead projector. Think of courses you are currently taking or have taken in the past, and then prepare slides that could accompany a short lecture on one of the class topics that interests you. For example, you could create a presentation that outlines the three principal causes of the First World War, or presents major issues in Shakespeare's *Macbeth*, or provides an overview of photosynthesis. In the box below, write the topic of your presentation:

Presentation Topic: _____

2. Determine the three subtopics you will discuss in your presentation. List these subtopics on the second slide of the presentation, and title that slide "Overview." For example, three topics for a presentation on major issues in Shakespeare's *Macbeth* could be "The Tragic Hero," "Dramatic Irony," and "Imagery." Write the three topics of your presentation in the box below:

Topic 1: _____

Topic 2: _____

Topic 3: _____

3. Start PowerPoint and create an outline of your presentation. Save the presentation as **My Lecture** to the location where you store your Data Files. Use the same format suggested for Independent Challenge 1 to organize your topics and subtopics.

4. Change the page orientation for the presentation to portrait, and then apply the presentation theme and color scheme of your choice.

5. Switch to Slide Master view and modify the appearance of the text in the placeholders and of the various elements that make up the slide design. For example, you can choose to delete some objects, change the fill colors of other objects, or add a new clip-art picture.

6. Add a clip-art picture to the presentation, then modify the clip-art image by removing selected objects or filling other objects with different colors.

7. On one slide, draw text boxes and shapes to show a process. For ideas, refer to the Lecture Presentation for Project Management you completed in this unit.

8. Save the presentation, print a copy of the presentation, and then close the presentation.

INDEPENDENT CHALLENGE 4

You have helped to organize a three-day convention for home-based entrepreneurs in your state or province. This convention will include seminars, booths for the entrepreneurs to promote their products or services, a keynote speech by your state governor or provincial premier, and plenty of opportunities for entrepreneurs to network. A few months prior to the convention, you will hold a meeting for local entrepreneurs to inform them about the conference and encourage them to participate. Follow the instructions provided to create and then modify the presentation that you plan to give at this meeting.

1. Create a new presentation in PowerPoint and then enter just the slide titles and text as shown in the completed presentation in Figure H-26.

2. Save the presentation as **Entrepreneurs Presentation** in the location where you store your Data Files.

3. Apply the Solstice theme, then apply the Blue tissue paper texture to the background.

4. In the slide master, remove the large white rectangle and the other small rectangle that appears after you have removed the large rectangle so the entire slide is filled with the texture.

5. Select the Apex color scheme.

6. Add clip-art pictures to some slides. Use the drawing tools to modify at least one of the clip-art images after you have ungrouped it. For example, the clip-art picture shown on Slide 4 in Figure H-26 was modified by removing a circle shape and then filling the flip chart shape. Use search keywords such as "seminar," "booth," "home," and "business" to find appropriate images. Note that the images you choose do not need to be the same as the images shown in Figure H-26.

7. Add the Pyramid List SmartArt graphic (in the List section) to slide 3, select the Inset SmartArt style, then select the color scheme of your choice.

8. On slide 8, insert a WordArt graphic using the style and settings of your choice.

9. When you are satisfied with the appearance of your slides, print them as handouts (six to a page).

10. Add an animation scheme to all slides and a custom animation scheme to the SmartArt graphic on Slide 3, then preview the presentation in Slide Show view.

11. Print, save, close the presentation, and then exit PowerPoint.

FIGURE H-26: Completed presentation in Slide Sorter view

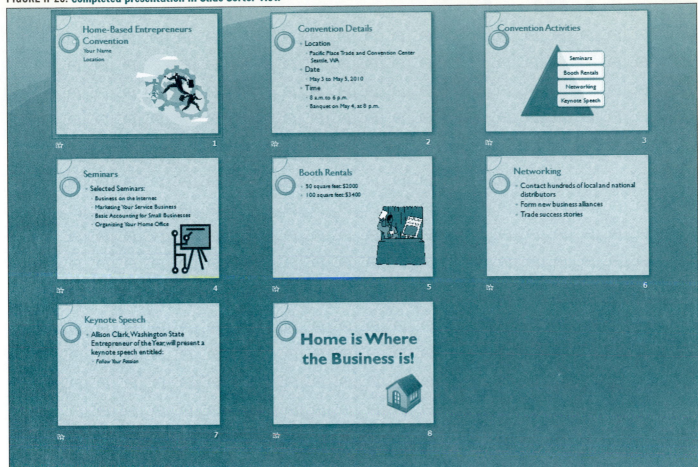

Visual Workshop

As part of a presentation on Saving the Wilderness that you are giving at a meeting of a local environmental group, you need to create the two slides shown in Figures H-27 and H-28. Enter the title and subtitle text on Slide 1, use the Concourse presentation theme and the Trek color scheme, select the Papyrus texture for the slide background, then work in slide master to increase the title text size to 54 pt on the title slide. For Slide 2, change the layout to Blank and the text color to Brown, then add text boxes and clip-art photos as shown in Figure H-28. Note that you need to search for "bear," "moose," and "bighorn sheep" to find the photos and then you need to crop and resize them as shown. Save the presentation as **Montana Wilderness** in the location where you store your Data Files for this book, print the two slides, and then close the presentation.

FIGURE H-27: Title slide

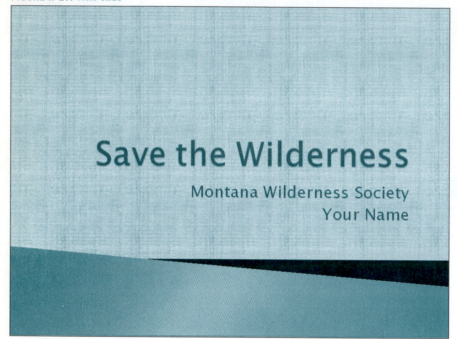

FIGURE H-28: Slide 2

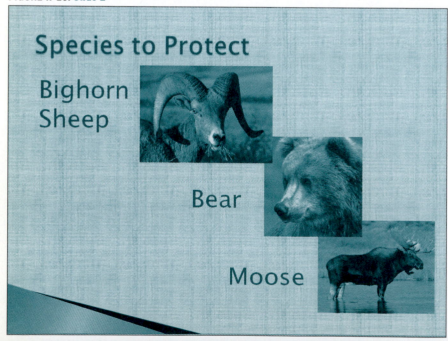

Microsoft
► # PowerPoint, Word, Excel, and Access
Projects

Unit I

Integration Projects III

In This Unit You Will Create the Following:

► ## Status Report

► ## Investor Orientation

► ## Class Party Presentation

You can integrate Office applications to present information in a variety of ways. For example, you can compile source materials in Access and Excel and then create a report in Word or a presentation in PowerPoint that includes objects from the source materials. You can also create an outline in Word and then send it to PowerPoint to create a presentation. Conversely, you can create a presentation in PowerPoint and send it to Word to create a report. You can also create links between objects from the various applications, and then you can update the links as new data becomes available. In this unit, you will integrate PowerPoint, Access, Excel, and Word to produce a report in Word and two presentations in PowerPoint.

Status Report for Total Health Clinic

You've been asked to present a status report on the programs run by the Total Health Clinic to the clinic's board of directors. To produce the report you need to **Format the Report in Word**, **Compile Source Materials**, **Add Excel and PowerPoint Objects**, and **Add a Report from Access**. The completed report is shown in Figure I-10 on page 205.

Activity:

Format the Report in Word

You need to open and format a document containing the text for the report and placeholders that indicate the location of objects you plan to import from Excel, Access, and PowerPoint in later lessons.

Steps:

1. Start Word, open the file **Status Report.docx** from the location where you store your Data Files, save the file as **Total Health Clinic June Report**, then scroll through the report to familiarize yourself with its contents and to view placeholders

2. Press **[Ctrl][Home]**, press **[Ctrl][Enter]** to insert a page break, press **[Ctrl][Home]** again, then press **[Enter]** once

3. Click the **Insert tab**, click the **Object button** in the Text group, scroll the list of object types, click **Microsoft Office PowerPoint Slide** as shown in Figure I-1, then click **OK**

4. Click the **title placeholder**, type **Total Health Clinic**, click the **subtitle placeholder**, type **June Status Report**, press **[Enter]**, then type your name

5. Click the **Design tab**, click the **More button** in the Themes group, select the **Metro theme**, click the **Background Styles button** in the Background group, select **Style 6** (second row, second column), click outside the slide, click the **Home tab**, click the **slide**, click the **Center button** in the Paragraph group, click the **Borders list arrow** in the Paragraph group, click **Outside Borders**, then click outside the slide

   A light gradient fill is applied, and the slide is centered and enclosed in a border as shown in Figure I-2.

6. Press **[Ctrl][G]**, type **3**, click **Go To**, click **Close**, click **Introduction**, click **Heading 1** in the Styles gallery, then apply the **Heading 1** style to the remaining document headings

7. Click the **Change Styles button** in the Styles group, point to **Colors**, then select **Metro**

8. Scroll up to page 2, click below **Table of Contents**, click the **References tab**, click the **Table of Contents button** in the Table of Contents group, then click **Insert Table of Contents**

9. Click the **Formats list arrow,** select **Formal** as shown in Figure I-3, click **OK**, then save the document

   All the headings formatted with the Heading 1 style appear. Once you have inserted objects from Access, Excel, and PowerPoint, you will update the table of contents to show the new page numbers.

Hint

The remaining document headings are Running Clinics, Lifestyle Seminars, Nutrition Workshops, and Summary.

FIGURE I-1: Selecting a PowerPoint Slide object

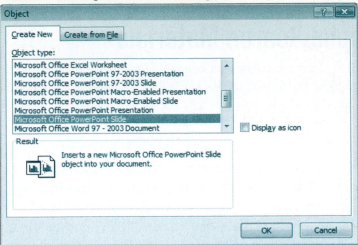

FIGURE I-2: Completed PowerPoint slide for the report title page

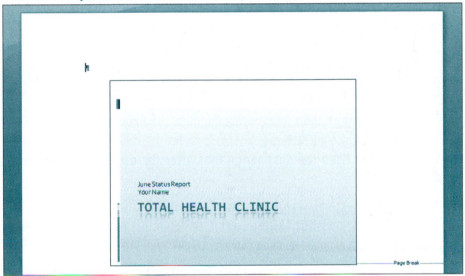

FIGURE I-3: Formal Table of Contents format selected

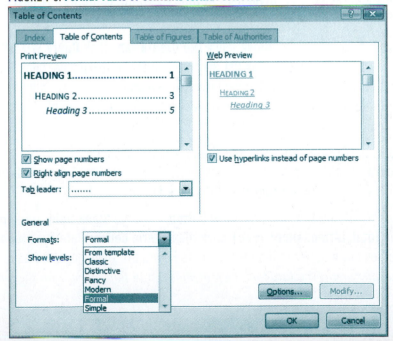

PROJECT 1

Activity:

Compile Source Materials

You need to open a database that contains some of the data required for the report, and then you need to modify the format of selected fields. You also need to publish an Access table in the Word report and create two queries.

Steps:

Trouble

To save a database with a new name, click the **Office button**, point to **Save As**, click **Access 2007 Database**, type the new filename, then click **Save**.

1. Start Access, open **Clinic.accdb** from the location where you store your Data Files, save the database as **Total Health Clinic.accdb**, double-click **June Running Clinic:Table**, click in the blank **Start Run Time cell** for Record 1, type **14.55**, then press **[Tab]**

   The number you entered is automatically rounded up to 15. You want to show decimals so you need to modify the format of the Number data type.

2. Click the **View button** in the Views group, click the **Number data type** next to Start Run Time, refer to the Field Properties area, click **Long Integer** next to Field Size, click the **list arrow**, click **Single**, click **Auto** next to Decimal Places, click the **list arrow**, click **2**, then repeat this procedure to change the format of the Number data type for the End Run Time field

3. Click the **View button**, click **Yes** to save the table, enter data for the Start Run Time and End Run Time fields and widen columns as shown in Figure I-4, then close and save the table

4. With June Running Clinic: Table selected, click the **External Data tab**, click the **Word button** in the Export group, click **Browse**, navigate to the location where you store your Data Files, click **Save,** click the **Open the destination files after the export operation is complete check box**, then click **OK**

   The table appears in a new Word document called June Running Clinic.rtf.

5. Select the table, press **[Ctrl][C]** to copy it, switch to the report in Word, select the placeholder text **[Running Times]** on page 3, then press **[Ctrl][V]** to paste

6. Select the pasted table, click the **Table Tools Design tab**, click the **More button** ▼ in the Table Styles group, select **Light Grid - Accent 6** (third row), press **[Ctrl][E]** to center the table, double-click any column divider to autofit the table contents, deselect the table, compare it to Figure I-5, then save the document

Hint

To save time, you enter only the beginning of the criteria followed by the wildcard character to tell Access to list all records in the Program Area field that contain "Life" as the first four letters.

7. Switch to Access, click **Close**, click the **Create tab**, click **Query Wizard** in the Other group, click **OK**, click the **Tables/Queries list arrow**, click **Table: Programs**, click the **Select All Fields button** >> , click **Next**, click **Next**, enter **Lifestyle Seminars** as the title, click the **Modify the query design option button**, click **Finish**, click the **Program Area Criteria cell**, type **Life***, click the **Run button** in the Results group, verify that three Lifestyle seminars are listed, then close and save the query

8. Click the **Create tab**, click the **Query Wizard button** in the Other group, click **OK**, select the **Programs table**, select all the fields in the table *except* the Program ID field, click **Next**, click **Next**, name the query **June Programs**, then click **Finish**

9. Click the **Home tab,** click the **View button**, click the **blank field** to the right of the Fee field, then type **Total: [Attendance]*[Fee]**, click the **Criteria cell** for Date, type **June***, click the **Run button** in the Results group, compare the query to Figure I-6, then close and save the query

   The query returns a list of all the programs run in June, along with the total revenue generated from each program.

FIGURE I-4: Data for the Start Run Time and End Run Time Fields

June Running Clinic

ID	Last Name	First Name	Start Run Time	End Run Time	Add New Field
1	Wilson	Melody	14.55	11.55	
2	Knutson	Olga	15.35	12.35	
3	Kirkpatrick	Wendy	15.45	11.45	
4	Svensen	Lars	14.25	12.35	
5	Ralston	Patty	16.35	14.35	
6	Mason	Brenda	16.55	12.45	
7	O'Brien	Sean	17.45	15.25	
8	Evans	Adele	12.55	12.25	
9	Markoff	Catherine	15.35	12.45	
10	Mason	Donna	14.35	11.25	
*	(New)				

FIGURE I-5: Formatted table in Word

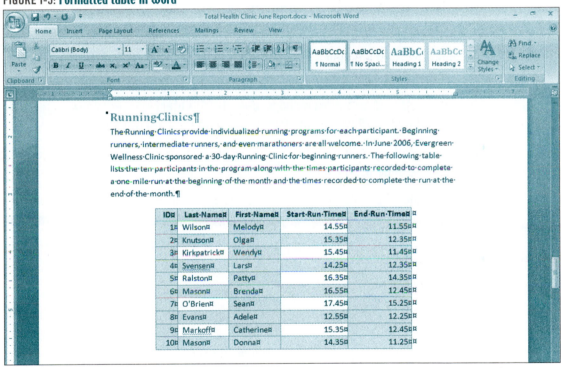

FIGURE I-6: June Programs query

June Programs

Date	Program Area	Attendance	Fee	Total
June 1	Running Clinic	12	$45.00	$540.00
June 4	Lifestyle Seminar	20	$75.00	$1,500.00
June 10	Running Clinic	25	$45.00	$1,125.00
June 20	Nutrition Workshop	40	$50.00	$2,000.00
June 25	Nutrition Workshop	38	$50.00	$1,900.00
*		0	$0.00	

Activity:

Add Excel and PowerPoint Objects

You need to analyze the Lifestyle Seminars query in Excel, calculate totals, and then copy selected cells to the [Attendance Figures] placeholder in the Word report. You then need to copy two PowerPoint slides from an existing presentation to the [PowerPoint Slides] placeholder in the Word report.

Steps:

1. Click **Lifestyle Seminars**, click the **External Data tab**, click the **Excel button** in the Export group, click **Browse**, navigate to the location where you store your Data Files, click **Save,** click the **Export data with formatting and layout check box**, click **OK**, click **Close**, then start Excel and open **Lifestyle Seminars.xlsx**

2. Click cell **F1**, type **Totals**, press **[Enter]**, type **=D2*E2** in cell F2, press **[Enter]**, copy the formula through cell **F4**, then click the **Accounting Number Format button** $ in the Number group

3. Select cells **B1:F4**, press **[Ctrl][C]**, switch to the report in Word, select the placeholder text **[Attendance Figures]**, then press **[Ctrl][V]**

4. Select the table, double-click any **column divider** to autofit the text, click the **Table Tools Design tab**, apply the **Light Shading – Accent 6** table style (top row), press **[Ctrl][E]**, click below the table, then compare it to Figure I-7

5. Click to the left of **Nutrition Workshops**, press **[Ctrl][Enter]** to insert a new page break, then delete the placeholder text **[PowerPoint Slides]**, but leave the paragraph mark

6. Start PowerPoint, open **Nutrition Workshops.pptx** from the location where you store your Data Files, then click the **Slide Sorter button** on the status bar to switch to Slide Sorter view

7. Verify that the title slide is selected, press **[Ctrl][C]**, switch to the Word report, press **[Ctrl][V]**, switch to PowerPoint, click **slide 3**, press **[Ctrl][C]**, switch to the Word report, then press **[Ctrl][V]**

8. Click and then right-click the **slide** you just inserted, click **Format Object**, click the **Size tab**, set the Width at **2.8"**, click the **Colors and Lines tab**, click the **Fill Color list arrow**, click the **Black box, Text 1**, then click **OK**

9. Repeat Step 8 to set the width of the first slide at 2.8" and add a border line, then deselect the slide

   The two slides appear side by side as shown in Figure I-8.

FIGURE I-7: Excel data copied to Word

Lifestyle Seminars¶

Joanne Moore presented four lifestyle seminars in May and June 2006. Each seminar provided advice to help participants initiate and maintain healthy eating and exercise patterns. Shown below are the attendance figures at the May and June lifestyle seminars.¶

Date¤	Program Area¤	Attendance¤	Fee¤	Totals¤	¤
May 1¤	Lifestyle Seminar¤	45¤	$75.00¤	$3,375.00¤	¤
May 15¤	Lifestyle Seminar¤	15¤	$75.00¤	$1,125.00¤	¤
June 4¤	Lifestyle Seminar¤	20¤	$75.00¤	$1,500.00¤	¤

Nutrition Workshops¶

Philip Warren facilitated two workshops on good nutrition to health practitioners in the Seattle area. Shown below are two slides from the presentation that Philip delivered at the workshop.¶

FIGURE I-8: Completed PowerPoint slides in Word

Nutrition Workshops¶

Philip Warren facilitated two workshops on good nutrition to health practitioners in the Seattle area. Shown below are two slides from the presentation that Philip delivered at the workshop.¶

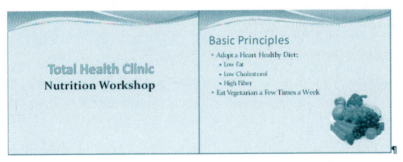

Summary¶

The Evergreen Wellness Clinic continues to provide valuable health and lifestyle services to a diverse group of clients in the Seattle area. The data shown below summarizes attendance figures for the month of June 2006.¶

¶

Activity:

Add a Report from Access

You need to create a report from the June Programs query, publish the report in Word, and format it attractively. Finally, you need to update the table of contents in Word and print a copy of the report.

Steps:

1. Switch to Access, click **June Programs**, click the **Create tab**, click the **Report button** in the Reports group, click the **AutoFormat** button in the AutoFormat group, select the **Metro** style, then adjust the columns so the report appears as shown in Figure I-9

2. Right-click **7065** at the bottom of the Total column, click **Properties**, click the **Format tab** if necessary, click the **blank cell** next to Format, click the **list arrow**, click **Currency**, close the Property Sheet, then close and save the report as **June Programs**

3. With the June Programs report selected, click the **External Data tab**, click the **Word button** in the Export group, click the **Open the destination file after the export operation is complete check box**, then click **OK**

    When the report is published in Word, all the formatting applied to the report in Access is removed. You can convert the data into a table so that you can quickly apply formatting.

4. Delete all of the first line (contains the date in very light print), scroll to the bottom of the document, delete the **last line** of text (contains the page number), press **[Ctrl][A]**, click the **Insert tab**, click the **Table button** in the Tables group, click **Convert Text to Table**, then click **OK** to accept the number of columns entered (6)

    By default, Word enters a number of columns equal to the maximum number of tab characters in any one line of text. The first column in the table is blank.

5. Click to deselect the table, move the pointer over the top of column 1 to show **⬇**, click once to select all of column 1, press **[Ctrl][X]**, select **$7065.00** at the bottom of the new column 1, press **[Ctrl][X]**, click in the blank cell below $1,900.00, then press **[Ctrl][V]**

6. Select the table, press **[Ctrl][C]**, switch to the report in Word, select the text **[Summary Report]** at the end of the report, then paste the table

7. Select the table, click the **Table Tools Design tab**, select the **Medium Grid 3 – Accent 4** table style in the Turquoise column, double-click any **column divider** to autofit the contents, then center the table

8. Scroll up to the table of contents, right-click the **table of contents**, click **Update Field**, click the **Update entire table option button**, then click **OK**

Additional Practice

For additional practice with the skills presented in this project, complete Independent Challenge 1.

9. Click the **Office button** 🔘, point to **Print**, click **Print Preview**, click the **Zoom button** in the Zoom group, click the **Many pages icon**, select **2 x 2 Pages**, click **OK**, compare the four pages of the report to Figure I-10, click the **Close Print Preview button**, save the document, print a copy, close it, then close and save all other files and programs

FIGURE I-9: Column sizes adjusted

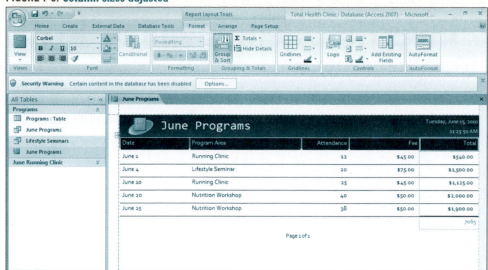

FIGURE I-10: Completed report in Print Preview

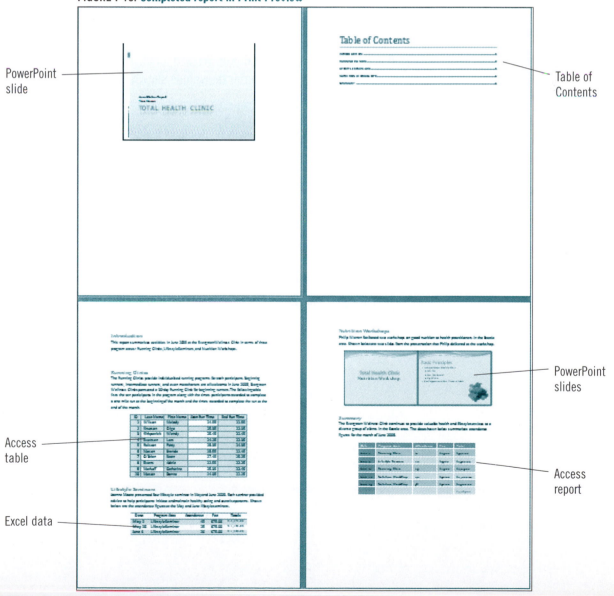

PowerPoint slide

Table of Contents

Access table

Excel data

PowerPoint slides

Access report

Investor Orientation for Orca Estates

You work for the Sales Manager of Orca Estates, a new resort development on the West Coast. You need to prepare a presentation to welcome investors and provide them with important information about the resort. For this project, you need to **Create a Database**, **Create a Chart**, **Create the Presentation**, and **Update the Presentation**. The completed presentation appears in Figure I-20 on page 213.

Activity:

Create a Database

You need to enter the data in an Access table and then copy the Access table to Excel and paste it as a link.

Steps:

1. Start Access, then create an Access database called **Orca Estates** and save it in the location where you store your Data Files

2. Switch to Design view, save the table as **Home Designs**, then enter the fields and data types shown in Figure I-11

3. Click the **Data Type list arrow** for Style, click **Lookup Wizard**, click the **I will type in the values that I want option button**, click **Next**, press **[Tab]**, enter the values shown in Figure I-12, then click **Finish**

4. Create a lookup field for Location containing the values **Cliffside**, **Forest**, and **Waterfront**

5. Enter the records for the table as shown in Figure I-13, close the table, click the **Create tab**, click the **Query Wizard button** in the Other group, click **OK**, add all the fields from the Home Designs table, name the query **Design Breakdown**, click the **Home tab**, then show the query in Design view

6. Sort the **Style** and **Cost** fields in **Ascending** order

7. Click the **Run button** in the Results group, close and save the query, then click the **Copy button** in the Clipboard group

8. Start Excel, click the **Paste list arrow** in the Clipboard group, then click **Paste Link**

9. Save the workbook as **Orca Estates Data** in the location where you store your Data Files

FIGURE I-11: Fields for the Home Designs table

Field Name	Data Type
Design ID	AutoNumber
Style	Text
Bedrooms	Number
Location	Text
Cost	Currency
Quantity	Number
Sales	Number

Home Designs

FIGURE I-12: Values for the lookup field

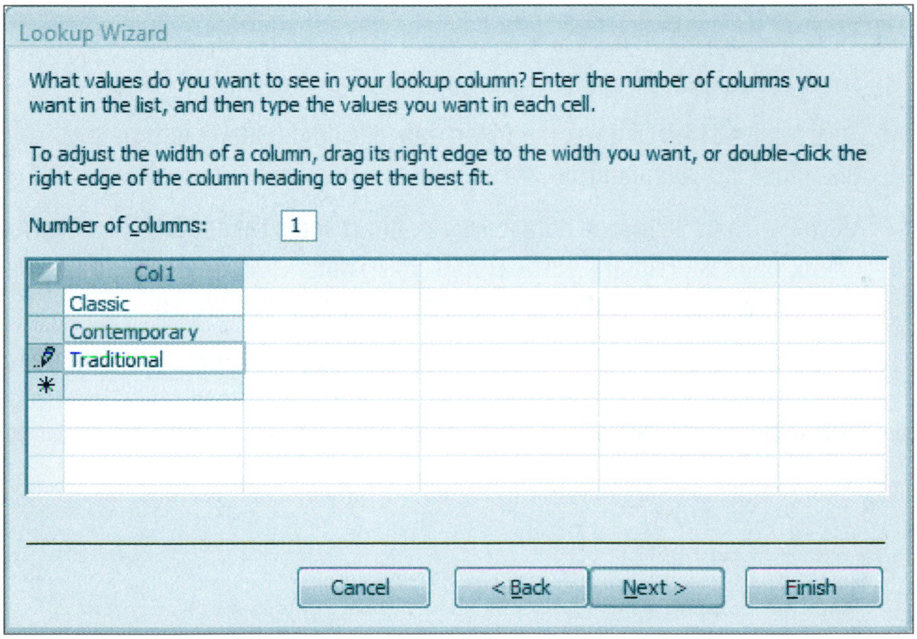

Lookup Wizard

What values do you want to see in your lookup column? Enter the number of columns you want in the list, and then type the values you want in each cell.

To adjust the width of a column, drag its right edge to the width you want, or double-click the right edge of the column heading to get the best fit.

Number of columns: 1

Col1
Classic
Contemporary
Traditional

Cancel   < Back   Next >   Finish

FIGURE I-13: Data for the Home Designs table

Home Designs

Design ID	Style	Bedrooms	Location	Cost	Quantity	Sales	Add New Field
1	Contemporary	3	Cliffside	$400,000.00	10	5	
2	Traditional	4	Waterfront	$600,000.00	6	3	
3	Traditional	4	Waterfront	$650,000.00	5	2	
4	Classic	2	Forest	$400,000.00	7	4	
5	Classic	4	Cliffside	$550,000.00	6	5	
6	Contemporary	5	Waterfront	$750,000.00	8	4	
7	Traditional	5	Waterfront	$780,000.00	8	4	
8	Contemporary	4	Forest	$550,000.00	5	3	
9	Contemporary	3	Cliffside	$600,000.00	7	4	
10	Traditional	5	Waterfront	$800,000.00	8	2	
(New)							

Activity:

Create a Chart

You need to create a column chart to display information about the resort development. In a later lesson you will copy the column chart and paste it as a link on a slide in the PowerPoint presentation.

Steps:

1. In Excel, click cell **H1**, type **Total Worth**, press **[Enter]**, type **=E2*F2**, press **[Enter]**, then copy the formula in cell **H2** through cell **H11**

2. Click cell **I1**, type **Total Sales**, press **[Enter]**, type **=E2*G2**, press **[Enter]**, then copy the formula in cell **I2** through cell **I11**

3. Click cell **F12**, click the **Sum button** Σ ▾ in the Editing group, press **[Ctrl][Enter]**, then copy the formula through cell **I12**

4. Format cells **E2:E11** and cells **H2:I12** with the Accounting Number Format style

5. Click cell **B14**, then enter the labels and calculations shown in Figure I-14

   When you copy data from an Access database and paste it as a link into an Excel workbook, you cannot use tools such as the Subtotals function to calculate totals.

6. Select cells **B14:D15**, click the **Insert tab**, click the **Column button** in the Charts group, then click the upper-left column style

7. Move the chart below the data, click the **Chart Tools Layout tab**, click the **Axes button** in the Axes group, point to **Primary Vertical Axis**, click **None**, click the **Legend button** in the Labels group, click **None**, click the **Data Labels button**, then click **Outside End**

8. Right-click one of the **data labels**, click **Format Data Labels**, click **Number**, click **Number** in the Category list, reduce the decimal places to **0**, click **Close**, click the **Home tab**, click the **Bold button** B in the Font group, then deselect the chart

9. Compare the completed chart to Figure I-15, then save the workbook

FIGURE I-14: Calculations of total worth

	A	B	C	D	E	F
1	Design ID	Style	Bedrooms	Location	Cost	Quantity
2	4	Classic	2	Forest	$400,000.00	7
3	5	Classic	4	Cliffside	$550,000.00	6
4	1	Contemporary	3	Cliffside	$400,000.00	10
5	8	Contemporary	4	Forest	$550,000.00	5
6	9	Contemporary	3	Cliffside	$600,000.00	7
7	6	Contemporary	5	Waterfront	$750,000.00	8
8	2	Traditional	4	Waterfront	$600,000.00	6
9	3	Traditional	4	Waterfront	$650,000.00	5
10	7	Traditional	5	Waterfront	$780,000.00	8
11	10	Traditional	5	Waterfront	$800,000.00	8
12						70
13						
14		Classic	Contemporary	Traditional		
15		$ 6,100,000.00	$ 16,950,000.00	$ 19,490,000.00		
16						
17						
18						
19						

Formula for B15:
=SUM(H2:H3)

Formula for C15:
=SUM(H4:H7)

Formula for D15:
=SUM(H8:H11)

FIGURE I-15: Completed column chart

	A	B	C	D	E	F
7	6	Contemporary	5	Waterfront	$750,000.00	8
8	2	Traditional	4	Waterfront	$600,000.00	6
9	3	Traditional	4	Waterfront	$650,000.00	5
10	7	Traditional	5	Waterfront	$780,000.00	8
11	10	Traditional	5	Waterfront	$800,000.00	8
12						70
13						
14		Classic	Contemporary	Traditional		
15		$ 6,100,000.00	$ 16,950,000.00	$ 19,490,000.00		

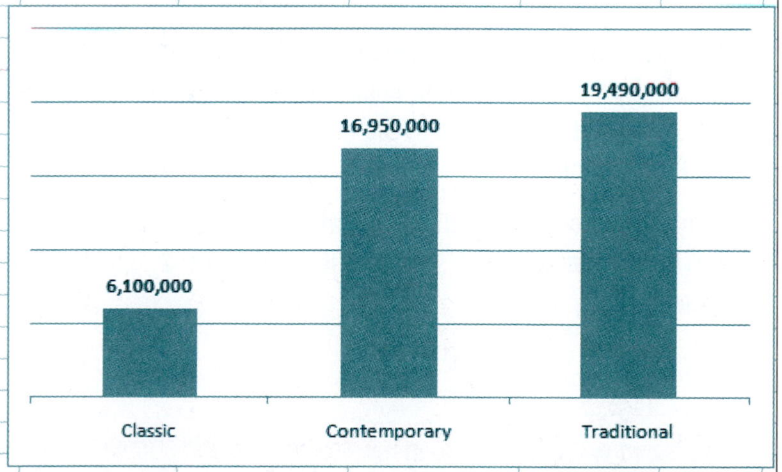

Activity:

Create the Presentation

The text for the PowerPoint presentation is already stored in a Word document. You need to import the Word text into a new presentation and then modify the presentation design so that a picture appears on every slide in the presentation except the title slide.

Steps:

1. Start PowerPoint, click the **New Slide list arrow** in the Slides group, click **Slides from Outline**, navigate to the location where you store your Data Files, select **Orca Estates.docx**, click **Insert**, then save the presentation as **Orca Estates Investor Orientation**

2. Click **Slide 1**, press **[Delete]**, click the **Layout button** in the Slides group, click **Title Slide**, click to the right of Investor Orientation on the slide, press **[Enter]**, then type your name

3. Click the **Design tab**, apply the **Paper** presentation theme, click the **Colors button** in the Themes group, click **Civic**, click the **Colors button**, click **Create New Theme Colors**, click the **Text/ Background – Dark 1 button** (the top selection), click **Green, Accent 5, Lighter 40%**, click **Save**, click the **Background Styles button** in the Background group, then click **Style 12**

4. Click the **View tab**, click the **Slide Master button** in the Presentation Views group, click the **slide next to 1** in the slide pane, click the **Insert tab**, click the **Picture button** in the Illustrations group, navigate to the location where you store your Data Files, then double-click **Arbutus.jpg**

5. Select the contents of the **Width text box** in the Size group, type **2.5**, press **[Enter]**, position the picture as shown in Figure I-16, click the **Slide Master tab**, then click the **Close Master View button** in the Close group

6. Move to Slide 4 in the presentation, switch to Excel, click the **column chart** if necessary to select it, press **[Ctrl][C]**, switch to PowerPoint, press **[Ctrl][V]**, then click anywhere on the slide to deselect the chart

   By default the chart is copied into PowerPoint as a link.

7. Click the **Design tab**, click the **Hide Background Graphics check box** in the Background group to select it, then size and position the chart on the slide as shown in Figure H-17

8. Make sure the chart is still selected, click the **Chart Tools Format tab**, click the **Text Fill list arrow** in the WordArt Styles group, click **Ice Blue, Text 2, Darker 90%**, click the **Home tab**, click the **Increase Font Size button** in the Font group A˚ until the font size is increased to **16 pt**, then click the **Bold button**

9. Right-click any column, click **Format Data Series**, click **Fill**, click the **Solid fill option button**, click the **Color button**, click **Dark Yellow, Accent 2, Lighter 40%**, click **Close**, then save the presentation

FIGURE I-16: Positioning the picture in the Slide Master

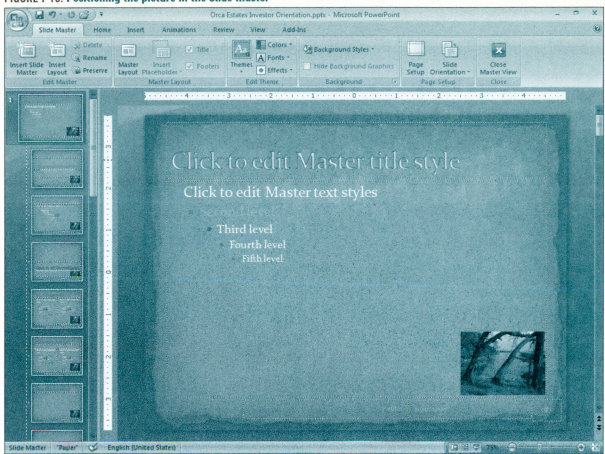

FIGURE I-17: Column chart sized and positioned

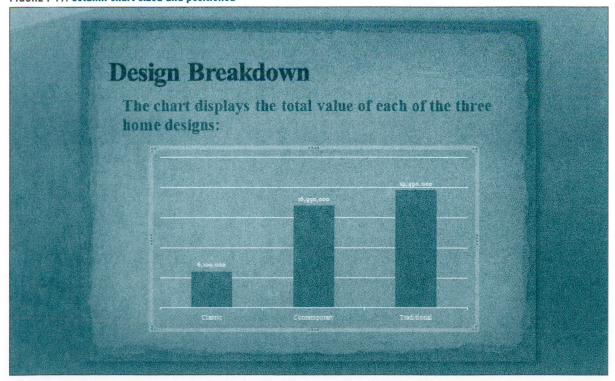

Activity:

Update the Presentation

You need to summarize data in the Excel worksheet, copy it, and paste it as a link on Slide 5. Then, you need to change data in the Access database and update the links in Excel and PowerPoint. Finally, you need to print a copy of the completed presentation.

Steps:

1. Switch to Excel, click cell **I14**, then enter and format the labels and formulas as shown in Figure I-18

   Make sure you enter formulas where indicated, not values, and that you enclose cells I14:J17 with border lines.

2. Select cells **I14:J17**, press **[Ctrl][C]**, switch to PowerPoint, go to **Slide 5**, click the **Paste list arrow** in the Clipboard group, click **Paste Special**, click the **Paste link option button**, then click **OK**

3. Apply the **Title Only slide layout**, then size and position the object as shown in Figure I-19

4. Verify that the Total Worth of all the homes in Orca Estates is **$42,540,000** and the total sales are **$21,220,000**

5. Show the **Home Designs table** in Access, increase the price of the homes in records **1** and **4** to **$700,000**, close the table, switch to Excel, then verify that the total in cells I12 and J17 is **$23,920,000**

   If the values do not update within a few minutes, click the Office button, point to Prepare, click Edit Links to Files, select the link, click Update Now, then click Close.

6. Switch to PowerPoint, then verify that the value for Total Sales has been updated to $23,920,000

7. Click the **Slide Sorter View button** on the status bar, click the **View tab**, click the **Fit to Window button** in the Zoom group, then compare the completed presentation to Figure I-20

8. Print a sheet of handouts (six slides to the page), then save and close all files and applications

Additional Practice

For additional practice with the skills presented in this project, complete Independent Challenge 2.

Clues to Use

Reestablishing Links

To reestablish links, you should start with the program that does not contain links and then open the remaining files in the order in which they are linked. For this presentation the order of files is Access, Excel, and PowerPoint.

FIGURE I-18: Total Quantity and Sales values

H	I	J	K
$ 3,600,000.00	$ 1,800,000.00		
$ 3,250,000.00	$ 1,300,000.00		
$ 6,240,000.00	$ 3,120,000.00		
$ 6,400,000.00	$ 1,600,000.00		
$ 42,540,000.00	$ 21,220,000.00		
	Number of Homes	70	
	Total Worth	$ 42,540,000.00	
	Number of Sales	36	
	Total Sales	$ 21,220,000.00	

Enclose all cells with a border line

=F12
=H12
=G12
=I12

FIGURE I-19: Excel object sized and positioned

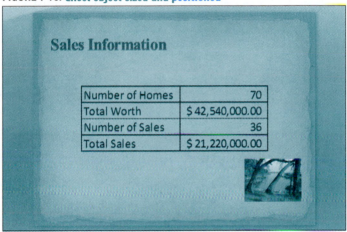

FIGURE I-20: Completed presentation in Slide Sorter view

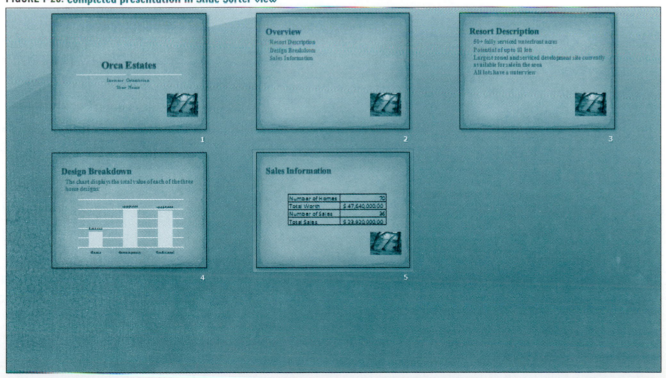

Class Party Presentation

You are organizing a class party to celebrate graduation from the business diploma program at Devan Community College outside Philadelphia. You need to create a presentation to inform class-mates about the party and a database to keep track of the students who plan to attend. For this pro-ject, you need to **Create a Form** and **Create the Presentation**. The completed presentation appears in Figure I-27 on page 217.

Activity:

Create a Form

You need to create a table in Access, and then create a form to enter information about students who plan to attend the party. The form includes the title slide from the presentation.

Steps:

1. Start Access, create an Access database called **Class Party** saved in the location where you store your Data Files, switch to Design view, save the table as **Attendees**, enter the fields and data types as shown in Figure I-21, then close and save the table

2. Click **Attendees: Table**, click the **Create tab**, click the **Form button** in the Forms group, apply the **Opulent** AutoFormat, then as shown in Figure I-22, reduce the widths of the text boxes

3. Start a new blank presentation in PowerPoint, type **Class Party** as the slide title, enter **Business Diploma Program, Devan Community College**, and your name on three separate lines in the Subtitle area, then save the presentation as **Class Party Presentation** in the location where you store your Data Files

4. Click a new blank presentation in the **Insert tab**, click the **Picture button** in the Illustrations group, navigate to the location where you store your Data Files, then double-click **Traces.jpg**

5. Click the picture, click the **Picture Tools Format tab**, click the **Recolor button** in the Adjust group, click the **Washout option** in the Color Modes section, right-click the **picture**, click **Save as Picture**, navigate to the location where you store your Data Files, type **Traces_Class Party** as the filename, then click **Save**

6. Delete the picture, click the **Design tab**, click the **Background Styles button** in the Background group, click **Format Background**, click the **Picture or texture fill option button**, click **File**, navi-gate to the location where you store your Data Files, click **Traces_Class Party.jpg**, click **Insert**, click **Apply to All**, then click **Close**

7. Switch to Slide Sorter view, press **[Ctrl][C]**, switch to Access, click the **View list arrow** in the Views group, click **Design View**, click the blank area to the right of the text boxes, then press **[Ctrl][V]**

8. Right-click the **picture**, click **Properties**, verify that the **Format tab** is selected on the Property Sheet, click the **list arrow** to the right of Clip next to Size Mode, click **Stretch**, close the Property Sheet, move and resize the picture as shown in Figure I-23, click the **Form Design Tools Arrange tab**, click the **Tab Order button** in the Control Layout group, click **Auto Order**, click **OK**, then close and save the form with the name **Attendees**

9. Double-click **Attendees** to open the form in Form view, use the form to enter data for the five attendees listed in Figure I-24, then close the form

FIGURE I-21: Fields for the Attendees table

Field Name	Data Type
ID	AutoNumber
First Name	Text
Last Name	Text
Contact Date	Date/Time
Attending	Yes/No
Contribution	Text

FIGURE I-22: Resizing form components

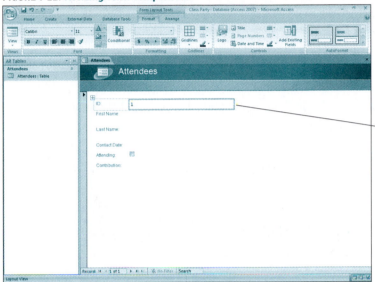

Drag the right border of the orange box to the left to reduce the width of all the text boxes

FIGURE I-23: Completed form in Design view

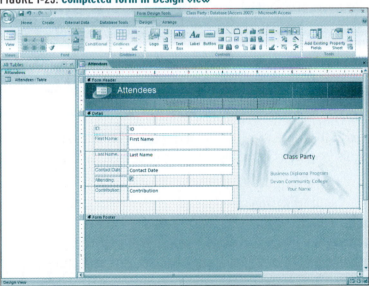

FIGURE I-24: List of attendees

ID	First Name	Last Name	Contact Date	Attending	Contribution	Add New Field
1	Mary	Jones	3/10/2010	☑	Appetizers	
2	Darren	Price	3/12/2010	☑	Chips and salsa	
3	Donald	Marches	3/15/2010	☐		
4	Polly	Quarles	3/14/2010	☑	Fruit Plate	
5	Karen	Watson	3/12/2010	☑	Vegetable platter	
*	(New)			☐		

CLASS PARTY PRESENTATION

Activity:

Create the Presentation

You need to complete the presentation, enter some of the data in Excel and Word, then copy the data to the presentation.

Hint

Be sure to add the blank slide 5 as shown in Figure I-25. with the skills presented in this project, complete Independent Challenge 3.

Steps:

1. Switch to PowerPoint, click the **Normal button** on the status bar, click the **Outline tab**, click after your name in the Outline tab, press **[Enter]**, press **[Shift][Tab]** to start a new slide, then enter the outline as shown in Figure I-25

2. Start Excel, save the workbook as **Class Party** in the location where you store your Data Files, then enter and format the data shown in Figure I-26 in cells **A1** through **B5**

   This data will be used in a chart that you create in PowerPoint.

3. Switch to PowerPoint, go to **Slide 4**, apply the **Title Only** slide layout, click the **Insert tab**, click the **Chart button** in the Illustrations group, click **Pie**, then click **OK**

   The PowerPoint and Excel windows appear side by side, a sample chart appears on the slide, and sample data appears in an Excel workbook. You want to replace the sample data with the data from the Class Party workbook.

4. Click cell **A1** in the Excel worksheet, click the **Class Party.xlsx button** on the taskbar, select cells **A1:B5**, press **[Ctrl][C]**, return to the Chart worksheet, click cell **A1**, press **[Ctrl][V]**, then close the worksheet

   The chart is updated with the data you copied from the Class Party workbook.

5. Return to PowerPoint, click the **pie chart**, click the **Chart Tools Design tab**, click the **More button** in the Chart Styles group, select **Style 26**, click the **Chart Tools Layout tab**, click the **Legend button** in the Labels group, click **Show Legend at Bottom**, click the **Data Labels button**, then click **Outside End**

6. Start Word, type **Date:**, press **[Tab]**, type **June 5**, press **[Enter]**, type **Time:**, press **[Tab]**, type **7 p.m. to ??**, press **[Enter]**, type **Place:**, press **[Tab]**, type **Meadowview Terraces**, then save the document as **Class Party** in the location where you store your Data Files

7. Press **[Ctrl][A]** to select all the text, press **[Ctrl][C]**, switch to PowerPoint, view **Slide 3: Party Details**, apply the **Title Only** slide layout, click below the title, press **[Ctrl][V]**, click the border of the copied object, then increase the font size to **40 pt**

8. Click the **Drawing Tools Format tab**, click the **More button** in the Shape Styles group, select **Subtle Effect – Accent 5**, click the **Shape Fill list arrow**, point to **Gradient**, select the **From Corner** gradient style (second row, last column), click the **Design tab**, click the **Theme Colors button** in the Themes group, click **Opulent**, size and position the object attractively on the slide as shown in the completed presentation in Figure I-27, then save the presentation

9. Go to Slide 5, apply the **Blank slide layout**, then add a WordArt object and a clip-art image similar to Figure I-27 (search for "balloons" in the Clip Art task pane)

10. View the presentation in Slide Sorter view, switch to 100% view, compare the completed presentation to Figure I-27, print the presentation as handouts six to a page, then save and close all files and applications

Additional Practice

For additional practice with the skills presented in this project, complete Independent Challenge 3.

FIGURE I-25: **Outline for the Class Party Presentation**

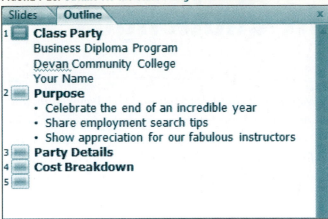

FIGURE I-26: **Data for Party Costs entered in Excel**

	A	B	C
1	Item	Cost	
2	Dinner Service	$ 2,300.00	
3	Decorations	$ 450.00	
4	Entertainment	$ 600.00	
5	Gifts	$ 800.00	
6			
7			
8			

FIGURE I-27: **Completed presentation in the Slide Sorter view**

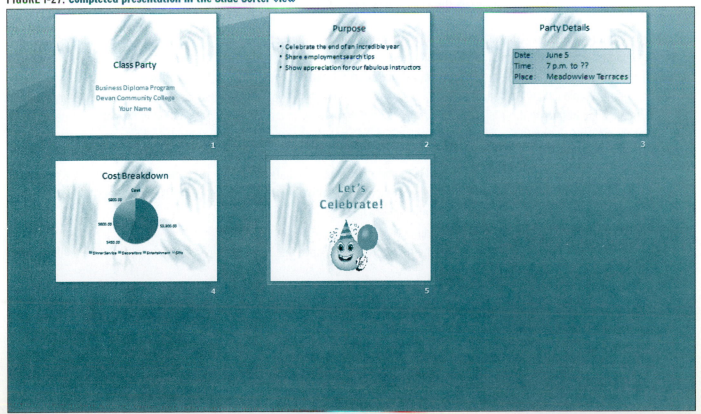

Independent Challenges

INDEPENDENT CHALLENGE 1

Create a multiple-page report in Word that includes objects from Excel, PowerPoint, and Access. Base the report on a business-oriented subject. For example, you could write a status report that describes activities over the past six months related to a company or organization of your choice, or you could write a report that proposes a change to a specific policy such as the employee dress code or the establishment of an employee recognition program. Follow the steps provided to create the report in Word and then to include objects from the other applications.

1. Determine the name of your company or organization and the type of activities it has engaged in over the past six months. For example, you could call your organization Vision Art Gallery and describe activities such as exhibitions, lectures, and auctions. Write the name and a brief description of the activities in the box below:

   Company Name: _____

   Description of Activities: _____

2. Start Word, then type text for the report. Include placeholders for objects that you will insert from other applications. Your report should include space for a worksheet or chart from Excel, a slide or two from PowerPoint, and a report from Access. You also need to include a Table of Contents.

3. Include your name and the page number in a footer.

4. Format headings with heading styles and generate a table of contents above the first page of the report text. Apply a new color scheme.

5. Save the report as **My Integrated Report.docx** in the location where you store your Data Files, switch to Excel, then create a worksheet containing data appropriate to a section of your report. You may also wish to use the worksheet data to create a chart.

6. Save the Excel workbook as **My Integrated Report Data.xlsx** in the location where you store your Data Files.

7. Copy the Excel worksheet and/or chart to the appropriate location(s) in your Word report. Format the worksheet with the table or chart design of your choice.

8. Create a PowerPoint slide somewhere in the report. You can choose to include the slide as your title page or in another location. Enter appropriate text and apply a presentation theme, select a new color scheme, then customize the background.

9. Start Access, create a database called **My Integrated Report Database.accdb** saved in the location where you store your Data Files, create a table called **My Report Data** that contains data relevant to your report, then create a query called **Query 1** and a report called **My Report** that highlights some aspect of the data. Refer to the database you created in Project 1 for ideas.

10. Adjust the column widths in the report, then apply the AutoFormat that corresponds with the color scheme you used in the Word report.

11. Export the report to Word (the file is saved as My Report.rtf), remove the date or any extra tab marks at the top of the page and the page number at the bottom of the page, convert the text to a table, remove any blank columns and adjust the location of the data where needed, then copy the table to an appropriate location in the report.

12. Format the table with an appropriate table style.

13. Update the table of contents, print a copy of the report from Word, save and close the report, then save and close all open documents and applications.

INDEPENDENT CHALLENGE 2

Create an on-screen presentation of six to eight slides that highlights sales information and recommends marketing strategies for a company or organization of your choice. For example, you could create a presentation for the continuing education department of a local college that presents the revenues from the last 10 courses offered and recommends a marketing plan for the courses that generated the most revenue. For ideas, check the business section of your local newspaper, surf the World Wide Web, or browse through the clip-art categories. Follow the steps provided to create a table in Access, charts in Excel, and the presentation in PowerPoint. Data in the Access table should be linked to the Excel worksheet and the Excel objects in PowerPoint.

1. Determine the name of your company or organization and the type of products or services that it sells. For example, you could call your company Organic Planet and describe it as an online grocer that delivers organic fruits and vegetables and health food products to households in the Dallas area. Write the name and a brief description of your company in the box below:

Company Name:_____

Description:_____

2. Start Access, create a database called **My Sales Presentation Database.accdb** saved in the location where you store your Data Files, and create a table consisting of at least four fields and 10 records. Call the table Sales. Include fields in the table that you will be able to use in charts. For example, a table for the Organic Planet presentation could include the following fields: Product, Category (e.g., Fruit, Vegetable, Dairy), Number of Sales, and Sale Price.

3. Create a query called My Sales Query that sorts the data by category. Copy the query and paste it as a link into Excel. Create two charts that illustrate sales information about your company. For example, you could create a pie chart that shows the breakdown of product sales by category and a column chart that compares product prices. Save the workbook as **My Sales Presentation Data.xlsx** in the location where you store your Data Files.

4. Switch to Word, create an outline for the presentation, then save the document as **My Sales Presentation Outline.docx** in the location where you store your Data Files. Following are some ideas to help you get started:

SLIDE #	SLIDE TITLE	TEXT
1	Company Name	Sales Presentation Your Name
2	Goal	Write a one- or two-sentence description of your company's goals.
3	Product Categories	Write a one- or two-sentence description of a chart that illustrates the breakdown of sales by category.
4	Product Sales or Location	Write a one- or two-sentence description of a chart that shows the breakdown of sales by location or overall sales, depending on the type of chart you have created.
5	Marketing Plan	Write two or three points describing your marketing plan.

5. Add additional topics to your outline, if you wish. Remember to format all the headings with the Heading 1 style and all the bulleted items with the Heading 2 style. If you work in Outline view, the text is automatically formatted with the appropriate headings.

6. Save the outline in Word, then close Word.

7. Create a new presentation in PowerPoint, then insert slides from the Word outline. Save the presentation in PowerPoint as **My Sales Presentation.pptx** in the location where you store your Data Files.

8. Remove the blank slide, apply the presentation design of your choice, and change the color scheme and background style. Apply the Title Slide layout to the title slide.

9. Switch to Slide Master view, and add a clip-art image to the slide master or modify any images included with the slide design.

10. In Normal view, paste the charts from Excel as links to the appropriate slides and format them as necessary to make them readable and attractive.

11. Print the presentation slides as handouts (for example, six slides to the page).

12. Change some of the values in the Access table, then update the charts in PowerPoint.

13. Print only the slides that are updated as a result of the new values you entered in the Access table.

14. Save and close all files and applications.

INDEPENDENT CHALLENGE 3

Create a presentation that proposes a special event, entertainment, or party to a group of your choice. For example, you can create your own class party presentation similar to the presentation you created for Project 3. Alternatively, you can create a presentation that proposes a class reunion, a company picnic, or a weekend seminar.

1. Create an outline in PowerPoint that includes slide titles with the following information:
   a. Type of party or event
   b. Purpose of the party or event
   c. Location, time, and cost
   d. Chart showing the cost breakdown
   e. Motivational closing slide

2. Use as many slides as you wish. For ideas, refer to the presentation you created for Project 3. Save the presentation as **My Party Presentation.pptx** in the location where you store your Data Files.

3. Format the presentation attractively. Include a picture as the background on each slide in the presentation. Note that you will likely need to adjust the coloring of the picture so that text appears clearly.

4. In Access, create a database called **Class Party.accdb** and save it in the location where you store your Data Files. Create a table to keep track of attendees, then create an attractive form for entering the data. In the form, modify the column widths and include a copy of the title slide of the presentation. Print a copy of the form for one attendee.

5. Enter the event details in Word, save the document as **My Party Details.docx** in the location where you store your Data Files, copy and paste the text into PowerPoint, then format the text to make it clear and easy to read. For example, you will need to increase the font size and then you may wish to format the text box with one of the preset shape styles.

6. Create a worksheet in Excel that shows the cost breakdown for the party, create a pie chart in PowerPoint, then copy the data from Excel and paste it into the worksheet for the chart. Paste the chart in PowerPoint, then format the chart attractively. Save the worksheet as **My Party Costs.xlsx** in the location where you store your Data Files.

7. Print a copy of the presentation as handouts. Save and close the presentation, close the database, then close all open applications.

INDEPENDENT CHALLENGE 4

You need to create a presentation to welcome new employees to Food Mart, a large chain of grocery stores in Toronto. Follow the instructions provided to create and then modify the presentation.

1. Open a blank PowerPoint presentation in Outline view, enter the slide titles and text for the presentation as shown below, then save the presentation as **Food Mart Orientation.pptx** in the location where you store your Data Files.

SLIDE #	SLIDE TITLE	LEVEL 1 TEXT
1	Food Mart	Employee Orientation Your Name
2	Overview	• Company History • Company Policies • Employee Benefits • Other Resources
3	Company History	• Established in 1980 by Marianne Harris
4	Sample Products	• Here are sample products in each of the eight categories carried by Food Mart:
5	Benefits	• Medical Plan • Dental Plan • Group Life Insurance • Group Disability Insurance
6	Human Resources	• Human Resources Department ° Local 3455 ° Open from 8:00 a.m. to 6:30 p.m.

2. Apply the Module presentation design to all the slides, select the Urban color scheme, then select background style 9.
3. Switch to Slide Master view, click the top slide, fill the black rectangle with Indigo, Accent 1, Lighter 80%, change the font in the Master Title Style placeholder to Comic Sans MS, then reduce the font size to 40 pt.
4. Open the Insert Clip Art task pane, search for "shopping cart," insert an appropriate clip-art picture, then size and position the picture in the upper-right corner of the slide master. Refer to Figure I-29 as you work. Change the fill of the black rectangle on the title slide master to match the other slides, then change the font color of the subtitle placeholder to match the title.
5. Close Slide Master view, open a blank worksheet in Excel, save it as **Food Mart Data.xlsx**, then enter the data shown below:

1980	1990	2000	2010
1	10	35	75

6. Create a column chart, click the Select Data button in the Data group, click Series 1, click Remove, click Series 2, click Edit, select cells A1:D1, click OK, then click OK.

7. Remove the legend, click Axis Titles, click Primary Vertical Axis Title, point to Rotated Title, type Stores, then press [Enter].

8. Copy the chart, go to Slide 3 in PowerPoint, paste the chart, click Stores, increase the font size to 18 pt, click one of the dates (e.g., 1980), then use the Mini toolbar to increase the font size to 18 pt.

9. Apply chart style 29, then size and position the chart as shown in the completed presentation in Figure I-29.

10. Start Access, create a database called **Food Mart Orientation Database.accdb** saved in the location where you store your Data Files, then create the table shown in Figure I-28.

11. Export the table to Word (the file is saved as Product Lines.rtf), then copy the table and paste it on Slide 4.

12. Apply the Themed Style 1 - Accent 1 table style, change the font size of the text in the table to 20 pt, adjust column widths, then size and position the table as shown in Figure I-29.

13. Switch to Excel, change the number of stores in 2000 to 50 and the number of stores in 2010 to 92, then verify that the chart is updated in PowerPoint.

14. View the presentation in Slide Sorter view, then compare it to the completed presentation shown in Figure I-29.

15. Print the slides in your presentation as a handout of six slides to one page.

16. Save and close the presentation, then close all open applications.

FIGURE I-28: Product Lines

Product ID	Product Name	Category	Add New Field
1	Shampoo	Cosmetics	
2	Strawberries	Produce	
3	Cheese	Dairy	
4	Chicken Strips	Meat, Fish, Poultry	
5	Cookies	Dry Goods	
6	Bread	Bakery	
7	Pens	Stationery	
8	Ice Cream	Frozen Foods	
*	(New)		

FIGURE I-29: Completed presentation in the Slide Sorter view

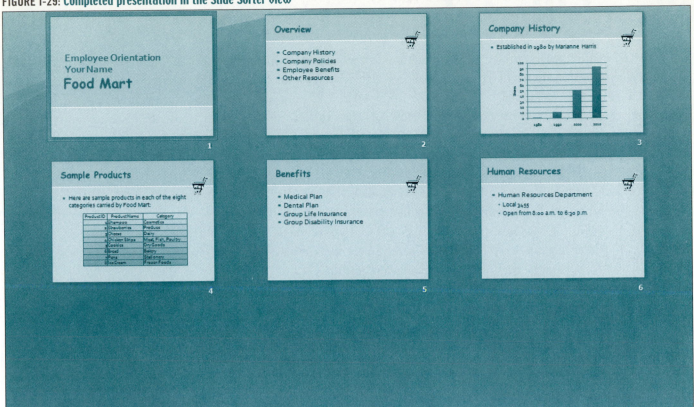

Visual Workshop

You've been asked to create a presentation on cultural tours of Europe. One of the slides in the presentation will be a pie chart that shows the breakdown of participants by tour category. Create the Tours table, as shown in Figure I-30, in an Access database called **Cultural Tours.accdb** saved in the location where you store your Data Files. Note that you need to select the Euro currency style. Create a query called **Tours Query** that sorts the records in ascending order by Theme. Copy the query table and paste it as a link into a new Excel workbook. Find the total revenue for each tour (Participants × Price), format the currency amounts with the Euro format, then create a pie chart that shows the percent of total revenue generated by each tour theme. (Note: At this point, your values will differ from Figure I-31.) Copy the pie chart and paste it as a link in a new PowerPoint slide. Add a title to the slide and format the slide and pie chart as shown in Figure I-31. Note that the Foundry theme and Background style 1 are applied to the slide. Style 27 is applied to the chart. Switch to Access, then change the number of participants in the Medieval Tuscany tour to 120. Verify that the pie chart is updated in PowerPoint. Save the Excel workbook as **Cultural Tours.xlsx** in the location where you store your Data Files, and save the PowerPoint presentation as **Cultural Tours.pptx** in the same location. Close all open applications.

FIGURE I-30: Tours Table

Tour	Tour	Theme	Country	Participan	Price
1	Ancient Rome	History	Italy	40	€3,500.00
2	Magical Provence	Culinary	France	30	€4,500.00
3	Rhineland Dreaming	Culinary	Germany	35	€4,200.00
4	Medieval Tuscany	History	Italy	80	€3,800.00
5	Van Gogh Odyssey	Art	France	25	€3,200.00
6	Mozart Madness	Music	Austria	35	€4,500.00
7	Renaissance Florence	Art	Italy	20	€2,800.00
8	Dutch Masters	Art	Netherlands	15	€3,200.00
9	The Impressionists	Art	France	20	€3,300.00
10	Megalith Builders	History	France	35	€3,800.00
* (New)					€0.00

FIGURE I-31: Completed slide

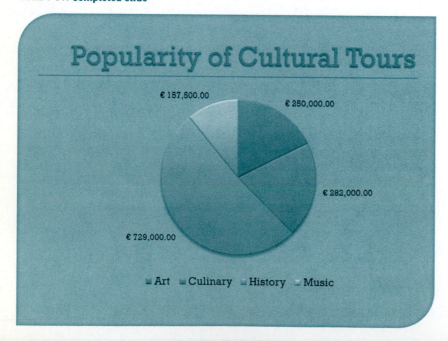

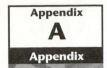

Restoring Defaults in Windows Vista and Disabling and Enabling Windows Aero

Files You Will Need:

No files needed.

Windows Vista is the most recent version of the Windows operating system. An operating system controls the way you work with your computer, supervises running programs, and provides tools for completing your computing tasks. After surveying millions of computer users, Microsoft incorporated their suggestions to make Windows Vista secure, reliable, and easy to use. In fact, Windows Vista is considered the most secure version of Windows yet. Other improvements include a powerful new search feature that lets you quickly search for files and programs from the Start menu and most windows, tools that simplify accessing the Internet, especially with a wireless connection, and multimedia programs that let you enjoy, share, and organize music, photos, and recorded TV. Finally, Windows Vista offers lots of visual appeal with its transparent, three-dimensional design in the Aero experience. This appendix explains how to make sure you are using the Windows Vista default settings for appearance, personalization, security, hardware, and sound and to enable and disable Windows Aero. For more information on Windows Aero, go to *www.microsoft.com/windowsvista/experiences/aero.mspx*.

OBJECTIVES   Restore the defaults in the
    Appearance and Personalization
    section
Restore the defaults in the Security
    section
Restore the defaults in the Hardware
    and Sound section
Disable Windows Aero
Enable Windows Aero

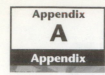
Restoring the Defaults in the Appearance and Personalization Section

The following instructions require a default Windows Vista Ultimate installation and the student logged in with an Administrator account. All of the following settings can be changed by accessing the Control Panel.

STEPS

- To restore the defaults in the Personalization section
    1. Click Start, and then click Control Panel. Click Appearance and Personalization, click Personalization, and then compare your screen to Figure A-1
    2. In the Personalization window, click Windows Color and Appearance, select the Default color, and then click OK
    3. In the Personalization window, click Mouse Pointers. In the Mouse Properties dialog box, on the Pointers tab, select Windows Aero (system scheme) in the Scheme drop-down list, and then click OK
    4. In the Personalization window, click Theme. Select Windows Vista from the Theme drop-down list, and then click OK
    5. In the Personalization window, click Display Settings. In the Display Settings dialog box, drag the Resolution bar to 1024 by 768 pixels, and then click OK

FIGURE A-1

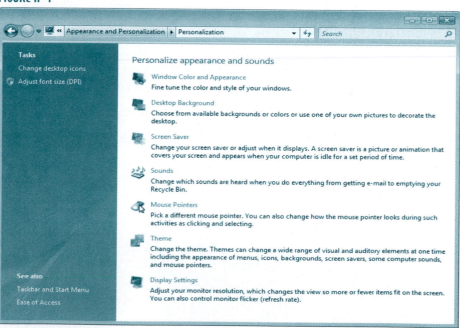

- To restore the defaults in the Taskbar and Start Menu section
  1. Click Start, and then click Control Panel. Click Appearance and Personalization, click Taskbar and Start Menu, and then compare your screen to Figure A-2
  2. In the Taskbar and Start Menu Properties dialog box, on the Taskbar tab, click to select all checkboxes except for "Auto-hide the taskbar"
  3. On the Start Menu tab, click to select the Start menu radio button and check all items in the Privacy section
  4. In the System icons section on the Notification Area tab, click to select all of the checkboxes except for "Power"
  5. On the Toolbars tab, click to select Quick Launch, none of the other items should be checked
  6. Click OK to close the Taskbar and Start Menu Properties dialog box

- To restore the defaults in the Folder Options section
  1. Click Start, and then click Control Panel. Click Appearance and Personalization, click Folder Options, and then compare your screen to Figure A-3
  2. In the Folder Options dialog box, on the General tab, click to select Show preview and filters in the Tasks section, click to select Open each folder in the same window in the Browse folders section, and click to select Double-click to open an item (single-click to select) in the Click items as follows section
  3. On the View tab, click the Reset Folders button, and then click Yes in the Folder views dialog box. Then click the Restore Defaults button
  4. On the Search tab, click the Restore Defaults button
  5. Click OK to close the Folder Options dialog box

- To restore the defaults in the Windows Sidebar Properties section
  1. Click Start, and then click Control Panel. Click Appearance and Personalization, click Windows Sidebar Properties, and then compare your screen to Figure A-4
  2. In the Windows Sidebar Properties dialog box, on the Sidebar tab, click to select Start Sidebar when Windows starts. In the Arrangement section, click to select Right, and then click to select 1 in the Display Sidebar on monitor drop-down list
  3. Click OK to close the Windows Sidebar Properties dialog box

FIGURE A-3

FIGURE A-4

FIGURE A-2

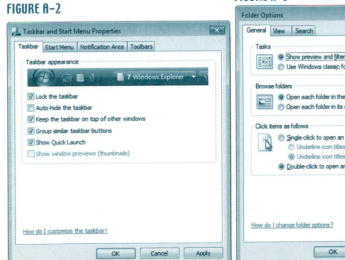

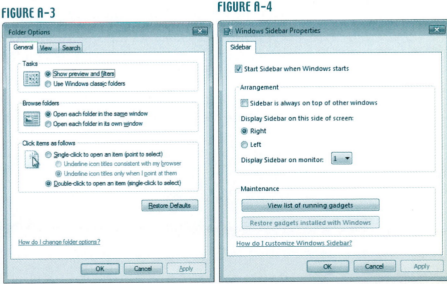

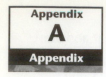

Restoring the Defaults in the Security Section

The following instructions require a default Windows Vista Ultimate installation and the student logged in with an Administrator account. All of the following settings can be changed by accessing the Control Panel.

- **To restore the defaults in the Windows Firewall section**

  1. Click Start, and then click Control Panel. Click Security, click Windows Firewall, and then compare your screen to Figure A-5

  2. In the Windows Firewall dialog box, click Change settings. If the User Account Control dialog box appears, click Continue

  3. In the Windows Firewall Settings dialog box, click the Advanced tab. Click Restore Defaults, then click Yes in the Restore Defaults Confirmation dialog box

  4. Click OK to close the Windows Firewall Settings dialog box, and then close the Windows Firewall window

- **To restore the defaults in the Internet Options section**

  1. Click Start, and then click Control Panel. Click Security, click Internet Options, and then compare your screen to Figure A-6

  2. In the Internet Properties dialog box, on the General tab, click the Use default button. Click the Settings button in the Tabs section, and then click the Restore defaults button in the Tabbed Browsing Settings dialog box. Click OK to close the Tabbed Browsing Settings dialog box

  3. On the Security tab of the Internet Properties dialog box, click to uncheck the Enable Protected Mode checkbox, if necessary. Click the Default level button in the Security level for this zone section. If possible, click the Reset all zones to default level button

  4. On the Programs tab, click the Make default button in the Default web browser button for Internet Explorer, if possible. If Office is installed, Microsoft Office Word should be selected in the HTML editor drop-down list

  5. On the Advanced tab, click the Restore advanced settings button in the Settings section. Click the Reset button in the Reset Internet Explorer settings section, and then click Reset in the Reset Internet Explorer Settings dialog box

  6. Click Close to close the Reset Internet Explorer Settings dialog box, and then click OK to close the Internet Properties dialog box

FIGURE A-5

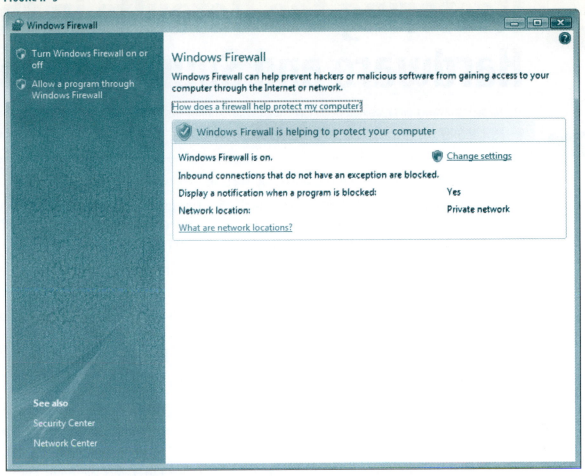

FIGURE A-6

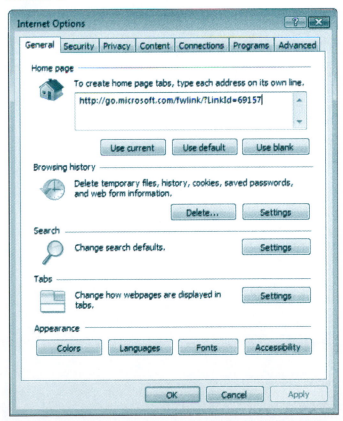

Restoring the Defaults in the Hardware and Sound Section

The following instructions require a default Windows Vista Ultimate installation and the student logged in with an Administrator account. All of the following settings can be changed by accessing the Control Panel.

STEPS

- **To restore the defaults in the Autoplay section**
    1. Click Start, and then click Control Panel. Click Hardware and Sound, click Autoplay, and then compare your screen to Figure A-7. Scroll down and click the Reset all defaults button in the Devices section at the bottom of the window, and then click Save

- **To restore the defaults in the Sound section**
    1. Click Start, and then click Control Panel. Click Hardware and Sound, click Sound, and then compare your screen to Figure A-8
    2. In the Sound dialog box, on the Sounds tab, select Windows Default from the Sound Scheme drop-down list, and then click OK

- **To restore the defaults in the Mouse section**
    1. Click Start, and then click Control Panel. Click Hardware and Sound, click Mouse, and then compare your screen to Figure A-9
    2. In the Mouse Properties dialog box, on the Pointers tab, select Windows Aero (system scheme) from the Scheme drop-down list
    3. Click OK to close the Mouse Properties dialog box

FIGURE A-7

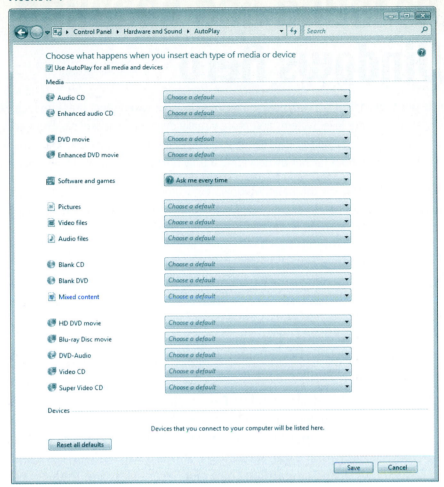

FIGURE A-8

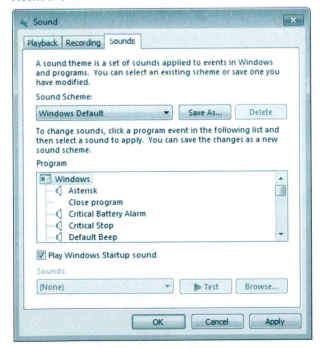

FIGURE A-9

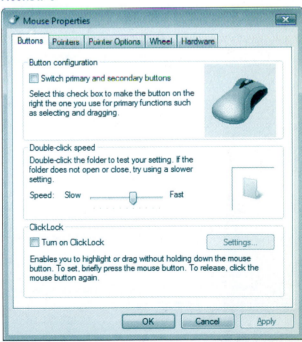

Disabling and Enabling Windows Aero

Unlike prior versions of Windows, Windows Vista provides two distinct user interface experiences: a "basic" experience for entry-level systems and more visually dynamic experience called Windows Aero. Both offer a new and intuitive navgation experience that helps you more easily find and organize your applications and files, but Aero goes further by delivering a truly next-generation desktop experience.

Windows Aero builds on the basic Windows Vista user experience and offers Mircosoft's best-designed, highest-preforming desktop experience. Using Aero requires a PC with compatible graphics adapter and running a Premium or Business edition of Windows Vista.

The following instructions require a computer capable of running Windows Aero, with a default Windows Vista Ultimate installation and student logged in with an Administrator account.

STEPS

- **To Disable Windows Aero**

We recommend that students using this book disable Windows Aero and restore their operating systems default settings (instructions to follow).

1. Right-click the desktop, select Personalize, and then compare yor screen in Figure A-10. Select Window Color and Appearance, and then select Open classic appeareance properties for more color options. In Appearance Settings dialong box, on the Appearance tab, select any non-Aero scheme (such as Windows Vista Basic or Windows Vista Standard) in the Color Scheme list, and then click OK Figure A-11 compares Windows Aero to other color schemes. Note that this book uses Windows Vista Basic as the color scheme

- **To Enable Windows Aero**

1. Right-click the desktop, and then select Personalize. Select Window Color and Appearance, then select Windows Aero in the Color scheme list, and then click OK in the Appearance Settings dialog box

FIGURE A-10

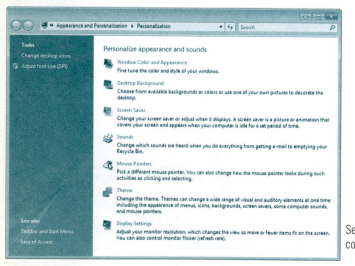

FIGURE A-11

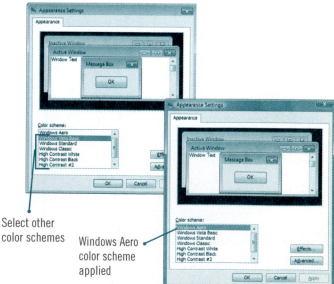

Index

►T